STEWARDSHIP

Also by Peter Block

The Empowered Manager
Flawless Consulting

STEWARDSHIP

Choosing Service Over Self-Interest

PETER BLOCK

Berrett-Koehler Publishers
San Francisco

Berrett-Koehler Publishers, Inc.

155 Montgomery St.
San Francisco, CA 94104-4109

Ordering Information

Orders by individuals and organizations. Berrett-Koehler publications are available through bookstores or can be ordered direct from the publisher at the Berrett-Koehler address above or by calling (800) 929-2929.

Quantity sales. Berrett-Koehler publications are available at special quantity discounts when purchased in bulk by corporations, associations, and others. For details, write to the "Special Sales Department" at the Berrett-Koehler address above or call (415) 288-0260.

Orders by U.S. trade bookstores and wholesalers. Please contact Publishers Group West, 4065 Hollis St., Box 8843, Emeryville, CA 94608; tel. (800) 788-3123; fax (510) 658-1834.

Orders for college textbook/course adoption use. Please contact Berrett-Koehler Publishers, 155 Montgomery St., San Francisco, CA 94104-4109; tel. (415) 288-0260; fax (415) 362-2512.

Printed in the United States of America

 Printed on acid-free and recycled paper that meets the strictest state and U.S. guidelines for recycled paper (50 percent recycled waste, including 10 percent postconsumer waste).

Library of Congress Cataloging-in-Publication Data

Block, Peter.
    Stewardship : choosing service over self interest / Peter Block. — 1st ed.
       p. cm.
    Includes bibliographical references and index.
    ISBN 1-881052-28-1 (alk. paper)
    1. Industrial management. 2. Industry—Social aspects.
I. Title.
HD31.B54 1993
658-dc20

                                          93-6597
                                         CIP

First Edition
    First Printing 1993

Editing: Leslie Stephen
Copyediting: Debra Costenbader
Word processing: Millie Rodriguez and Sherry Sprague
Indexing: Linda Webster
Cover design and book design: Barbara Gelfand
Cover painting: John Nieto

To Barbara for offering hope, and caring so
gently about all things that matter,

To Joel for telling the truth, and being
willing to embrace the night.

CONTENTS

FOREWORD

by Joel Henning

This is a book about optimism and harsh reality. This is a book about helplessness and leadership. This is a book about democracy and tyranny. It is about the human spirit and profit, about survival and prosperity.

It is written at a time when the peoples of the world actively yearn for freedom and the chance to create a life that has both purpose and possibility, a life that has hope. It is strange that the institutions that are yielding to this tide are primarily in the public sector, governments who have understood their primary mission to be the creation and maintenance of stability. From Poland to China the show goes on, with all the pain and chaos necessary to the creation of a new order.

We in the United States and, I suspect, our close allies in Western Europe look on with a smug arrogance and declare victory over the "evil empire" we have done battle with since World War II. It is true enough that the fall of these totalitarian governments is a moment for celebration and that the world sleeps easier as the threat of military confrontation and nuclear annihilation recedes. Yet I find myself troubled by our giddy response. While we have been quick to see how the creation of "drab gray societies" in these communist nations led to their collapse, we see no relevance to our own lives and institutions. In a fundamental way this book is about the application of the learnings emerging from this global revolution to our own business institutions. These "drab gray societies" wagered their survival on central control and the supposed promise of safety for their citizens. Whatever their intention, in the end they strangled the human spirit, wilted faith and hope among the population, and created helplessness. If we can grasp that many of our own institutions have made the same wager and are in the process of reaping the same rewards, we can choose to create alternatives to the "drab gray societies."

Where are these institutions? Many of us go to work in them every day; from 8:00 to 5:00 we earn our daily bread laboring for them; they are the institutions that create our wealth as a nation and as individuals; they are the institutions of business and commerce both large and small. In many cases we can find them in the public sector, in our schools and government buildings.

In some ways we are a nation profoundly conflicted about what we believe. We live with political institutions that celebrate the rights of individuals to express themselves, to assemble, to pursue happiness and individual purposes, to pick their own political leaders. We pay enormous attention to the rights and procedures of due process. At times we seem to be on the edge of anarchy and yet we tenaciously cling to our political beliefs and rituals with all their flaws and contradictions. Yet when we enter the factory door or the lobby of the business cathedrals in our major cities, we leave our belief in democratic principles in the car. The halls and chambers of these buildings have flourished on a very different set of beliefs and rituals.

The first day of my first serious job—one I had to get dressed up for—the orientation began with the boss telling the group of new hires, "This is not a democracy." The alternative to democracy was not precisely named but it didn't take long to get the idea. When I arrived that first day of work I was full of fear, naiveté, optimism, and hope in the future. I wanted to make a contribution. What I was introduced to in orientation was harsh reality. What harsh reality made clear was that hope and optimism were somewhat irrelevant and that compliance and fitting in counted. It was an honest presentation. I got it and, for a while, I tried hard at it. I became passionate about complying. I discovered all the rules, the written and unwritten. I abided by all of them—with commitment.

I "dressed for success" as defined by the corporate culture. My passions for social change faded and I started taking seriously that the point was to move up the ladder. Perhaps the high point of my passion for fitting in was a call to the vice-president of human resources to inquire what kind of car I should purchase to be appropriate in my new corporate home. It was years ago and yet the early memories are vivid. Much of what came after was merely repetition. I had become the boss and found myself telling new hires, "This is not a democracy." The show goes on. What was important in those events was the learning of deeply held beliefs and faith on which businesses for the most part had bet their survival and prosperity. Although not complete, three articles of faith capture much of what the religion was and is about.

The first is the most powerful, equivalent to an ancient religious creed. In the case of most corporations the beginning line is, "I believe in Compliance...." It is so pervasive and it is meant to be. This is serious stuff. The message is everywhere, from how we draw organization charts to endless manuals on company policies and procedures. We elevate and revere those who carry the heavier responsibility for insuring compliance. We believe that the burden of insuring compliance deserves everything from large offices which are always at the top to special parking places which are at the bottom connected by special elevators. CEOs, corporate officers, and their kind have become the bishops and cardinals, the keepers of the faith. And so edicts are issued, values and vision statements are published, and the faithful attend services to be edified in the finer points of doctrine and to make appropriate commitments. Now it is called training rather than going to church. What is this all about? It is about living out the belief that compliance is everything and upon this rock we will build our future. In this world political correctness or silence replaces freedom of speech; public assembly, not sponsored by those above, becomes grounds for dismissal; demands for due process become insubordination; and disagreement with those above becomes "you're not a team player." The most basic democratic principles somehow become the "enemy" in a community where we have bet our survival on compliance.

The second article is derived from the first: Watching is better than doing. In a world committed to compliance the primary means of making such a value operational is to insure there are plenty of people watching, being ever vigilant in the name of alignment. Watching becomes an activity of extraordinary value. Enter endless staff groups and management roles. The first five years of my consulting life I never met the people who actually did the work and I never thought about it. I spent endless hours with managers and staff persons. It never occurred to me that none of the people I was with ever produced a product or service that actually stood the test of the marketplace. In many cases the people who did the work were in distant lands, not easily accessible. What is most disturbing in hindsight is it never occurred to me that there was anything wrong with this picture. Of course it made sense that the wealth, privilege, and power were distributed among those who watched, monitored, and audited the people who did the work. It is really not such a surprise to see the manufacturing base of the country being transferred to the Far East and Central America. It is the simple living out of our belief that "doers" are not all that important. If we can reduce wages, worker compensation costs, and irritating union activity—why not? Nobody is suggesting that we send the HR, finance, legal, or systems functions off shore. Watching has come close to establishing a corporate aristocracy. They live in palaces far removed from the masses of workers, they vie for the favor of the king or queen in hopes of a new title, they enjoy privilege beyond the reach or dreams of the common worker—the doer—the one who actually produces the product or service for which we pay. This is more the land of monarch and divine right than the world of democracy where each is born with the right to life, liberty, and the pursuit of happiness. This is the world that looks to great leaders to provide vision, structure, and meaning for the spiritually and the intellectually impoverished. It is not the world of simple democracy that sees each individual as capable and responsible for pursuing their own happiness—their own pursuit of purpose, meaning, and structure. In most corporations, leadership and management have become a class—not a simple set of tasks which are accessible to all who would seek them.

The third article of faith is that in the event of breakdown or failure, try harder. It is the Vince Lombardi lesson. Businesses and corporations in trouble almost always respond to crisis by doing more of what they have already done. When the going gets tough the tough get going. What that generally means is trying harder at compliance. It may get packaged differently. Generally it takes a program format. Programs on excellence, quality, values, empowerment, strategic planning, leadership, and so on and so on and so on. It could be called hope through repackaging. The point is still getting control. As Janis Joplin once noted, "It's the same damn thing," or words to that effect. The prayer book may be revised, the language may be changed, or facial expressions more tender, but the core remains intact.

The point is simple. These great institutions which produce our wealth, which put meals on our table, provide shelter for our families, medical care, and all the other pieces that make up our lives, have made a bet. The bet has been on an idea. The idea is that compliance and control are the best means to insure future survival and prosperity. Of course a benevolent spirit is to be part of the execution of the idea, but compliance is still the idea. It didn't work in Eastern Europe. It created a "drab gray society." It worked for a while, but a lot of bad ideas work for at least a short time. In the end what overcame the governing institutions was an act of the spirit. It was purposeful, dedicated, impassioned human beings longing for something better than a world of safety through compliance. What is the application to business and industry who have also bet on compliance? Success in the future will depend on businesses that produce products and services that give an innovative and unique response to the customer or client in the marketplace.

Success in the future will depend on organizations that can create new knowledge that results in innovative products and services in the marketplace. Success in the future will depend on people who have a passion for the business, who generate new ideas, ways of doing things that result in new knowledge that results in innovative and unique products in the marketplace. If these are the demands of future survival or prosperity, do we want to place our bet on compliance, watching, and trying harder?

This book offers an alternative; it is not about extolling the virtue of trying harder at what we have been doing. It is not a repackaging job. It is about revolution. Not violent revolution, but a revolution of ideas. It places its hope in democratic principle. It is not a book simply about relationships; it is a book that calls into question the governance structures and systems of our economic institutions. It attempts to make relevant to our economic survival the integration of the best of the human spirit with the demands for survival in the marketplace. Nothing is as powerful as an idea, from them all that we know has taken form. From concrete products—bicycles, computers, hula hoops, toothpaste—to political institutions—democracy, communism, socialism, the rule of law—they all started with an idea. What makes this book important is the introduction of a new idea into the marketplace of business and industry.

Not only is this work an alternative, it is, as well, unique. It is the antithesis to the current thesis in our management and organizational theory. So much of what we read today in examining the factors that promise to make our economic institutions viable is more repackaging than new and substantive proposal. So much of it is merely redesigned practice to carry out old beliefs. Even the values of democracy can be perverted to become technique—oppression through participation. Not here! Peter confronts us at the level of belief. He understands that the struggle to be faced is not with the technology of management techniques. It is with the whole notion of management and its relation to our future economic survival and viability. He confronts the possibility that if we don't examine the beliefs upon which we are "betting the family farm," our faith may become a product of our methods. It is in that examination that Peter makes explicit for the first time the fundamental relationship between political values and economic viability. What he may see more clearly than any predecessor is that we are at risk. As Lincoln noted, "A house divided against itself will not stand." So to live in a country where we shed blood to preserve democratic political institutions while creating our economic institutions based on antithetical values can lead us to no good end. Raising and making explicit this challenge is the significant contribution of this work.

I recommend this work to you. For those who have taken the time to read the foreword and are already troubled that the book or I may not understand the need for control and so on—not to worry. Anarchy is not the solution to our current economic woes. Nor is more control. For those who may consider this "soft stuff" and therefore of no value, I can only suggest a reading before reaching such a conclusion.

A final word about the author, my friend and mentor. I have no wish to make a hero of him; it would be a disservice to the ideas contained within this book. But this I will say in tribute to him and this work. He has always known what was important to him: telling the truth, passion for his work, taking responsibility for his own life, and making some contribution to the world that would relieve in some way the suffering of others. It is from these values and his own wonderful gift for writing and thinking that this book has come. It is the best of him and a major accomplishment.

PREFACE

Our task is to create organizations that work, especially in a world where everything constantly seems up in the air. We know that fundamental change is required. We keep talking about cultural change, but this will not be enough if we stay focused on changing attitudes and skills. No question that beliefs and attitudes need to change, but unless there is also a shift in governance, namely, how we distribute power, and privilege, and the control of money, the efforts will be more cosmetic than enduring.

The need for something different partly grows out of us as individuals. There resides in each of us the desire to more fully integrate our lives. We must feel fragmented, because we talk about ourselves as if we were cats with several lives. "This is my work life," "this is my personal life," "this is my spiritual life." In compartmentalizing our lives, we are constantly setting aside parts of ourselves, even at times giving ourselves away. This fragmentation is also reflected in our organizations. There are all the debates between being people-oriented and task-oriented, hard-nosed and soft-nosed, values-driven and results-driven.

The central idea of this book, stewardship, has the potential to reintegrate parts of ourselves and move beyond the debates in our organizations. In this way it is a book of reconciliation. Stewardship focuses our attention on aspects of our workplaces that have been most difficult to change, namely the distribution of power, purpose, and rewards. It is these dimensions of organizations that need to be re-formed if we are to become whole in our efforts to strengthen ourselves. We are each engaged in discrete exercises to help our organizations lose weight, become more flexible, and stay hopeful. We have a program for everything. Cost reduction, continuous improvement, customer service, cycle time, quality, learning, visioning, process control, team building, empowerment, diversity, school improvement, reinvented government. Implemented independently, each one meets its goals, yet a major part of our lives still seems unchanged. We remain watchful of people who have power over us; we feel that the organization is the creation of someone other than ourselves, and that the changes we want to make still need sponsorship and permission from others at a higher level.

We need a way of reconciling the promise of our programs with the experience of our day-to-day lives so that the Queen Mary truly changes direction.

Stewardship

Stewardship is the umbrella idea which promises the means of achieving fundamental change in the way we govern our institutions. Stewardship is to hold something in trust for another. Historically, stewardship was a means to protect a kingdom while those rightfully in charge were away, or, more often, to govern for the sake of an underage king. The underage king for us is the next generation. We choose service over self-interest most powerfully when we build the capacity of the next generation to govern themselves.

Stewardship is defined in this book as the willingness to be accountable for the well-being of the larger organization by operating in service, rather than in control, of those around us. Stated simply, it is accountability without control or compliance.

Service

The underlying value is about deepening our commitment to service. We have the language of service. We serve our country, we call ourselves a service economy, we choose public service as a profession, we have committed to serve customers. What is missing is the experience of service. Our experience is too often to find ourselves surrounded by self-interest, especially inside our institutions. The ways we govern, manage, and lead are a testimony to self-interest. Authentic service is experienced when

▼ There is a balance of power. People need to act on their own choices. Acts of compliance do not serve those around us or the larger organization. Dominance also fails. We also do a disservice to others when we make decisions for them. Even if we are right.

▼ The primary commitment is to the larger community. Focusing constant attention on the individual or a small team breeds self-centeredness and entitlement.

▼ Each person joins in defining purpose and deciding what kind of culture this organization will become. We diminish others when we define purpose and meaning for them, even if they ask us to do so.

▼ There is a balanced and equitable distribution of rewards. Every level of an organization shares in creating its wealth and expanding its resources. When an organization succeeds in its marketplace, money and privilege need to be more evenly distributed among levels if our commitment to service is to have any integrity.

Without these elements, no genuine service is performed.

These notions of service and stewardship, however, are not the basis of how we currently run our organizations. They do reflect some of our intentions about how to govern, but not the reality.

Some of the elements are often in place. We frequently see innovative pay systems, self-managing teams, total quality efforts, partnerships, customer attentiveness, and inverted pyramids. They are rarely, however, put together in a pervasive governance strategy. As a result, we end up too often working against ourselves. We share control with the left hand and take it back with the right. One moment we are on the fast track toward participation and the next moment we are instituting more controls.

The intent of this book is to translate these ideas about power, community, purpose, and privilege into a whole strategy for governing our companies and institutions. Stewardship becomes then a governance strategy. It is the search for the means of experiencing partnership and empowerment and service. This book offers a guide map for this search. Discovering how to govern, to insure the well-being and survival of our organizations, is how we create meaning in what we do. This is the spiritual stream we stand in.

Stewardship encompasses concerns of the spirit, but it also must pass the test of the marketplace. It must be practical and economic. It must be low cost and good for customers as well as employees. Our organizations constantly stand on this intersection of spirit, community, and the marketplace. The unique intention of this book is to offer the means by which there can be a reconciliation of what is good for the soul, good for a customer, and good for the health of the larger institution.

This book, then, is for those of us living questions of purpose and survival. It is not written from the point of view of consultants, experts in managing change, and experienced practitioners worried about changing others. The book takes the viewpoint of core workers, staff people, supervisors, managers, and executives. People who are in the middle of it all. It is for activists in school reform, health care, government under fire, as well as businesses in the private sector. It is for people who have decided that their organization needs reforming, and have doubts whether what they are doing now is enough. The book builds on an earlier book, *The Empowered Manager.* That book's basic ideas of empowerment and individual responsibility are melded into the current ideas of stewardship and service. However, where *The Empowered Manager* focused primarily on the individual, this book focuses on the policies, practices, and structures that constitute the organization.

This book is divided into three parts. Part I, Trading Your Kingdom for a Horse, is about the basic concept and the promise of stewardship and the limitations of leadership. It dramatizes the choices we face and the high wire we dance upon. Part II, The Redistribution of Power, Purpose, and Wealth, gets practical. It is for the engineer in each of us that asks at some point in every conversation, "Enough theory, what does it look like? What do we do differently tomorrow, first thing at 7:00 a.m.?" I don't know why the engineer in us gets up so early. In this second part resides the vision of stewardship in action. Special attention is given to staff groups like finance and human resources. Part III, The Triumph of Hope over Experience, goes into some of the details about how to get there. What is a logical sequence for thinking about the reform process? Also it is about how to handle cynics and victims and people who do not want to take the trip. It often does not matter what the trip is, there are just some people that do not want to take it.

A comment about the design of the book. Alongside the text of the book, there are inserts of anecdotes, short stories, quotes, and key sentences from the text itself. This is intended as a book within a book. If the main text gets slow, you always have the inserts and quotes to chew on. This treatment is also a way of balancing the rhythm of the text with voices more profound than mine. And you will notice words set vertically on certain pages. This is to visually open up the book and also to let you know where you are; if you should want to return to a particular spot, they are there to help you find your way back.

At the end of the book there is a Lost and Found section. This takes the place of a bibliography and acknowledgments. Bibliographies value only the written word. I wanted a way to honor those who live out, through actions, their contribution and have not taken the time to write. So included in the Lost and Found section are the people who contributed to the ideas in this book plus many people who are putting these ideas into practice. The section is called Lost and Found because they are among my favorite places to go. There is something very hopeful about Lost and Found departments. Someplace to go in search of something missing or in this case, something more.

O my Will...Preserve me from all petty victories!...That I may one day be ready and ripe in the great noontide...a bow eager for its arrow, an arrow eager for its star—a star, ready and ripe in its noontide, glowing, transpierced...Spare me for one great victory!

Friedrich Nietzsche,
Thus Spoke Zarathustra

Finally a word about the painting that graces the dust jacket. It is a painting of an archer by John Nieto, a well-known, contemporary American artist. The painting speaks to the best intentions of this book. The archer's feet are so planted as to be almost a part of the ground. Practical and connected to reality. The bow and the arrow are aimed at the heavens. The arrow carries within it clear intentions, the sky a place of infinite view and vision. The colors of deep purple and fierce yellow offer a hint of what is unknown, they speak to adventure. These are at the heart of the offering that is this book.

All of the above by way of welcome.

Connecticut
March 1993

Peter Block

PART I

TRADING YOUR KINGDOM FOR A HORSE

Few rulers in literature can top Shakespeare's Richard III for self-centeredness and inhumanity. Dismounted on the battlefield, with his life in the balance, he cries out, "A horse! a horse! my kingdom for a horse!" At that moment, he would gladly give up all the wealth and power he had accumulated for a practical means that would insure his survival.

Each of us is in the same spot—facing the same choice. Our marketplace is the field of battle, and we have to decide whether to hold on to the power and privilege we have worked so hard to acquire, or to pass it on in exchange for a better chance for survival.

1

REPLACING LEADERSHIP WITH STEWARDSHIP

This book is about how our institutions are managed and governed.

There is a longing in each of us to invest in things that matter, and to have the organization in which we work be successful. Our task is to insure that when we step aside, our job, or at least our organization, still exists for the next generation. No easy task in this environment.

This book is also about living out democratic values, using the workplace as the focal point. One of its goals is to quicken our efforts to reform our organizations so that our democracy thrives, our spirit is answered, and our ability to serve customers in the broadest sense is guaranteed.

The evidence that our organizations are not working well is fully upon us. Something stark has happened to our institutions that we were not quite ready for. The changes seemed to come in waves and private industry took the first hit. Most businesses got the point in the 1970s and 1980s: if they did not find a way to serve their markets more quickly, with higher quality and lower costs, they would not endure. Granted, some have still not gotten the point. Hospitals and other health care providers were next in receiving their wake-up calls. We see the beginnings of the changes being undertaken in that hospitals now have marketing departments, hold meetings about market segmentation, call doctors "customers," and call patients "guests." If you do not like your meal in the hospital, all you have to do is call room service.

Schools are at the front of the most recent wave of reform. A radical version of the changes to come will have your eleven-year-old child be given four thousand dollars and a bus ticket and told to go shopping for the best education she can get. Private capitalists are racing into the business of elementary education, and in many systems each school building now has site-based management teams that are planning new beginnings with teachers, parents, and local business people. Making government work is next. Perhaps you will get your next driver's license from an ATM machine in the mall, or have your own customer service representative at the Internal Revenue Service. And, who knows, your local fire department might become a franchise operation with headquarters in Daytona Beach, Florida.

The changes we witness are an outgrowth of several fundamental crises facing our organizations. Crises always come packaged in economic terms first. And economically our schools, our health care systems, our government agencies, our private businesses and industries are under enormous pressure. They are all getting smaller as fast as they can. Eighty percent of new jobs in this country come from organizations with less than one hundred employees. The largest five hundred companies in the U.S. have not created one net new job since 1974. Our manufacturing capability is being exported to low-cost labor countries. And on it goes.

None of this is news. In fact we are weary of hearing about it. The problem with all the emphasis on economics is that economics is not the real problem. If we keep describing the problem as one of economics and the need for more money, it will lead us to the same actions that created the problem in the first place. Spending more money on health care, more money on education, more money to support higher prices and buy greater protection for business, more money for social problems, will only deepen our concern, given our lack of faith in the ability of these institutions to spend the money in a useful way. Money is a symptom, money is never the real issue. Money is a language. It is easily measured, so it is easy and convenient to talk about.

An economic crisis for any organization means it is failing in its marketplace. In some fundamental way it is unable to serve its customers. And if it is unable to serve its customers, it means it has failed to serve its own internal people. The way organizations mobilize to serve customers and their own people has to do with the definition of purpose, the use of power, and ultimately the distribution of wealth. Purpose, power, and wealth are the chief concerns of the system and process traditionally called *management*. Better to use the term *governance*. *Management* is a cool, neutral term. It has a professional flavor to it and would treat power as a problem in social engineering. The political nature of institutions is finessed when we talk of management. The term *governance* gets more to the point. We are accustomed to equating power and purpose and wealth with the process of government. Using a term like *governance* recognizes the political nature of our lives and our workplace. Hope for genuine organizational reform resides in reshaping the politics of our work lives, namely how we each define purpose, hold power, and balance wealth.

Stewardship is the set of principles and practices which have the potential to make dramatic changes in our governance system. It is concerned with creating a way of governing ourselves that creates a strong sense of ownership and responsibility for outcomes at the bottom of the organization. It means giving control to customers and creating self-reliance on the part of all who are touched by the institution. The answer to economic problems is not more money; it is to focus on quality, service, and participation first. This is what will put us closer to our marketplace. It is the connection with our marketplace that is the answer to our concerns about economics.

We know there is a need for reform, we are less clear about how to achieve it. Most of our theories about making change are clustered around a belief in leadership. We think that leadership is the key to fitting organizations to their marketplace and fitting people to their organizations. If the organization fails, it is the leader's head that we want. It is this pervasive and almost religious belief in leaders that slows the process of genuine reform. This book about stewardship offers an approach to reform that puts leadership in the background where it belongs.

We cannot be stewards of an institution and expect someone else to take care of us.

Stewardship begins with the willingness to be accountable for some larger body than ourselves—an organization, a community. Stewardship springs from a set of beliefs about reforming organizations that affirms our choice for service over the pursuit of self-interest. When we choose service over self-interest we say we are willing to be deeply accountable without choosing to control the world around us. It requires a level of trust that we are not used to holding.

In its commitment to service, stewardship forces us then to yield on our desire to use good parenting as a basic form of governance. We already know how to be good parents at work. The alternative, partnership, is something we are just learning about. Our difficulty with creating partnerships is that parenting—and its stronger cousin, patriarchy—is so deeply ingrained in our muscle memory and armature that we don't even realize we are doing it.

In addition to engendering partnership, genuine service requires us to act on our own account. We cannot be stewards of an institution and expect someone else to take care of us. Regardless of how parental our environment may be, we decide whether to support efforts to treat us like children, which expresses our wish for dependency, or whether to keep deciding that we serve the organization best by creating a place of our own choosing. The well-worn word for this is empowerment.

Stewardship is the choice for service.
We serve best through partnership, rather than patriarchy.
Dependency is the antithesis of stewardship and so
empowerment becomes essential.

The way we govern our institutions grows out of the stance we take on each of these dimensions. How we define purpose, how we create structure, how we pay people, how we set goals and measure progress—all grow out of the beliefs we have about control, and about safety, and about self-interest. These are the essential questions about governance. And they are more profound than simply asking who is at the top of our organization or what management style enjoys popular support at the moment.

CHOOSING PARTNERS

In deciding how to govern, one critical choice is between patriarchy and partnership. Patriarchy expresses the belief that it is those at the top who are responsible for the success of the organization and the well-being of its members. A measure of patriarchy is how frequently we use images of parenting to describe how bosses should manage subordinates in organizations. If our intent is to create workplaces that provide meaning, and are economically sound and strong in the marketplace, we need to face the implications for having chosen patriarchy for the governance system inside our organizations. The governance system we have inherited and continue to create is based on sovereignty and a form of intimate colonialism. These are strong terms, but they are essentially accurate. We govern our organizations by valuing, above all else, consistency, control, and predictability. These become the means of dominance by which colonialism and sovereignty are enacted. It is not that we directly seek dominance, but our beliefs about getting work done have that effect.

The governance system we have inherited and continue to create is based on sovereignty and a form of intimate colonialism.

We pay a price for our top-driven, parenting, patriarchal governance system:

▼ Democracy cannot thrive if we only experience it for a moment of voting every two to four years. If day in and day out we go to a workplace that breeds helplessness and compliance, this becomes our generalized pattern of response to the larger questions of our society, and in fact most other aspects of our lives.

▼ In a high-control environment, what is personal and sacred to us is denied. Autocratic governance withers the spirit.

▼ In the marketplace we operate in now, centralized control cannot create product, guarantee quality, or serve customers. This is true for both a whole economy as in Eastern Europe or Russia, as well as for the single organization where we work.

Partnership carries the intention to balance power between ourselves and those around us. It brings into question the utility of maintaining consistency and control as cornerstones of management. It comes from the choice to place control close to where the work is done and not hold it as the prerogative of the middle and upper classes. It also flows from the choice to yield on consistency in how we manage, and thus to support local units in creating policies and practices that fit local situations.

CHOOSING EMPOWERMENT

Another choice is between dependency and empowerment. Dependency rests on the belief that there are people in power who know what is best for others, including ourselves. We think the task of these leaders is to create an environment where we can live a life of safety and predictability. Dependency also holds those above personally responsible for how we feel about ourselves (we want that positive feedback) and for how much freedom we have. I will never forget hearing a supervisor say to his boss, "I want my freedom, if it is all right with you." Dependency is the collusion required for patriarchy and parenting to endure.

If we were not looking so hard for leadership, others would be unable to claim sovereignty over us.

We cannot be leaders without followers, and we cannot be good parents unless we have good children. This dependent mindset justifies and rationalizes patriarchy and keeps it breathing. If we were not looking so hard for leadership, others would be unable to claim sovereignty over us. Our search for great bosses is not that we like being watched and directed, it is that we believe that clear authority relationships are the antidote to crisis and ultimately the answer to chaos.

Empowerment embodies the belief that the answer to the latest crisis lies within each of us and therefore we all buckle up for adventure. Empowerment bets that people at our own level or below will know best how to organize to save a dollar, serve a customer, and get it right the first time. We know that a democracy is a political system designed not for efficiency, but as a hedge against the abuse of power. Empowerment is our willingness to bring this value into the workplace. To claim our autonomy and commit ourselves to making the organization work well, with or without the sponsorship of those above us. This requires a belief that my safety and my freedom are in my own hands. No easy task, therefore the adventure.

Choosing Service

Ultimately the choice we make is between service and self-interest. Both are attractive. The fire and intensity of self-interest seem to burn all around us. We search, so often in vain, to find leaders we can have faith in. Our doubts are not about our leaders' talents, but about their trustworthiness. We are unsure whether they are serving their institutions or themselves. When we look at our peers and our neighbors, we see so much energy dedicated to making sure each gets all of their entitlements. The nuclear family now includes one parent, one partner, children, a financial consultant, a lawyer. We ourselves are no different. We are so career-minded, even though there are so few places to go. Or we have surrendered to life-style and dream of the day we will have our own business...a small but profitable guesthouse-marina-landscape nursery-travel agency-human services conglomerate. We were born into the age of anxiety and become adults in the age of self-interest.

The antidote to self-interest is to commit and to find cause. To commit to something outside of ourselves. To be part of creating something we care about so we can endure the sacrifice, risk, and adventure that commitment entails. This is the deeper meaning of service.

One need ask only one question: "What for?" What am I to unify my being for? The reply is: Not for my own sake.

Martin Buber,
*The Way of Man,
According to the
Teaching of Hasidism*

Let the commitment and the cause be the place where we work. It is not so much the product or service of our workplace that will draw us out of ourselves. It is the culture and texture and ways of creating community that attract our attention. Our task is to create organizations we believe in and to do it as an offering, not a demand. No one will do it for us. Others have brought us this far. The next step is ours. Our choice for service and community becomes the only practical answer to our concern about self-interest.

WE DON'T ACT ON WHAT WE KNOW

What is beguiling about our situation is that we already know a lot about service, about partnership, and about empowerment. The books have been written (I wrote one), the experiments have been conducted, and the results are in. We know, intellectually and empirically, that partnership and participation are the management strategies that create high-performance workplaces. Virtually every medium to large organization showcases the success it has had with self-management, quality improvement efforts, partnerships, autonomous operations, and giving superior service to customers.

Some short examples.

▼ General Motors took its plant in Fremont, California, which had a history of strife and poor performance, and reopened it in partnership with Toyota and the United Auto Workers union. Through this partnership, this plant became one of the most successful in the company, and with essentially the same workforce.

▼ Xerox has taken itself from a history of quasi-militaristic management to formally create district partnerships in each of its field operations. They have brought together the service, sales, and business functions to create a triumvirate, with no single function predominating. A district office, without a single chief. Who would have thought...?

▼ AT&T has its American Transtech. In the late 1970s, Larry McMasters took a unit of the treasurer's office in corporate AT&T, and with heavy employee involvement and empowerment, created an independent, self-sustaining business in Jacksonville, Florida. Over ten years later, through several changes in leadership, some much less participative than Larry's, the culture of involvement sustains itself.

▼ Stew Leonard's is a supermarket whose major asset is Stew Leonard. He wrote the book on partnerships with customers, making money by giving them what they asked for.

In addition to most organizations' having their own pockets of innovation, there is a busload of executives, authors, and consultants traveling around this country to conferences and seminars, telling their stories of workplaces transformed, bureaucracies flattened, employees involved, customers honored, and quality awarded. They are all true stories, with primarily happy endings.

So what's the problem? The problem is that despite this load of knowledge and evidence, there has been disturbingly little fundamental change in the way business, government, health care, and education manage themselves. Even the organizations that are out telling their stories have enormous difficulty in capitalizing on their own experience. One or two plants may be accomplishing miracles, but within the same division, the other fifteen plants still operate business as usual...high command, high control, results acceptable, trying to make a living and doing the best they can. You can go back to 1971 in Topeka, Kansas, where a Gaines Pet Food plant created deep participation, with teams doing their own purchasing and controlling their own work process. They even designed rooms with round corners to symbolize their intention to honor the circle of the team. The plant was successful in its quick start-up, and in the productivity and quality it achieved for many of its early years. It became a showcase, charged people for coming to hear the story, even launched several of its originators into consulting careers. What it did not do was have much influence over the way the multitude of other General Foods plants were managed around the world.

We are so actively engaged in change, yet certain fundamentals remain untouched. Like an old western movie set where a cowboy actor, elbows flapping, pistol smoking, sits on a stationary horse, painted scenery passing by on rollers. Every executive and manager in America has given at least one speech in the last year on the need for change. Every company in America has implemented at least one program intended to empower, one to improve quality, one to embrace customers, and one to "right-size" as a means to flatten its stomach and reduce body fat. These efforts are sincere and each taken alone is generally successful. Something larger, though, like the cowboy's wooden horse in front of the camera, remains unmoved.

What remains untouched is the belief that power and purpose and privilege can reside at the top and the organization can still learn how to serve its stakeholders and therefore survive. When an innovative experiment challenges this fundamental belief about how to govern, one of two things usually occurs. Either the organization rejects the local experiment and it is power and privilege as usual, or an effort is made to drive the experiment across the bottom four layers of the whole institution, never really touching the real centers of control. The way we try to transform large groups of human beings bound together by common goals, with leadership as a big part of the solution, is our wooden horse. Our strategies and beliefs about how to change are not designed to serve, but are the very acts that can keep us frozen. The purpose of this book is to explore what is required to foster changes in our institutions that are truly fundamental and long lasting. If we are not careful, we too quickly lose faith even in the change efforts that we ourselves initiate.

THE LEADERSHIP QUESTION

The search for authentic reform, and the answer to the question why we have such difficulty implementing what we know, begins by questioning our current notions about leadership. Though there is great appeal to the concept of leadership, it will not take us the distance we need to travel. It is not easy to question something that we have been searching for most of our lives, but it is the right starting point.

The strength in the concept of leadership is that it connotes initiative and responsibility. Good friends in hard times. It carries the baggage, however, of being inevitably associated with behaviors of control, direction, and knowing what is best for others. The act of leading cultural or organizational change by determining the desired future, defining the path to get there, and knowing what is best for others is incompatible with widely distributing ownership and responsibility in an organization. Placing ownership and felt responsibility close to the core work is the fundamental change we seek.

To state it bluntly, strong leadership does not have within itself the capability to create the fundamental changes our organizations require. It is not the fault of the people in these positions, it is the fault of the way we all have framed the role. Our search for strong leadership in others expresses a desire for others to assume the ownership and responsibility for our group, our organization, our society. The effect is to localize power, purpose, and privilege in the one we call leader.

Focusing power and purpose at one point in an organization, usually the top, has over time the impact of destroying the culture and very outcomes we sincerely intend to create. One of the clearest examples is our efforts to control nature and exercise dominion over the earth. We have split the atom, cleared our forests, and taken fossil fuels from beneath the ground and placed them in the engines of industrialization. But these triumphs over nature have left us vulnerable, and we do not yet know whether we have the will or the wealth to repair the environment we have wounded.

It is much the same with leadership as an organizing concept. The act of a few, in charge, defining the future, controlling the path, and knowing what is best for others, interferes with its own desire for cultural change as much as it fosters it.

We have the right language about change. We know it is a process and not a program. We know it takes time and training and is evolutionary. We know it requires commitment, not coercion. But then we begin to talk about leadership. It is at this point that we revert to our underlying beliefs about control and direction, and our intent for authentic and lasting change gets undermined.

When the chairman was a Protestant, the Protestants were disappointed; when the chairman was a Catholic, the Catholics were disappointed. If we ever have a woman as chairman, the women will be disappointed.

Earl Shorris,
Scenes from Corporate Life

In the 1960s and early 1970s, we rarely used the term leadership. We talked about managers and managing. Leadership seemed too ill-defined, too much a personality trait and not enough a set of professional skills. You could train managers, how could you train leaders?

The 1980s saw the idea of leadership emerge. Every writer defined leadership, every company listed leadership as a training need, a nation looked for leadership and wondered where it had gone. The attraction of the idea of leadership is that it includes a vision of the future, some transforming quality that we yearn for. Managers get things done, but without heart and passion and spirit. Leaders bring spirit, even integrity, into play.

The wish for leadership is in part our wish to rediscover hope and, interestingly enough, to have someone else provide it for us. We hold on to the belief that hope resides in those with power. In response to this need, we create modern folk heroes. Executives who have turned companies around. Those who have saved Xerox, Harley Davidson Motorcycles, Johnsonville Sausage. Those who have built Federal Express, Apple Computer, Hewlett Packard. Our concern for education has created teachers and principals who stood tall and delivered.

These people write books, are documented on eight-hundred-dollar training videos, and become keynote speakers at conferences. All well and good, they have earned their recognition. That is not the point. The point is does this attention to leadership and leaders serve us? We pay a price for attributing to people in power the ability to transform whole institutions.

▼ The leaders we are looking for have more effect in the news than in our lives.

▼ Great leaders reinforce the idea that accomplishment in our society comes from great individual acts. We credit individuals for outcomes that required teams and communities to accomplish.

▼ Our attention becomes fixated on those at the top. We live the myth that if you do not have sponsorship from the top, you cannot realize your intentions.

▼ People in power who succeed begin to believe their own press. They begin to believe that their institution's success was in fact their own creation.

Is anyone capable of providing us the leadership we are looking for? And if not, is it the failing of the people in power, or is it the problem in the nature of our expectations?

THE UNDERBELLY OF LEADERSHIP

There is something in the way leaders define themselves that inevitably becomes self-congratulatory and over-controlling. We expect leaders to choose service over self-interest, but it seems the choice is rarely made. Successful leaders begin to believe that a key task is to recreate themselves down through the organization. To make their beliefs and actions reproducible. They begin to wonder, "How do I instill in others the same vision and behaviors that have worked for me?" At the moment, this question may seem to the leader like a sincere desire to be of service, but to an observer, it has the stamp of self-interest.

Men **who cannot conceive a happiness of their own accept a definition imposed upon them by others.**

Earl Shorris,
*Scenes from
Corporate Life*

This becomes clear when you read about the way executives describe the basis for their success. One example is the president of a chemical company: we will call him John and the company Atlantic Chemical. His story is an example of how we can do the right thing, put in place the right pieces and programs, yet have the fundamental relationship of parenting leader and dependent organization remain unchanged.

John took over Atlantic Chemical and initiated its turnaround by creating an empowering, people-oriented environment. He decided that the competitive advantage he had, in what was essentially a commodity business, was the attitude of his people. His strategy was to

▼ Flatten the organization by two to four levels, giving everyone more control over what they do.

▼ Create a participative culture, and force the issue with those who did not support a participative style.

▼ Fully inform people about the business and how it was doing in the industry.

▼ Implement pay systems geared to real outcomes and earnings.

▼ Eliminate the trappings of privilege.

▼ Be clear in defining quality in customer-response terms, both internally and externally.

And more. All of which made sense. And worked for the business. He led a struggling division of a large company into becoming a profitable independent business.

The steps that John took were intelligent and of service to the business, but somewhere in the midst of this John began to see himself as more and more central to the success of the business. Undoubtedly encouraged by others, an effort of a different nature began. John started to believe he not only knew what was best for the business, but also the best ways for people to behave; he began to believe that direction and soft coercion were needed from him to create the desired behaviors. He decided then to define the specific behaviors required to be successful at Atlantic. Consultants were brought in to create ways of measuring those behaviors and questionnaires were used to give feedback on those behaviors.

A workshop called "Managing the Atlantic Way" was used to reinforce John's vision and all employees were required to take this course. John continually talked about the need for him to repeat his vision and behaviors for the company over and over and over again, until people got it and believed it. Everyone was appraised each year, measured against whether they were managing the Atlantic Way.

The universal element in John's story is that people in charge begin to think that the way to achieve and institutionalize change is to

- ▼ Define the behaviors required.
- ▼ View themselves as essential to the change.
- ▼ Use education as indoctrination.
- ▼ Redo appraisals to insure compliance.

This is the way strategy turns into dogma. Our notion of leadership, which embraces these actions, too easily focuses ownership at one point. It encourages the replication of one belief system and tends to be very narrow in giving credit for success. Atlantic Chemical's success is now John's success. The governance at Atlantic Chemical remains one of parenting, even if the content of "Managing the Atlantic Way" has major segments on the importance of partnership.

Just **because you own the land, doesn't mean you own the people.**

Philippine land reform saying

The interest we have in people like John is the attraction each of us has to lead and be led. The concept of leadership does not leave much room for the concept of partnership. We need a way to hold on to the initiative and accountability and vision of the leadership idea, and to abandon the inevitable baggage of dominance and self-centeredness.

STEWARDSHIP

THE STEWARDSHIP ANSWER

The alternative to leadership is stewardship. Not a perfect concept, but an entryway into exploring what fundamental change in our organizations would look like and what strategies are conducive to lasting change.

Stewardship asks us to be deeply accountable for the outcomes of an institution, without acting to define purpose for others, control others, or take care of others. Leadership is very different. When we train leaders, the topics of defining purpose, maintaining controls, and taking care of others are at the center of the curriculum. We were raised to believe that if we were to be accountable, we needed the authority to go with it. How many times have we heard the cry, "How can you hold me accountable, without giving me authority?"

Stewardship, as the term is used here, questions the belief that accountability and control go hand in hand. We can be accountable and give control to those closer to the work, operating from the belief that in this way the work is better served. Instead of deciding what kind of culture to create, and thus defining purpose, stewards can ask that each member of the organization decide what the place will become. Stewardship also asks us to forsake caretaking, an even harder habit to give up. We do not serve other adults when we take responsibility for their well-being. We continue to care, but when we caretake, we treat others, especially those in low power positions, as if they were not able to provide for themselves. In our personal relationships we have begun to understand the downside of caretaking, and the dominance that defining purpose for others can represent. What we have not yet done is to apply these concepts to the structure of how we govern. Many individual "leaders" understand the issues, and have the desire to serve, in the best sense, but the machinery of how we manage is filled with prescription and caretaking.

We are reluctant to let go of the belief that if I am to care for something I must control it. If I have stewardship for the earth, I must exercise dominion over the earth—this sort of thinking undermines our intentions. Like the logic that leads to the conviction that the way to protect animals is to put them in the zoo. Behind bars, on view to the caretakers. Now, I have nothing against zoos and aquariums. I like a good shark tank, as well as the next person. But this connection between accountability and control needs to be broken. There needs to be a way for me to be accountable for the earth without having to control it. To be accountable for outcomes of an organization without feeling I must control them.

We are reluctant to let go of the belief that if I am to care for something I must control it.

The desire to see stewardship as simply a different form of leadership is to miss the political dimension of the distinction. When we hold on to the wish for leaders, we are voting status quo on the balance of power. Looking for leadership is some blend of wanting to get on top or stay on top, plus liking the idea that someone up there in my organization or society is responsible for my well-being.

STEWARDSHIP AND BUILDING ORGANIZATIONS

Because it exercises accountability but centers on service rather than control, stewardship is a means to impact the degree of ownership and responsibility each person feels for the success of our organizations, our society, and our lives.

Ownership and responsibility have to be felt strongly at every level—from bottom to top—for democracy to succeed, spiritual values to be lived out, and customers to be served well. Stewardship gives us the guidance system for navigating this intersection of governance, spirituality, and the marketplace.

THREE CHALLENGES OF GOVERNANCE
What is troubling about ideas like stewardship is that even though they are intuitively appealing, they seem removed from the heart of the way we run our organizations. There needs to be a clear connection between the idea of stewardship and achieving concrete

results for the organization. If we do not have a strong business reason to initiate significant reform in our institutions, no real change will take place. Here are three strong business issues that any governance strategy must address for the organization to survive.

DOING MORE WITH LESS

How do we keep making productivity gains? We have fewer and fewer people, and the demand from users and customers stays the same or increases. Cost pressures are enormous, especially in health care and government. In addition to cost, there is the question of quality. What method of governing is most likely to give the gains in quality we need? Quality in part requires the right measures and improvement tools, but fundamentally it comes from individual choice. One person deciding how much ownership and responsibility to take for the quality of product, quality of service, quality of contact with a customer.

LEARNING TO ADAPT TO CUSTOMERS AND OUR MARKETPLACE

We have awakened to the existence of customers, but only barely. Customers want a unique response. They want us to make an exception in response to the specifics of their requirements.

A consistent response to a customer will no longer insure our survival. Customers want a response that is unique to their requirements.

Customer service runs deeper than friendliness, listening skills, and positive attitude. Customers want more control over the relationship with us. They want to choose who serves them, they want influence over the terms of the sale, they want choice in the way the product or service is delivered to them, they want to contact one person, even though their answer may require the cooperation of four different departments. Again, what system of governance is most likely to give the person at the point of contact with the customer the resources, knowledge, and mindset to give the right response?

Then there is the cycle time it takes us to offer a new product or service. Our survival will be dependent on our ability to bring a new service to customers in three months instead of fifteen, to introduce change in the classroom this year instead of next. Can a belief system that demands control, consistency, and predictability deliver short cycle time and highly adaptive responses to clients who have greater and greater choices over where to go to get their needs met?

CREATING PASSION AND COMMITMENT IN EMPLOYEES

Given the challenges, we know we need employees who have chosen to take ownership and responsibility for the success of the organization. Indifference or compliance is a form of passive aggression. People who leave their minds at home and bring their bodies to work will destroy us.

We need commitment from people when we can no longer offer them much security.

What is difficult is that we need commitment from people when we can no longer offer them much security. We cannot promise them lifetime employment, because they may outlive us. Or the unit may disappear. Or we might even change our minds about them. The environment is too unstable to promise a future. We have been forced to betray the mid-century contract that if you work hard and deliver, we will take care of you. We need to create a workplace that evokes commitment that is not based on a false promise.

The fundamental question, then, is what strategy of governance can best control costs, deliver quality, adapt quickly to customers, shorten cycle time, and keep employees driving toward these targets?

Only by rediscovering what it means to commit ourselves to acts of service will these business demands be met. Each member needs to believe the organization is theirs to create if any shift is to take place in how customers are served, students are taught, patients are healed. Cost control and quality improvement are questions of individual accountability and ownership. Strategies of control and consistency, for all their strengths, tend to be expensive, are slow to react to a marketplace, and drain passion from human beings. With the element of service at its core, stewardship creates a form of governance that offers choice and spirit to core workers so they, in turn, can offer the same to their marketplace. When governance has the texture of service, it calls for a like response from those governed. Leadership-based governance, no matter how loving the leader, swims upstream in giving choice and optimism to those at the bottom. A governance based on stewardship's mixture of accountability with partnership, empowerment, and service will give us the means for taking the experimental programs and pocketed successes we now have in our hands and making them more widespread and ingrained as a way of doing business. If we use leadership to disseminate the successful experiments, they will wither from the attempt.

The **first order of business is to build a group of people who, under the influence of the institution, grow taller and become healthier, stronger, more autonomous.**

Robert K. Greenleaf,
Servant Leadership

Setting goals for people, defining the measures of progress toward those goals, and then rewarding them for reaching them does not honor their capabilities. In its most benign form, our control becomes some variation of supervision by a loving parent. Stewardship asks us to serve our organizations and be accountable to them without caretaking and without taking control. And in letting caretaking and control go, we hold on to the spiritual meaning of stewardship: to honor what has been given to us, to use power with a sense of grace, and to pursue purposes that transcend short-term self-interest.

If we take this to heart, this means we are all stewards, but we do not define ourselves by the amount of responsibility we have or how central we are in the eyes of other people. Stewardship in an institutional setting means attending to the service brought to each employee, customer, supplier, and community. To be accountable to those we have power over. This is accountability congruent with the redistribution of power, privilege, and purpose. This means initiating political reform so as to govern in service of those doing the work.

2

CHOOSING PARTNERSHIP OVER PATRIARCHY

Most of our organizations are geared to solve problems of quality and cycle time and adaptability through strategies of control and consistency. Primary responsibility for these strategies lies with top management. Vision, direction, and leadership are expected to come from the top. If these are lacking, those at the top are held responsible. This approach to governance is best characterized by the concept of patriarchy. In its softer forms patriarchy behaves like a parent. In its harsher clothing, we call it names like "autocrat."

CREATING ORDER

Patriarchy is not about leadership style; it is a belief system first and foremost, shared to some extent by us all. Its fundamental belief is that in order to organize effort toward a common goal, which is what organizations are all about, people from top to bottom need to give much of their attention to maintaining control, consistency, and predictability.

CONTROL
Control means that there is a clear line of authority. Decisions about policy, strategy, and implementation are the domain and prerogative of the leader. People at the middle and the bottom exist to execute and implement. In the

PATRIARCHY

context of patriarchy, the definition of service for those in charge is to provide clear goals, well-defined jobs and responsibilities, and mechanisms to make sure all are headed in the right direction. The definition of service for the subordinate is to commit to this direction and to be accountable to those above. Not too complicated, we live it every day.

CONSISTENCY

Consistency means that we need a common way of managing ourselves across the organization. Key policies and practices in areas such as compensation, budgeting, approval authority, information systems, and levels of responsibility of certain managerial jobs need to be similar, whatever your specific function might be.

The primary task of the staff functions of finance, information systems, legal, human resources, and centralized technical groups is to maintain control and consistency across functions. The staff people lead in the creation of policy, they seek the approval of those at the top, and they audit to insure that the policies and strategies are being correctly implemented.

PREDICTABILITY

Patriarchy is also fueled by its need for predictability. If you cannot define outcomes in advance and cannot measure the outcomes, you cannot proceed. The belief is that things that cannot be measured cannot be controlled, and they are therefore unmanageable. Some even feel that if something cannot be measured, it does not exist. (So much for love.) Patriarchy feels about surprises much the same as nature feels about a vacuum.

The risk in relying too heavily on predictability is that basic purpose gets displaced. Strong emphasis on predicting outcomes drives our attention to things that can be measured. This in itself doesn't need to be a problem...we need to know outcomes. A heavy hand, however, leads people to give more attention to the measurement than to the service or product or outcome. We see it in schools when we care more about grades than we do about learning. An extreme example is the principal who personally upgrades student SAT answers to improve his school's scorecard. The moment we decide that scoring is everything, we lose sight of the game, and learn to manipulate the score.

On the surface, patriarchy may appear to be a common sense and logical approach to governance...top leaders in control and responsible for strategy, policy, and rule-making, with staff groups assuring consistent implementation, all in pursuit of predictable, measurable results. From another angle, though, it is possible to see how patriarchy's demands for control, consistency, and pre-dictability become its own obstacle.

DISTRIBUTING OWNERSHIP AND RESPONSIBILITY

The unwitting outcome of our belief in control, consistency, and predictability is that ownership and responsibility for solving the challenges of cost, customer satisfaction, and employer commit-ment are localized primarily at the top of the organization. The practical application of the principles of stewardship hinges on this point. Do you need a strong sense of ownership and responsibility from people doing the core work of the organization? Is this essential to the survival of your unit? If the answer is no, then just get better at the way you govern now. If you need ownership and responsibility from core workers, patriarchy cannot get you there. It steals accountability from the middle and the bottom of the organization. As soon as people at the top, in all good faith, devise ways of control-ling costs, insuring good customer service, and motivating their workforce, time will have passed and ownership and commitment will have to be persuaded, bought, or demanded. Too often, they will have initiated a program that will collapse of its own weight. As soon as the

In business, men do not arrive at totalitarian methods because they are evil, but because they wish to do the good in what seems to them the most efficient way, or because they wish merely to survive, or with no more evil intent than to prosper.

Earl Shorris,
Scenes from Corporate Life

organization's leaders, with support and tactics supplied by their staff functions, demand consistency across the board, they have in effect attempted to legislate accountability.

Coercive strategies to create ownership and responsibility are expensive and difficult to implement. Legislated accountability creates compliance and caution and prevents the short cycle time and unique response to customers that were intended in the first place. The meaning of service gets subverted when it is defined as treating your boss as your most important customer. This is an inversion of institutional purpose. This process is also what creates bureaucracy, which demands policy and procedure in the name of consistency. Patriarchy creates the bureaucratic mindset, the choice for a low-risk operation. High control creates low risk. Legislation creates compliance. A passion for predictability makes a quick and unique response to a customer practically impossible. When patriarchy asks its own organization to be more entrepreneurial and empowered, it is asking people to break the rules that patriarchy itself created and enforces.

*W*hen patriarchy asks its own organization to be more entrepreneurial and empowered, it is asking people to break the rules that patriarchy itself created and enforces.

This is like calling for a horse, without giving up the kingdom. A convoluted prescription for reform.

Governance structures and strategies aimed at control, consistency, and predictability work well in stable, predictable environments. In some sense, they made us great and have brought us to this point. It is these patriarchal beliefs, though, that form the operating reality for most of our institutions—with power, privilege, and rewards concentrated at the top. It is patriarchy itself that breeds self-centeredness and self-interest and gives rise to the ponderous kind of internal political environment we call bureaucracy. What is intriguing, though, is that even though we see the costs of patriarchy, and spend half of our lives complaining about those above us in the hierarchy, we still think leadership is necessary to organize effort and get work done. Our complaint is generally not about the weaknesses of patriarchy as a system of governance, it is that we believe we need a better patriarch.

PARTNERSHIP AS THE ALTERNATIVE

Most of us know and experience daily the limitation of command and control. Part of the reason we continue to operate this way is that we are unsure of the alternative. This is partly because we have never experienced the alternative. The situation brings to mind Bertrand Russell's statement: "The problem with Christianity is that it has never been tried." Same with the alternative to patriarchy.

We are unsure what to even call what we are seeking. Entrepreneurship, intrapreneurship, empowerment, partnership, employee involvement, total quality management, continuous improvement. All have in common the wish to minimize bureaucracy, cut costs, and better serve clients and customers. The ideas of stewardship, empowerment, and partnership are useful because they clearly carry within them the intention of doing something about the distribution of power. If the issues of real power, control, and choice are not addressed and renegotiated, then our efforts to change organizations become an exercise in cosmetics.

The principles of stewardship bring accountability into each act of governance, while partnership balances responsibility. It is the commitment to partnership that gives the meaning of stewardship, as used here, a different complexion. We have a long history of practicing stewardship by taking a parenting stance, where the steward takes responsibility for the well-being of others, often the financial well-being. Stewardship has also taken on teaching and disciplinary responsibilities. For a parent in a family with children, these responsibilities fit. In an organization, where those around us are all adults, taking responsibility for others' performance, learning, and future is a caretaking role that undermines the most effective distribution of ownership and responsibility. This is why partnership is so critical to stewardship. It balances responsibility and is a clear alternative to parenting. The questions "How would partners handle this?" and "What policy or structure would we create if this were a partnership?" are the two most useful questions I know in the search for the alternative to patriarchy.

BALANCING POWER

Partnership means to be connected to another in a way that the power between us is roughly balanced. Stewardship, the exercise of accountability as an act of service, requires a balance of power between parties to be credible. When we talk of supplier-customer partnerships, of marketing-manufacturing-research partnerships, what we are seeking is to recognize the interdependence of the parties and replace control with cooperation. Partnership is the opposite of parenting, and when we are dealing with adults, people over eighteen years of age, stewardship and parenting do not mix. If there is no balance of power, then the name stewardship is simply a new word for an old form of control, even though it may be a loving and caretaking variety. Partnership acknowledges our absolute interdependence.

Partnership occurs when control shifts from

Manager to the core worker.
Supplier to the customer.
Doctor to the patient.
Teacher to the student.
Caseworker to the citizen.

Free consent...is the most basic political act. It enables men to negotiate a social contract that includes a degree of reciprocity between the government and the governed. The giving of consent implies the withdrawal of it, placing limits on power, allowing the recalcitrance of man its opportunity.

Earl Shorris,
*Scenes from
Corporate Life*

This is the way our concern for costs and consistency can be transformed into a concern for quality and response time.

Real accountability and service seek equity in relationships. This is why efforts at implementing stewardship usually begin with some kind of team building activity. Team building is a good way of creating partnership in small groups; it can take the form of renegotiating the relationship between boss and subordinate, or creating open dialogue and clear expectations within a work group or across departmental boundaries. The intent, though, is to do more than improve communication, it is to create a balance of power.

Accountability exchanged in both directions. Demands and requirements flowing both ways.

FOUR REQUIREMENTS OF PARTNERSHIP

Partnership is a broad business strategy, and it can also be expressed in very specific ways. There are four requirements that need to be present to have a real partnership.

EXCHANGE OF PURPOSE

Each party has to struggle with defining purpose, and then engage in dialogue with others about what we are trying to create. Patriarchy has those at the top define purpose for the organization. The traditional process is that management creates its vision, and then the enrollment process begins. Those in the middle and below are told the vision, reminded why it is critical, and given wall plaques, desk cubes, and plastic cards. The middle and below are then asked to enroll in the vision. Sign a card, register in a leather bound book, autograph a picture. The question asked of those below the top is, "What are you going to do to support this vision?" Enrollment is soft-core colonialism, a subtle form of control through participation. Nothing has changed in the belief in control, consistency, and predictability, only the packaging is different.

Partnership means each of us at every level is responsible for defining vision and values. Purpose gets defined through dialogue. Let people at every level communicate about what they want to create, with each person having to make a declaration. Let the dialogue be the outcome. The same process holds for relationships with customers, suppliers, and other stakeholders. Each has a voice in discussing what they want the institution to become.

RIGHT TO SAY NO

Partners each have a right to say no. Saying no is the fundamental way we have of differentiating ourselves. To take away my right to say no is to claim sovereignty over me. For me to believe that I cannot say no is to yield sovereignty. If we cannot say no, then saying yes has no meaning. There are, of course, limits on this. In any community there will always be different levels of authority. The boss will have 51 percent, the subordinate 49 percent. This means that when all is said and done, others will have the right to tell us what to do. This has no effect on our right to say no, even to say it loudly. The notion that if you stand up you will get shot undermines partnership. Partnership does not mean that you always get what you want. It means you may lose your argument, but you never lose your voice.

JOINT ACCOUNTABILITY

The third cornerstone of partnership is joint accountability. Each person is responsible for outcomes and the current situation. There is no one else to blame. Partners each have emotional responsibility for their own present and their own future. Bosses are no longer responsible for the morale, learning, or career of their subordinates. Bosses resign their caretaking role. The outcomes and quality of cooperation within a unit are everyone's responsibility. Each is responsible for maintaining faith, hope, and spirit. In contrast, patriarchy attempts to legislate accountability. Accountabilities are listed, measured, and documented, then purchased by tying them to the pay system. More on this later, but the central point is that if people want the freedom that partnership offers, the price of that freedom is to take personal accountability for the success and failure of our unit and our community.

Partners each have emotional responsibility for their own present and their own future. Bosses are no longer responsible for the morale, learning, or career of their subordinates.

ABSOLUTE HONESTY

Finally, absolute honesty is essential for partnership. Sounds so obvious, but in practice it is difficult. Patriarchal governance creates the social distance and vulnerability that cause us to work so hard to avoid the truth. Patriarchy creates a parent-child relationship between bosses and subordinates, and parents and children don't expect to tell the truth to each other. In a partnership, not telling the truth to each other is an act of betrayal. One of the benefits of redistributing power is that people feel less vulnerable and are more honest.

NO ABDICATION

A word of caution. There is a tendency in each of us when moving from a position of dominance to one of more equality to step back and create a vacuum. When the idea of assertiveness entered our consciousness a few years ago, many males were told they were too aggressive. Our way of doing something about this was to fold our arms, set our jaw, and step back and say, "All right, if you think I am too aggressive, fine. It's all yours." We withdrew, we withheld, we watched in silence. For some of us, this is our favorite learning posture. Give a talk these days to middle-aged white males who did not choose to be in the room, and you will see that silent watching, with folded arms and set jaws, is indeed their favorite learning position. This is passive aggression. This is abdication. Abdication for an individual manager is the first step to supporting anarchy as a governance strategy.

Partnership maintains contact. Fifty-fifty responsibility. Fifty-one—forty-nine with bosses, if you want to be exact, since we still have bosses. Our subordinates need to discover and explore their autonomy, but with us in the room. The difficult part is to maintain contact without control. We often don't know how to have a conversation where neither side is in control. We need to learn to ask questions. To make simple direct statements. To live with not getting our way. To be a boss without playing a role.

We are able to see dominance in other people so much more easily than we see it in ourselves. And so we are blind to the very thing we are trying to change. Withdrawal, though, is not the answer; it is just a defense against seeing clearly how deeply the desire and habit for dominance runs in each of us.

PARTNER IN CHARGE

Partnership does not do away with hierarchy and we still need bosses. People at higher levels do have a specialized responsibility, but it

is not so much for control as it is for clarity. Clarity of requirements. Clarity about value-added ways of attending to a specific market.

There is nothing inconsistent between practicing stewardship and partnership and being a boss. Stewardship is the willingness to hold power, without using reward and punishment and directive authority, to get things done. Leadership performs much the same duties, but is simultaneously concerned with the acquisition and centralization of power. Notice how we keep having to modify the term. We call for good leadership, strong leadership, visionary leadership, participative leadership. Each still represents centralized ownership and thereby centralized power.

Our belief systems about governance inside our organizations still lean in the direction of command economies even though we have ample evidence that as an economic system, command economies cannot serve markets. A surrealistic example is the Trebbie car in East Germany. Until December 1989, East Germans had no choice about what car to buy. It was buy a Trebbie or nothing. Service, product quality, and customer relations had no meaning and no market value. There was a fifteen-year waiting period for a car. You were grateful to get one, if and when it came. The day in December 1989 that East Germany switched to a market economy and the customer could choose what car to buy, sales of Trebbies stopped. Cold. In almost a moment, the operation shifted from a fifteen-year backorder to bankruptcy.

The Trebbie is a powerful symbol of the vulnerability of command economies and the vulnerability of command management systems. Yet we still believe that within one institution, power at the top can serve customers. Partnership is the willingness to give more choice to the people we choose to serve. Not total control, just something more equal. Stewardship maintains accountability for keeping things under control, but does not centralize the power or the point of action. As soon as you centralize the point of action at a higher level, you take away real ownership and responsibility from those closest to the work, the touch labor.

3

CHOOSING ADVENTURE OVER SAFETY

The practice of stewardship requires putting information, resources, and power in the hands of those people closest to making a product, designing a product or service, and contacting a customer. Changing policies, processes, and structure in service of placing knowledge, resources, and power in the hands of those doing the work is what is meant by changing the governance system. This is political reform inside our own organization. It brings us face-to-face with the issues of empowerment and dependency.

Many a manager has opened the door to their employees, and no one walked through it. Most of us chose safety when we took the job, and when the open hand of partnership is offered to us, we know there is a price to be paid. The price is uncertainty and anxiety. We are reluctant to close the chapter on safety and begin the one on adventure.

We choose dependency when we avoid ownership and responsibility by never confronting our own wish for safety and the importance we give our own self-interest. The most common way we maintain dominant and dependent relationships is by clinging to the idea of entitlement.

ENTITLEMENT IS EMPOWERMENT RUN AGROUND

All the recent attention to empowerment has reinforced, unintentionally, our zeal for entitlement. Believing that now empowered we can do exactly what we want, and get all that we ask for, is simply trying to win at the new game. Doing our own thing is a self-serving act. As subordinates we can use empowerment as a weapon. In the name of empowerment I have heard people ask for

- ▼ More pay.
- ▼ Larger budget.
- ▼ More people, more empire.
- ▼ Freedom to pursue strictly personal projects.
- ▼ Greater recognition and privilege.
- ▼ Immunity from disappointment from those above.
- ▼ A risk-free environment.

Wrong. Just because we have been encouraged to find our voice and stand up without getting shot, it does not mean that we are

Few men desire liberty; most men wish only for a just master.

Sallust (86-34 B.C.)

going to get all we ask for, nor can we expect to be protected. Partnership is a commitment to a dialogue, not an act of concession. Stewardship is based on reciprocal commitments. No licenses issued.

In coming out of a high-control governance system there is tendency to take advantage of the choice handed us. Partly to test the sincerity of the offer, partly as small acts of revenge. Some other ways people exploit their freedom:

▼ If a decision is made we don't agree with, we begin to undermine that decision, either actively or passively.

▼ We do not take responsibility for promises others in our unit have made. The belief that no one else can represent my viewpoint is a subtle form of anarchy.

▼ In expressing our opinion, we expect immunity from other people's anger. I was in an elevator with some middle managers following a general management meeting. In the meeting the president disagreed with one of them and had been pretty outspoken about it. The

manager in the elevator said, "I'll never speak up and get punished like that again." I thought, "You weren't punished, he was simply irritated. No blood, no arms taken, no careers aborted. Someone in power just got angry." Calling others' anger punishment is a form of manipulation.

At the heart of entitlement is the belief that my needs are more important than the business and that the business exists for my own sake. The careerism and exploding accumulation of material goods of the 1980s will be with us for a long time. Just because the calendar signals a new decade does not change our mentality and expectations. At some point each of us has to discover that our self-interest is better served by doing good work than getting good things. The more our job and our survival is on the line, the easier it is to make this discovery. In this way hard times are an ally.

Entitlement also rests on the belief that something is owed us because of sacrifices we have made. Granted, working under patri- archal governance does require sacrifice, and we feel something grand is due us for having given away a part of ourselves. What is hard to accept, though, is that, whatever we think we sacrificed, it was a choice that we made. We have to reclaim what we gave away. No one owes it to us. In fact, the more the organization gives us for what we may not have earned, the more entitled we feel. Entitlement is claiming rights that have not been earned. Entitlement diminishes self-esteem and restrains freedom. It is the inevitable outcome of caretaking. The only way to reclaim what we have lost is through acts of commitment and service to some larg- er entity than ourselves—in this case, our workplace.

CHOOSING EMPOWERMENT

The decision to pursue the principles and practice of stewardship is an issue of business strategy, but at its core, it is first a matter of individual choice. Managers can create the social architecture and practices to support partnership and empowerment, but individu- als have to make the decision to reclaim their own sovereignty, and this is no small matter either.

SURVIVAL IN OUR OWN HANDS

For each of us as individuals, empowerment means placing ourselves in the position of being creators of the organization to which we belong. Empowerment is embodied in the act of standing on our own ground, discovering our own voice, making our own choices. Regardless of the level of power and privilege we hold. It stems from our choice of the mindset that tells us that we have within ourselves the authority to act and to speak and to serve clients and those around us. We do not need permission to feel or to take what matters into our own hands.

DEFINING PURPOSE

In addition to enabling us to find our voice, empowerment means that we each have the right to define purpose for ourselves. Purpose has to do with the defining kind of culture we live within, not just with deciding what business we are in or what goals to pursue. We are deciding moment to moment what kind of culture we want to create. No need to wait for top management to declare their vision. By the time we get clear on the vision of those above, it will be too late. Like computer technology...the moment it hits the marketplace, it is obsolete. If those above have a vision, we want to know it and support it, but it does not substitute for our own.

COMMITMENT

Empowerment carries with it an obligation, and that is that we commit ourselves. It requires an emotional investment. To act now, to live with consequences, with failure. To give up our wish for safety. Taking responsibility is at the heart of claiming our freedom. The commitment has to be to the community within our workplace, not just to our own interests or our own career. Our answer to the question, "Are you here to build a career or to build an organization?" has to be clear and without hesitation...we are here first to build the organization.

Each of us has to create our own effort, conduct our own experiment, name our own child. We will experience our freedom the moment we take our assignment, our job, and make it our own.

When we move from being a participant to being a creator. What makes work fun is the act of re-creation. Recreation. That is why recess was one of our favorite subjects in school. It was the moment during the day where we could claim some small remnant of sovereignty over our actions. It is everybody's task to create a vision and translate these intentions into concrete practices.

𝒟o you call yourself free? I want to hear your ruling idea, and not that you have escaped from a yoke.

Friedrich Nietzsche,
Thus Spoke Zarathustra

We each create our purpose with or without the support of those who run our organization. We do not need sponsorship from above to do the right thing. All we really need from bosses is tolerance or indifference. The only reliable leadership for transforming cost, quality, and service is our own. It begins the moment we claim the change as ours to make. Not necessarily ours alone, but ours nevertheless.

STEWARD TO THOSE ABOVE US

Instead of expecting our leaders to give us direction, our job, then, is to teach those above us how an effective community is created. We become the customers of our bosses, and the job of the customer is to teach the supplier how to do business. We create in our own unit what we would like to see embodied in the whole organization.

If it is our task to teach partnership, empowerment, and service to those above us, it is the task of those above us to give us focus, to give us aim into the marketplace. They have a wider view; they have usually been in our business longer and have more experience. They have the luxury of a longer time perspective. When they stop being so busy watching us, they can think about the next three years while we agonize over the next three hours. We need our leaders to interpret the marketplace and the environment to us, to give us the boundaries within which we can create community, to tell us what is required to sustain ourselves economically and in offering our product and service.

When people in the middle and below (emotionally, that is all of us) are given clear focus and knowledge of the playing field and its boundaries, they will teach those above how stewardship can be lived in the pursuit of specific purpose.

We may have lost faith that this can happen. We equate partnership and even democracy with indecision, special interests, self-centeredness, and potential chaos. We have much more experience with patriarchy than with democracy. To say that we are deeply democratic in practice is to smooth over the real centralization of power that exists. That is why each organization has to discover participation and partnership for itself.

One final note. The goal of political reform in our workplaces is not to find new people to occupy leadership positions. The current ones are just fine. In fact they are increasingly aware that they cannot meet their goals without significantly changing the ways their organizations are governed. They can see that dependent subordinates and elaborate control systems do not serve customers, do not really control costs, and do not bring innovative answers to quality problems. They can see that more autonomy is needed lower down in the organization. They may be cautious in doing anything about it, but they see it. An example is Bill Ellis, the head of Northeast Utilities. When asked why he was interested in empowerment, his answer was, "When I noticed that the people in Eastern Europe were shooting their leaders, I started to pay attention."

To say that we are deeply democratic in practice is to smooth over the real centralization of power that exists.

STEWARDSHIP BEGINS AT HOME

A major obstacle to reform is our tendency to externalize the problem. As soon as we begin to talk about realigning power and privilege, we think of those who won't. We know them, we work for them, they work for us.

A friend of mine who works for a big telecommunications company was asked to devise ways for people at the bottom of the organization to take more ownership for the success of the business. One of his recommendations was to eliminate reserved parking for the top executives...a symbolic gesture to communicate we are all part of the same team working toward the same goal. He suggested this to Bob, the general manager, and Bob's response was, "If you ask for my parking space now, you will want my salary later. I don't want to give you my salary, I know you don't want to give your people your salary. The answer is no." Bob got the point and gave an honest response. (My answer to Bob would have been, "You can keep your salary, it is your privilege and prerogatives that we want.")

What is important is not that people like Bob won't yield, it is that Bob speaks for each of us. We each have enormous ambivalence about our own choices. We don't want to have to choose between acting on our beliefs or our ambition. We want to go to heaven, but we don't want to die.

One way we avoid dealing with our own doubts is by focusing on the doubts of others. Conversations about empowerment always seem to turn to a discussion of how we are going to change other people. These outward glances at some point need to turn inward. Bringing our own spirituality into the workplace is an inward journey. The revolution begins in our own hearts. It is the conversation about the integrity of our own actions that ultimately gives us hope.

There is little we can do about the integrity of other people's actions. Others' actions are there to distract us. Yet so much of the management literature is still written about how to analyze and control other people. Even though Bob, and others like him, stand in our way, there is little we can do about him. We are not going to change him. The harder we fight him, the stronger he gets. We do have to take a stand with Bob, but he is not the real problem. We are the starting point. Over and over again. We are the ones who are slow in getting the point of our own aspirations.

The spirit demands an inward focus. It needs the conversation about what we are doing to interfere with serving our markets and constituents. It worries about the clarity of our own intentions rather than the impact of others' actions. The focus outward, looking for the difficulty in others, is how we betray ourselves. We need to keep one eye on the marketplace, for that is the ultimate focus of our accountability long term. But we cannot exercise accountability to the marketplace without also demonstrating internal accountability and answering our own questions about how we are living out our purpose. Our impact on our governance systems is directly related to

OUR COLLUSION

It is possible that the origins of
totalitarianism lie neither in the
aberrations of history nor in the
failures of economic systems to
maintain living standards, but in
man himself. If so, the primary
task of freedom is no less than
for man to overcome his own
nature, and to do his business in
a way befitting a creature
capable of transcending himself.

Earl Shorris,
Scenes from Corporate Life

the extent to which we are able to live
out our own purpose...especially in the
midst of the politicized and patriarchal
environments that we choose to be part
of. What is difficult about social change
is to stay focused on the intimate connections between our own ability to
embody our intentions both inwardly, in
our own consciousness, and externally in
the way we express our beliefs in our
institutions.

The effort to reform the governance
system of our own institution is tied first
to our personal system of self-gover-
nance. Tied to the way we manifest our belief in consistency, control,
and predictability in our own actions...even as we distrust our own
feelings, our own intuition, our deeper knowing, even our own spirituality. For example, we generally agree that we want to eliminate
bureaucracy. Bureaucracy is patriarchy in the extreme, with people
being overly cautious, choosing safety over risk, being more interested in self than in service, exercising control for its own sake. No
amount of effort to change these qualities around us will be effective until we have confronted these qualities in ourselves. Part of
what sustains patriarchy/bureaucracy is our own caution, our own
wish for safety, our own self-service and desire for control.

It is not that we have created the patriarchy around us. What we
have done is colluded with it. We cannot mature inside a culture
without having internalized aspects of it. Our ability to change our
political environment begins with the understanding of how we have
helped create it. Our consciousness is where the revolution begins.
Fifty percent of the work we need to do is on ourselves. The other 50
percent is to focus outward and use ideas like stewardship to
redesign the practices, policies, and structures that institutionalize
what we wish to become.

4

CHOOSING SERVICE OVER SELF-INTEREST

Stewardship holds the possibility of shifting our expectations of people in power. Part of the meaning of stewardship is to hold in trust the well-being of some larger entity—our organization, our community, the earth itself. To hold something of value in trust calls for placing service ahead of control, to no longer expect leaders to be in charge and out in front.

There is pride in leadership, it evokes images of direction. There is humility in stewardship, it evokes images of service. Service is central to the idea of stewardship.

A MODEL OF STEWARDSHIP

The idea of service through stewardship has been with us forever in a religious context. The Bible directs us to care for the earth. Many of our religious institutions have practiced stewardship for ages, primarily as an exercise of financial responsibility. Stewardship committees today function as fund-raising groups, and sometimes they also have a voice in deciding how to distribute funds to worthwhile causes in the community. Corporate stewardship has come to mean financial responsibility for both the institution and the community it lives in. Stewardship for our purposes, though, goes beyond financial accountability and beyond being accountable for the right use of the talents given to us. Stewardship here has a political dimension in that it is

A poignant metaphor of "stewardship" has emerged. Especially recently—the idea that humans are the caretakers of the Earth, put here for the purpose, accountable, now and into the indefinite future, to the Landlord.

Carl Sagan, speaking about the environment

also concerned with the use of power. One intent of stewardship is to replace self-interest with service as the basis for holding and using power.

It is not surprising we should look to religious models for ways of thinking about the right use of power. Our best religious leaders have flourished through the ages in part because they have understood how to exercise accountability and activism in service to their followers. Mahatma Gandhi is one of the best examples in this century of integrating the religious and the political so well. Gandhi identified three elements making up his brand of service-based power, which he called trusteeship. Granted Gandhi sets a rather high standard, but his principles expand our understanding of stewardship's political meaning.

POWER IS GRANTED FROM THOSE BELOW

The community creates the opportunity for a person to be in a position of power. Power is bestowed upon us by those we "lead." We do not claim power, it is not passed on to us by others in power, we have no inherent right to power, whether by birthright, talent, or even achievement. If we serve those who put us in our position, then in an organization the recipients of our service and trusteeship are the core workers. They are the community, and they are the ones we become accountable to. We may be appointed by a board, or an executive, but they are given their authority as much by the people doing the work as by any other set of owners.

OUR CONTRIBUTION IS OUR HUMANITY

The obligation of accepting a position of power is to be, above all else, a good human being. Not to be a good leader, not so much to maintain order and fight back chaos, not to know what is best for others…these are the qualities of being a good parent. If you are a boss, the people working for you definitely have expectations of you to be their good parent, but this is not stewardship.

Stewardship is the willingness to work on ourselves first, to stay in intimate contact with those around us, to own our doubts and limitations, and make them part of our dialogue with others. Our humanness is defined more by our vulnerability than our strengths. This is something different from leading from the heart, or walking our talk, or articulating a vision.

WHAT IS TRUE IS KNOWN TO EACH OF US

Trust comes out of the experience of pursuing what is true. What is true lies within each of us. Stewardship is founded on the belief that others have the knowledge and the answers within themselves. We do not have to teach other adults how to behave. Going back to the Atlantic Chemical example in Chapter 1, John does not have to define for his employees what the desired behaviors are, or to send each person through a workshop on "Managing the Atlantic Way." Or to spell out for middle managers what their new role will be in an empowered environment. More parenting. John's task is to be clear about his own experience and attend to his own learning. This is what will be contagious.

Our survival depends on our taking the idea of service to constituents and making it concrete in our governance systems. The quality and customer service movement has the right idea but is implementing it through patriarchal governance strategies. Service-based governance strategies mean the redistribution of power, privilege, purpose, and wealth. All the team building, improvement teams, and skills training in the world will not create service if the institutional questions of choice and equity never change. This is why organizations have such a difficult time taking advantage of their own successful experiments. It would force them to redistribute power and ultimately privilege.

TEACHING REVOLUTION
TO THE RULING CLASS

We serve when we build capability in others by supporting owner-ship and choice at every level. We cannot continue to govern through patriarchy and say that we just want to be of service. When we act to create compliance in others, we are choosing self-interest over service, no matter what words we use to describe our actions. Service-givers who maintain dominance, aren't. Stewardship at the organizational level has to directly address the redistribution of power, and the redesign of fundamental management practices. Not for their own sake, but in service of the redistribution of felt ownership and felt responsibility.

A colleague, Sarah Polster, after hearing some of my views about empowerment, once said, "You are teaching revolution to the ruling class." The phrase stayed with me. There is something both unset-tling and very true about it. The truth is that we are, in fact, talking about a revolution. Revolution means a turning. Changing direction. The act of revolving. It means the change required is significant, obvious even to the casual observer. Obvious, for example, even to customers. It is more comforting to talk about evolutionary change. Evolutionary change means that everything is planned, under con-trol, and reasonably predictable. In every group I work with, at some point someone will raise their hand and declare, "Aren't we really talking about evolutionary change? We don't want to throw the baby out with the bath water." That baby gets a lot of baths. The problem with evolutionary change is that it is virtually unnoticeable to the participants. You have to look back over many generations to see any difference. If you want to make changes that go unrecognized, pick an evolutionary path. Patriarchy's attempts to change itself have been traditionally evolutionary, the choice of self-interest.

The revolution is for organizations to become the place where our personal values and economics intersect. Reforming our organizations so that our spirit is answered, and our ability to serve customers in the broadest sense is guaranteed. Stewardship is the strategy that embodies this goal. Stewardship enables the use of power with grace.

What is unique about this revolution—and gives us hope—is that it is being initiated by the ruling class, the managerial class. Stewardship is a revolution initiated and designed by those in power.

THE RULING CLASS

It is only a bit of an overstatement to say that the ruling class in our culture is our managers and executives. They are the class of people who drive much of what we do. They control the majority of our resources, they are the heroes of the American dream. We have no royalty, no powerful church. It is the executives of our organizations who have paved our streets with gold.

Patriarchy's attempts to change itself have been traditionally evolutionary, the choice of self-interest.

We have all created this ruling class. We have separated those who manage the work from those who do the work. In attempting to professionalize the role of managing, we have created a class of managers. We talk of management prerogatives. We invent special management privileges. We train the managerial class in our MBA programs. If you do not believe this ask the graduates of MBA programs about their expectations. They want to start at the top, and move up from there. And why not? We glamorize management, and treat it as a job title, even a profession, not as a set of functions. Management tasks and skills have been husbanded and herded into specific jobs. High-status, highly valued jobs which have developed their identity by excluding lower levels from exercising certain rights and privileges.

We have intentionally structured our organizations so as to exclude lower levels of an organization, those doing the core work, from planning, organizing, and controlling their own work. We admonish managers to put down their calculators, take off their lab coats, put on a tie, and get to the business of watching others work. And we have titles and labels that separate the management class from the working class: exempt/non-exempt, salaried/hourly, manager/individual contributor. These classifications of employees grew out of the industrial age, which put a premium on specialization, clearly defined roles, economies of scale, and large-is-beautiful thinking.

Ruling Class

The managerial class begins at the second level of supervision and extends upwards. This is where control is exercised and consistency demanded. The managerial class also includes most staff functions. They have become the eyes and ears of management. To enforce management intentions through policing and auditing and monitoring activities. Surveillance. External consultants extend the class further. They pursue their economic interests by aligning themselves with the concerns of the managerial class. The pursuit of economic self-interest through the maintenance of control is the essence of the managerial class.

Two problems with having a managerial class are that it is too expensive and it creates obstacles to improving quality, to giving customers what they want, and to succeeding in a volatile and unpredictable marketplace. A strong class structure makes an organization incapable of offering real service. The more levels in an organization, the slower the response time. The more watching and inspecting, the less responsibility people need to take for the quality of their work.

Having a managerial class, aligned with strong staff groups and separated in a hundred ways from those doing the work, is a major obstacle to empowerment and partnership. Having a group of people whose job is to watch and monitor steals accountability and responsibility from those doing the work. We can neither legislate nor engineer accountability. Having others define for us our accountabilities, measure us against them, and pay us in accordance with their measurements creates a culture of caution and compliance. Compliance is the antithesis of the emotional ownership that real accountability means. If we need an employee who takes personal responsibility for making a product, reducing cycle time, serving a customer, we cannot get there through better systems of directing, planning, and controlling.

Getting better at patriarchy is self-defeating. Having one group manage and one group execute is the death knell of the entrepreneurial spirit. We so often speak of employee involvement and participation, but they are not enough. Those doing the work need to have responsibility for managing the work. And this happens most effectively at the initiation of the managers.

What is required for real stewardship is the reintegration of managing the work with doing the work. This is empowerment. This is partnership. This is the right use of power.

RANK WITHOUT PRIVILEGE

Stewardship not only affects the use of power, but it also confronts the way we hold privilege. If we use power as an act of service, then we are required to let go of the idea that we should be waited upon. We can no longer hold on to privileges. We each type, make coffee, make travel reservations at work, we clean and cook at home. It has come to this.

If you start to embrace the right use of power, then you begin to redistribute privilege as well, and this is a very tender area. Holding on to privilege is an act of self-interest, the antithesis of service and stewardship. If we wish to send ownership and responsibility down to the people close to the work, then we are required to send along privilege as their companion.

ADVISE AND CONSENT

If our organizations are to survive, the redistribution of purpose, power, and privilege will have to take place with the involvement and consent of those who in some ways stand to lose the most, the managerial class. And this is basically what choosing service requires. Examine any experiment in self-management or work redesign, and you will discover that some supervisor, middle manager, or executive chose to relinquish their own control and prerogatives in service of the higher-order goal of doing what is right and good for the unit. This is the act of stewardship that constitutes genuine reform. This is the manager acting as social architect and sponsor of

The history of mankind on its road to redemption [is] a process involving two kinds of men, the proud who, if sometimes in the sublimest form, think of themselves, and the humble, who in all matters think of the world. Only when pride subjects itself to humility can it be redeemed; and only when it is redeemed, can the world be redeemed.

Martin Buber,
The Way of Man, According to the Teaching of Hasidism

political reform, designing ways to transfer to those doing the work the responsibility for the planning, guiding, and monitoring that was formerly theirs alone.

Taken seriously, this transfer of responsibility produces a shift in the political structure of the workplace. It confronts each of us with the choice of where to give first priority: to build an organization or to pursue self-interest? Stewardship is for those managers and workers who are willing to risk the class distinctions and privilege that signified their careers, in the pursuit of living out a set of values and creating an organization where each member has a sense of ownership and responsibility.

CONNECTING THE HEART AND THE WALLET

The revolution is also about the belief that spiritual values and the desire for economic success can be simultaneously fulfilled. Stewardship taken seriously is not just an economic strategy or a way to achieve higher levels of productivity or to succeed in a marketplace. It is also an answer to the spirit calling out.

Spirituality is the process of living out a set of deeply held personal values, of honoring forces or a presence greater than ourselves. It expresses our desire to find meaning in, and to treat as an offering, what we do. To embrace stewardship is to discover that all this is possible as a member of the working and middle class. Doing work that has meaning need not be reserved as a luxury or fringe benefit for the ruling class, or postponed until later in life. Offering people at the bottom more choice and control over what they do gives them the means to find purpose at work. But suggesting that people live out their personal beliefs without a shift in the governance system is using participation as a means of getting people to adapt more cheerfully to their helplessness. If all we do is seek input from time to time and engage in strategic or situational involvement,

She: **What do you do for a living?**
He: **I work for a company that makes bottle caps, but it's not as exciting as it sounds.**

From an unremembered movie

our invitation to participate becomes manipulation. Patriarchy as usual with a human touch.

The other side, economics, is where the war is currently being fought. Survival is now a question as never before. Higher quality of goods and services, lower costs, and rapid innovation determine survival. The governance system we grew up with cannot deliver quality, costs too much, and is ill-suited to meet the need for rapid change.

Patriarchal institutions cannot serve their customers. Therefore they essentially fail in the marketplace, and economics is the measuring rod for their failure. Schools only teach a portion of their students, government perpetuates helplessness and futility in its constituents. Health care providers, volunteer organizations, business and industry all seem to hang in the balance. The marketplace for each institution is its reality. To embrace stewardship, choosing service over self-interest, is to join the testing ground for integrating personal and economic values and making the spirit concrete and practical.

THE POINT

Stewardship depends on a willingness to be accountable for results without using control or caretaking as the means to reach them. This demands a choice for service with partnership and empowerment as basic governance strategies. Here are actually six points which capture the essence of these ideas. If you can make it through these, the practical and specific are right around the corner.

POINT ONE

We want to affirm the spirit. There is a longing in each of us to invest our energy in things that matter. In a high-control environment, what is personal and sacred is left at the door. We need a way to govern that affirms the person as truly central to the business. We have always spoken the right words—people are number one—but patriarchy cannot deliver on the promise. Patriarchy can

Summary

take care of us, but caretaking is not affirmation. Leaders can definitely treat us well, but affirmation comes only from the person taking responsibility and owning their own actions.

POINT TWO

Some of the fundamental beliefs we have about how to run organizations and organize work aren't working. We have grown up with the belief that control, consistency, and predictability are essential. Even our efforts to implement employee involvement, empowerment, inverted pyramids, and self-management are driven by the requirement for control, consistency, and predictability.

This paradox represents our struggle in choosing between patriarchy and partnership.

Partnership springs from the belief that balancing power and accountability is the basis upon which to govern and upon which to bring about reform.

POINT THREE

There is the dominant belief that leadership should come from the top and bosses are in some way responsible for their employees' performance and morale, much as loving parents are responsible for their children. A corollary is the idea that organizational change efforts should start at the top and cascade down.

Holding to this line of thought represents the choice of dependency over empowerment.

Empowerment means that each member is responsible for creating the organization's culture, for delivering outcomes to its customers, and especially for the quality of their own experience. This is the adventure.

POINT FOUR

We have separated the managing of the work from the doing of the work. We have created a class system inside our institutions. There is a management class and an employee or worker class.

The management class enjoys privileges and prerogatives and is taught management skills. The worker class has fewer privileges and prerogatives and is taught operational or basic skills.

This two-class system reflects the choice of self-interest over service.

A commitment to service requires us to reintegrate the managing and the doing of the work.

POINT FIVE

Despite our belief in the need for change, the actions most often disappoint. Part of the problem is that you cannot solve the problem by using the same management strategies that created the problem. What is happening is that most organizations are trying to *engineer* and *direct* the movement toward customer service, quality improvement, and cost containment. The very system that has patriarchy as the root problem uses patriarchal means to try to eliminate its symptoms. This is the dark side of leadership.

POINT SIX

We have implemented and perpetuated work structures, financial control systems, information systems, performance appraisal and reward systems, and other management practices that reinforce the class system and reenact in a thousand ways the primacy of consistency, control, and predictability. These practices also keep ownership and responsibility focused at the top. They are designed to control costs and produce consistent, predictable results. They are obstacles to quality and service. They are the tangible aspects of the political system we have set out to reform.

PART II

THE REDISTRIBUTION OF POWER, PURPOSE, AND WEALTH

Often our focus on change is aimed at better communication, working as a team, meeting to decide how to cut costs, and giving recognition for exceptional contributions. These actions do not change the rules, they simply help us better adapt to the same game. For the game to change, hard currency has to change hands. In organizations, hard currency is rearranging who makes choices, who defines culture, who determines the measures, and who shares in the wealth.

It is in our willingness to pass around the tools of real value that our sincerity is clarified. It is now time to get practical.

▼ ▼ ▼

A Case Study:
Sometime Later in the Week

This is both a break in the action and a test. At the conclusion of this drama of industry in action, you will be asked two questions: "What is the problem?" and "What is the solution?"

THE NEED

February 11—My requirements seem simple enough. All winter I had been staring at two telephone poles and their wires winding up the center of my front yard. I finally call the power company to request that the power line to my house be put underground. They tell me that a field technician would have to make a site visit to determine feasibility and cost. I will have to call the field technician between 7:00 and 9:00 in the morning or 3:00 and 4:00 in the afternoon. The field technicians cannot call me, they have too many requests and are in the field.

THE PLAYERS

February 12—I call the field technician. He is busy. I say it is urgent, he comes to the phone. I ask when can he come to the house? He says that this week is booked and he does not schedule next week until Thursday. Besides, the phone company needs to be there at the same time because it is their pole. I ask who coordinates with the phone company? The customer, he says.

February 25—Arthur, the field technician, walks the property. The phone company is in attendance. I ask, "Can we put this power line underground?" Arthur replies, "Don't see why not, but it is not the field technician's call." I ask, "What will it cost?" Arthur says, "It is hard to tell, depends on the length of the distance from the street." Patiently, I ask, "Can you measure the distance?" Arthur measures, says it is 400 feet from the street. The power company covers the first 150 feet, the rest requires a customer contribution. I ask, "When can it be done?" Arthur doesn't know. He has to go back to the office and calculate the cost and requirements and have the line foreman look at it. He agrees to send me the customer contribution letter. When I pay the money, he can see about scheduling the work. That's fine.

THE SQUEEZE

Four weeks pass. No letter. No word from Arthur. The electrician, contractor, phone company, and cable company all agree this is typical. Hassling does not help. I call Arthur, he is busy. I say it is urgent, he comes to the phone. "Arthur, where is my customer contribution letter? Has the foreman been to the site? When can we schedule the work?" Arthur says he has been busy locating lines. The letter takes about ten minutes to write, but he has been busy locating lines. I ask what can I do to make this a priority? Arthur suggests I call his boss, Mr. Phillips. He is the one having Arthur locate all those lines. He says he will try to get to my job soon.

I call again in four days, he says the letter went out that very day, even as we speak. I ask what the process is once I pay and return the letter. He says I need the meter moved, hooked up to the panel in the basement, and inspected by the town building inspector. Next, get the phone company to put in a new pole, and then contact Arthur, who will have the line foreman schedule the work.

April 5—I get the customer contribution letter. It is called a "customer contribution" to emphasize the point that my payment only covers part of the cost of the job. I make my contribution.

April 8—The meter is approved. The new pole is in place. The contractor who is doing other work on my house says they have been trying to get Arthur going with no success. I call Arthur. He is not available. I say it is urgent, Arthur comes to the phone. I ask what is now needed to get my line in. He says I need to dig the trench, and the foreman has to inspect it. Then beginning on

Thursday, the foreman schedules the work for the following week. Arthur says if I dig the trench by Thursday, the foreman will inspect it on Friday and the crew will be there on Monday to lay the line, rebuild the pole, and remove the old transformer. I agree to have the trench dug by Thursday. I ask what else is required, he says the phone company and cable company have to be there to put their lines in the trench before we can cover it up. All need to be there on Monday at 8:30 a.m. I ask Arthur if he will coordinate with them, since he is doing this with them all the time. No, Arthur says the power company does not get involved in scheduling with other utilities, that is the customer's responsibility. So I contact them all and get them ready to go on Monday.

April 15—The trench was dug by Thursday. Monday morning, on site are the contractor, the electrician, the cable company, the telephone company, the backhoe operator, and a worker to refill the trench. Six people, organizing their schedules around the power company, ready to go at 8:30 a.m. The power company does not show. I call Arthur, he is in the field. Locating lines. At 1:00 p.m. my gang of six gives up waiting. To a person they say this is typical. The phone company and cable company lay their lines, even though we have not got an official o.k. from the power line foreman. At 3:00 p.m., one of the carpenters working on the job sees the yellow truck of the power company. He goes out to see what is happening, and the truck takes off, no contact.

THE CRISIS

April 16—At 7:00 a.m., I call Arthur. He is tied up. I say it is urgent. Arthur comes to the phone. I ask, "What happened?" He doesn't know, he was out locating lines. I ask when he could find out. He puts me on hold and contacts the line foreman. Arthur comes back and says the line foreman inspected the job on Monday and the trench is fine. I say that the work was scheduled for Monday morning, what happened? He had promised that the inspection would be done the prior Friday. Arthur says he never said that, he claims he had said the inspection would be done Friday or Monday. If I had scheduled all those people there Monday morning, it was my mistake. I ask, "When can we get this scheduled?" Arthur puts me on hold, comes back and says the foreman will try to schedule the job "sometime later in the week." I lose it. I tell Arthur that I cannot ask six people to be available "sometime later in the week." He says the foreman told him that four of his linemen were in commercial driver's training class this week, so he is shorthanded. Sometime later in the week they would try to get to the job. I shout to Arthur, "I am a customer, Arthur. Is there anyone in your company who will treat me like a customer?" Arthur thinks for a moment. I can tell it is a difficult question. He says, "If that is what you want, maybe you should try Mr. Graham, supervisor of line foremen." I call Mr. Graham, who does in fact treat me like a customer. In an hour he has called me back and scheduled the job for Thursday, April 18, at 8:30 a.m. Thursday comes, so does the power company, the electrician, the contractor, the tractor operator, and worker and the job gets done.

THE TEST

Now for the test. Since we have so little time together, we will make it multiple choice. First, what is the problem?

1. Arthur is an unmotivated worker. He brings his body to work and leaves his mind and his heart at home.

2. Arthur lacks training in customer relations and empowerment.

3. The power company lacks teamwork and coordination between departments. The customer is left to navigate between the silos in the company.

4. The problem is a lack of clear goals. Arthur's boss, Mr. Phillips, has not made it clear to Arthur how to balance locating lines versus satisfying residential customers.

5. Mr. Phillips lacks supervisory skills. Arthur's time is too tightly controlled and Arthur is given no real freedom or responsibility to satisfy customers.

6. The appraisal process does not give adequate emphasis to timeliness or customer service.

7. The power company does not have a strong corporate culture. Arthur has not been enrolled in top management's vision and values, which are to delight customers.

8. The power company has not made the commitment to total quality. Their "Quality through Excellence" program has somehow missed Arthur.

9. Being a public utility and a virtual monopoly, there is no real economic incentive for Arthur to get it going.

10. Where is the problem? The job got done. The customer got what he wanted. Why is everybody in such a hurry?

11. All of the above. Therefore, none of the above.

12. Other.

POSSIBLE SOLUTIONS

Now that the problem is defined, we need an action plan. Your solution will grow our of your assessment of the problem. Here are some general categories of solutions.

TRAINING

Most companies are investing heavily in training to change Arthur's behavior. Arthur gets trained, Mr. Phillips gets trained. The training can be on total quality, customer focus, team development, dealing with difficult subordinates.

Sign here if you think training is the answer. _____

COMMUNICATION

Many places have efforts to communicate heavily with Arthur and Mr. Phillips. Meetings are held about the new era of competition, the importance of the customer, the new values and the change in culture that is required. Videotapes of top management are made for emphasis and those who cannot attend.

Sign here for better communication. _____

CLEAR STANDARDS AND REWARDS

Expectations of both Arthur and Mr. Phillips could be made clearer. Minimum response times could be set for Arthur. The power company's performance appraisal process could focus more on customer service. The customer, me, could be sent surveys on satisfaction and these could be used in Mr. Phillips and Arthur's evaluation. In addition, pay and rewards would then be geared to customer outcomes and the new values.

Sign here for better standards and rewards. _____

WORK REDESIGN AND SELF-MANAGEMENT

Another bundle of solutions involves changing practices and redesigning work. Arthur's unit could be organized around the customer. One-stop shopping for me. Arthur would be part of a team where each member would have the capability to locate a line, price a job, remove a transformer, inspect a trench, schedule an installation, and communicate with other utilities.

Sign here for restructuring work. _____

All of these actions will help. Their impact will be limited, though, unless the more fundamental beliefs about governance are examined. The power company now operates on the belief that to achieve high performance they need

▼ Each department doing one thing and doing it well.

▼ Clear boundaries between what the power company does and what the customer is responsible for.

▼ All customers treated the same.

▼ Sharply defined jobs, so Arthur knows exactly what to do.

▼ Sophisticated ways of measuring costs and pinpointing accountability. Arthur is measured on lines located.

▼ Bosses that plan and workers that do.

▼ Training done in a cost-efficient way.

▼ Employees informed about other operations on a need-to-know basis.

▼ Job security for employees.

These all sound reasonable. These elements constitute governance and are the norm in our culture. However, the belief in this way of operating is why it takes two months and fourteen phone calls to get a power line placed in a trench. Initiating training, · communicating, and creating new rules and new structures, without changing the beliefs about control and consistency, are incomplete solutions. They will yield temporary benefits. They are useful, but not enough to capture a marketplace, or make the power company as competitive as it will soon need to be. Interestingly enough, this power company has begun to make major changes, they just have not reached Arthur. (All names have been changed to protect the guilty.)

This story introduces the next part of the book. Explored in some detail is the complexity of how to run our organizations so that the power lines get in the trench quickly. For those of you who want the complete answer in short form, the case study continues after Chapter 13.

▼▼▼

5

DEFINING THE
STEWARDSHIP CONTRACT

Stewardship is a way to use power to serve through the practice of partnership and empowerment. This is the alternative to the conventional notions of "strong leadership" for implementing changes. The intent is to redesign our organizations so that service is the centerpiece and ownership and responsibility are strongly felt among those close to doing the work and contacting customers.

In the desire to get our intentions more concrete, two things may occupy our minds. One is the destination. What would stewardship look like in practice in our own unit, our own organization? The second preoccupation is with the journey, the way to get there. How to engage people in redesign and reform so that people are engaged in the re-creation of their own workplace? Both the journey and the destination are important. Don't choose between them. People who are into power tend to over-focus on the destination. Goals, milestones, outcomes, bottom line. People into personal growth tend to over-focus on the journey. Quality of work life, participation, feelings, team building. Both are essential, but you have to start somewhere. Let's start with the destination.

Principles for the Practice

Think of yourself as a social architect engaged in the redesign of a governance system. Stewardship is a set of design principles, a template from which a whole range of management practices can be molded. These principles need to be integrated and customized for your world before the practices will be truly useful. Jumping too quickly to specific practices, and where they are working, is a short cut that yields disappointing results. Copying others' best practices is mimicry, not learning and discovery. Benchmarking what others do well is useful for raising our aspirations and setting a higher standard, but this process can become a compliant and dependent form of learning. Creating our own practices is the basis of ownership and responsibility. Stewardship has us become skillful in articulating its principles and then insisting that people construct the house in which they live. The house must be situated within certain boundaries, but there are many choices on how to construct it.

Governing on the basis of stewardship would operate on the following nine principles.

MAXIMIZE THE CHOICE
FOR THOSE CLOSEST TO THE WORK

This holds both for our efforts at improvement and redesign and for the way we do business day to day. Core workers get involved in the creation of policies and practices and have a hand in customizing what is handed down to them. In any change effort, the first set of questions has to do with what the requirements of key customers are. The next series asks what those doing the work require to meet those customer requirements. The people doing the core work are active in answering both sets of questions. No expert consultants or staff people coming up with the workplace of the future. The intent is to put decision making and the authority to act right where the work gets done. Core workers need the freedom of action to control costs, enhance operations, and give customers more control over the relationship. The choice we offer people is what creates accountability.

REINTEGRATE THE MANAGING
AND THE DOING OF THE WORK

Management becomes a set of tasks and activities, not a full-time job title. Everybody manages, although some have a wider view and a longer time perspective. The notion of management prerogatives disappears. There is no privileged class of people. Everyone does work that brings value to the marketplace. And everyone should do some of the core work of the organization part of the time. Sell to a customer, teach a class, sew a pair of jeans. The higher the level in the organization, the more critical this becomes.

The choice we offer people is what creates accountability.

LET MEASUREMENTS AND CONTROLS
SERVE THE CORE WORKERS

This means the measures will be designed by those to be measured. Be realistic about predictability. Value longer-term, qualitative measures. Even if you cannot measure it, it might still be worth doing. Measure business results and real outcomes, stop measuring people's behavior and style in getting there.

Control is maintained by team and peer agreements. We negotiate performance contracts with our peers and with bosses and subordinates as the means for assuring that commitments get fulfilled. These contracts are between partners, so the expectations go both ways, with equal demands. The intent is to eliminate coercion as the basis for getting results. These performance contracts are not tied to pay or punishment, though they may be tied to termination in extreme cases. We can fire someone if they do not deliver, but we stop trying to improve performance by manipulating sanctions, privilege, or pay.

YIELD ON CONSISTENCY ACROSS GROUPS,
AND SUPPORT LOCAL SOLUTIONS

Embrace consistency only when the law, regulations, or external demands require it. Give unique, local solutions the benefit of the doubt. Have executives and staff groups prove the need for consistency, instead of having supervisors and work teams prove the need for an exception. In the case of genuine needs for consistency, such as particular reporting formats or conforming to certain health and safety requirements, have teams of workers determine how to meet them.

SERVICE IS EVERYTHING

People are accountable to those they serve. Service is aimed at customers and subordinates. Evaluations, feedback, the very definitions of roles and services offered, come out of conversations with customers and subordinates. Bosses are no longer customers, they are suppliers. This produces real, hard-nosed accountability and exemplifies the core distinction between leadership and stewardship. Leadership has often claimed to be in service of those they lead, but the leader's "service" took the form of giving direction and protection. Stewardship serves through the form of giving a basic structure and supporting self-direction.

Bosses are no longer customers, they are suppliers.

DE-GLORIFY MANAGEMENT AS A JOB TITLE AND DE-MYSTIFY THE STAFF FUNCTIONS

This means a minimum of management and staff jobs. Management and staff groups exist primarily to contribute to people doing the core work. Have staff groups and managers justify their role on the basis of value added to the core work process. Let core workers have a strong voice in determining the value that managers and staff groups add. Staff groups in effect sell their services to teams of core workers. If core work teams do not want the service or want to get it elsewhere, they are free to do so. Let concerns about cost and consistency be part of the negotiations, not a reason for staff people to get their way. Another way of saying this is to let line people decide what kind of services they want to receive. No one should be able to make a living simply planning, watching, controlling, or evaluating the actions of others.

END SECRECY

Support the idea of full disclosure. It requires giving complete information and telling the truth all the time. Knowledge is power, so give it away. This means training all employees so as to create business and customer literacy. Full disclosure and full information are the rule, so that people understand the consequences of the decisions they are making.

No one should be able to make a living simply planning, watching, controlling, or evaluating the actions of others.

Full disclosure also means to openly discuss bad news and difficult issues. No protecting or positioning allowed. The more sensitive the issue, the more it needs discussing, especially in groups. We express our trust in our institution by the amount of information we allow to become public. The military notion of telling people only on a need-to-know basis is how patriarchy maintains its grip. Full disclosure also requires that people do their own communicating. If our goal is to tell the truth, we do not need professionals to tell us how to get our message across.

DEMAND A PROMISE

There is a price to be paid by those given more choice over their work, and that price is a promise. People engaged in the redesign of their governance need to commit to act in the interests of the whole organization. Freedom and commitment are in every case joined at the hip.

REDISTRIBUTE WEALTH

The reward systems need to tie everyone's fortunes to the success of the team, unit, and larger organization. Paying for outstanding individual performance becomes a minor element of pay. Eliminate individual rankings and ratings. Self-interest is fed by individualism and overcome by community. Design the compensation system so that core work teams can make significant bonuses when they make exceptional contributions. The reward system needs to recognize that all employees are owners and all are managers. Our goal should be to pay everyone as much as possible. The constraint is that everyone's pay has to be earned each time by delivering real outcomes that are valued by customers.

The other side of this principle is that no one becomes an economic winner unless the organization is financially healthy. This gives real bite to the idea of community and it also reflects the reality of the marketplace. No automatic increases for business as usual.

These principles become the template or stencil with which we re-create our workplace. What follows is a description of how to begin to apply stewardship to change the governance and reform the politics of our institutions. This begins to define a blueprint for integrating spirit, democratic values, and marketplace performance.

THE STEWARDSHIP CONTRACT

The first requirement of stewardship is to honor the mandates of the larger institution without either caretaking or demanding consistency and control from those we have power over, namely those we serve. Our fear in following this path is our fear of anarchy. Our tendency has been to associate giving up control with abdication. The elements of the stewardship contract both define and set limits on what we control. The process of defining the contract sets the requirements and the boundaries of the playing field for partnership to be played out. It is better to postpone empowerment, self-management, total quality, and the like until there is clarity about our customers, value added, key results, basic structure and constraints, guiding principles, and difficult issues.

If any individual cannot support this contract, they do not join the effort.

Negotiating a stewardship contract is a means for clarifying the particulars. What this means is that if any individual cannot support this contract, they do not join the effort. The contract spells out the conditions of membership in the work unit. If stewardship is service to something larger than ourselves, what that "something larger" is needs to be known, before people can commit. It is the boss's job to define this contract. This is true whether you are the boss of a large organization or a one-person unit, where that person is you.

There are five elements of the stewardship contract.

CORE MISSION FOR THE UNIT

What services and products does the unit offer and not offer? Who are its customers and, especially, what is the unique value added for them? No matter where we are in the organization, even if we are a monopoly and no one else does what we do, we need to think as if we had competition and others could be serving our clients. So, compared to all others in the world who do what our group does for a living, what is the unique thing we bring our clients? It could be in our product or service itself, it could be in the way we work with clients. As people in power, we are entrusted with making the core mission visible and known to our people, and to holding it sacred.

Some answer the question of core mission by saying, "We want to be the best, world-class, number one." This is not service speaking, it is self-centeredness. It reflects being concerned more with our ranking than with our offering. There is nothing wrong in wanting to be number one, there is just nothing unique about it. Think more in terms of the guarantee we make to the client, a feature of our product or service, our commitment to a solution, the way we integrate our efforts on the client's behalf. Each unit needs to look at its own strengths and decide for itself the importance of such benefits as short turnaround time, innovative solutions, being first with new technology, understanding the customer's reality, offering low cost. Pick one. Being all things to our customers is being nothing special. This is important, and most of us who serve internal customers have not yet found a satisfactory answer to this question. Our uniqueness is the reason people will pay us to continue our work and is our hedge against hard times. Stewardship helps to define and protect this quality as a treasure.

MISSION

FINANCIAL ACCOUNTABILITY AND RESULTS

We are stewards for the operational and economic health of the unit. Every organization has to be economically self-supporting, either through selling something, fund raising, or taxing somebody. Each of us is accountable to a banker, we deliver outcomes in return for cash. That means the place has to work and deliver results. The boss has a right and obligation to define the outcomes that are required. This is one of our key hedges against anarchy or governance by entitlement. We give choice and flexibility to those below us, and in turn we exact a promise of certain outcomes. Stewards are accountable for defining those results. The results here have to do with specific outcomes. Financial, quality, client outcomes. Not the means to get there. We define sales volume, we abstain from defining number of sales calls.

The trick here is to be accountable without being controlling. Patriarchy has always justified control on the basis of accountability. Being on the line gives me the hunting rights to plan, organize, and control. This is the heritage stewardship refuses. What is entrusted to us, we in turn will entrust in others. We are clear about outcomes and fully inform people about the operation, so that they know the consequences of their actions. The faith required of us is that the machine will run without our having to constantly keep tending it.

STRUCTURE AND CONSTRAINTS

Defining the stewardship contract involves choosing a basic structure that fits the task and mission and environment of the organization. A sense of how the unit fits its market is needed to make this choice, so it falls within the boss's domain. This includes the choice about how much to flatten the structure.

If as the boss we are convinced that we should structure the unit in multifunctional teams, or around customers, geographic areas, a whole piece of the manufacturing process, business units—as opposed to organizing by functions—then we should present this determination as a given to our unit. It is the boss's wider view of the whole system and the environment that gives them a special voice in determining structure.

The process also involves setting limits. There will always be constraints on the services and products we offer. AT&T gave enormous choice to its phone centers on how to run each outlet, but they were required to have a standardized look to each store and sell only AT&T products, at a certain price. Xerox created district partnerships, operating increasingly as their own businesses, but they had to sell the full line of Xerox products.

A supervisor in the regulatory unit of a drug company named these principles for her unit:
- **No more privileges.**
- **No umbrella protection from me.**
- **We each take ownership and accountability.**
- **Stop treating me, your boss, as your client. Focus on external clients.**
- **Start getting your own clients.**
- **No more blaming other groups, no more victims.**
- **We will act as if we have competition for our services.**

There may be organizational and political constraints to the redesign effort. Such as don't mess with the pay system. Or we are going to build the relationship with the union and live within the contract as it exists now. Or flatten the structure, but leave the vice-president level intact (true story). Constraints stated clearly in the beginning reduce cynicism later.

BASIC GOVERNANCE STRATEGY

Stewardship means taking a clear stance in support of partnership and empowerment. As bosses we need to define what partnership means to us. The principles that begin this chapter and the requirements listed in Chapter 2 are two examples of this. These constitute the principles upon which the reform will take place. The redesign work then needs to adhere to these principles. Without a commitment and definition of partnership, people at every level will too often just recreate the patriarchy they have grown up with. They will ask for better parenting instead of seeking some more fundamental change. Developing partnership principles of our own is part of the homework preceding any change effort.

At times your people will accuse you of being autocratic in setting constraints and demanding partnership. When they make this accusation, confess. Plead guilty. Tell them nobody is perfect. But do not give in. If you had not initiated this reform, little would change. The people who are all of a sudden very fussy about how reform gets started do not want partnership. They want you to be a better parent, or they want to be the parent themselves.

FOCUSING ATTENTION

Given the wider perspective we have as a boss, it is the right use of the position to focus attention on where to begin the redesign effort or, if it has already begun, where to take it next. This is acting as a spotlight. It gives light without changing what it illuminates.

Focusing attention has two elements.

IDENTIFY THE DIFFICULT ISSUES

We need to learn how to point to problems without having to solve them. It is a misuse of our power to take responsibility for solving problems that belong to others. Our task is to keep a constant dialogue going about problems and ask people to diagnose and resolve them. The key is to tell the truth about difficult issues. Examples are poor response to customers, weaknesses in the work process, conflicts among co-workers, cost and quality concerns, avoiding responsibility for outcomes, inefficient use of new technology, widespread cynicism and caution, making a lot of task force meetings appear as if change is taking place.

It is a misuse of our power to take responsibility for solving problems that belong to others.

Our task is to discuss difficult issues without extending threats or protection. Parents have learned to present problems and then to identify consequences if the problems are not solved. This is good parenting. Not good partnering. Coercing outcomes, directly or indirectly, from those who work for us is what got us in to difficulty in the first place.

We can also take responsibility for others by protecting them. Softening the difficult issues by the language we choose. Some people do not have problems anymore, they just have "opportunities." Talking about problems and pain as "opportunities" is patronizing and controlling. Partners do not try and influence one another's responses by the way they position their own comments. "Positioning" language reinforces social distance. It is based on the belief that I am better able to handle difficult information than others, so I must be strategic and careful in what I say. Softening and positioning difficult issues is a subtle way of maintaining dominance. Stewardship has us act in way that trusts others to face and live with the difficult issues, even when there is no solution.

CHOOSE WHERE TO BEGIN

The second part of focusing attention is choosing where to begin. Wherever you are in the process, what is the next aspect of governance you want to reevaluate? It may be rethinking the basic work process, redoing quality measures and monitoring, or revamping personnel practices, or budgeting and financial practices. In a later chapter, various practices that need redesign will be outlined. What matters here is that it is helpful for the boss to identify what needs attention next.

Membership in an organization means we have chosen and accepted this playing field. This choice and acceptance becomes our contract. Our desires for compensation, self-expression, participation...whatever we want from a place...are viable only so long as we can commit to the mission, results, constraints, principles, and difficulties of the larger institution. If we cannot support these requirements and boundaries, then we should leave. If our subordinates cannot commit to this contract, they should leave or we should fire them, even if it takes three lawyers and three years. Agreement on the elements of the stewardship contract is the foundation for partnership and the basis for community. Stewardship offers more choice and local control in exchange for a promise. The promise the larger organization requires needs to be clear right at the beginning.

The stewardship contract is the balancing pole, the middle way between dominance and abdication. We avoid abdication by asking commitment to the elements of the contract. Our wish for dominance is constrained by our willingness to allow the stewardship contract to define the limits of what we will control. The boss chooses restraint the moment the subordinate chooses commitment.

The hard part is to confront self-interest and irresponsible actions right away. A certain percentage of people will abuse their freedom, take advantage of a loose structure, or be disruptive with their peers. There is nothing about stewardship that goes easy on this. Sometimes in the spirit of participation, managers pull back too far. If we confront dysfunctional behavior, we get accused of being insincere in our efforts to give up control. We are told we are not walking our talk. Don't buy it. There is tyranny in the claim that we cannot confront people or even express anger when we are partners. The fact that some will not be responsible does not mean we are going to revert back to patriarchy. We are just going to ask certain individuals or teams to face the problem.

6

Upsetting Expectations: The Emotional Work of Stewardship

At the same time we contemplate our strategy and chart our next steps, our thoughts are also on how to deal with the people around us to build support for our intentions and the process we have in mind. This is the beginning of the journey toward stewardship. The starting point, as with all change, is to get clear within ourselves. We need to be sure that we are personally choosing stewardship and not acting out of obligation or a desire to please.

It is hard to know at times whether we have chosen or borrowed the words we use and the path we pursue. We can assure ourselves that the choice is real when

▼ We have found a good business or organizational reason for proceeding. This includes identifying the difficult issues facing our unit.

▼ We can clearly define our customers and can identify the unique value we bring them.

▼ We can be specific about the results we need to stay healthy and meet our obligations to those who finance us.

▼ We have named, in our own words, the principles we commit to and will guide any change.

These actions have us define a stewardship contract with ourselves. So, with this contract as the context and a reassurance against our concerns about anarchy and chaos, we are ready to learn the meaning of surrender.

Surrender has never been my favorite word. I always thought it had only one meaning, which was to lose and be defeated. There is also a spiritual meaning to the word. To surrender is to accept that there is a waxing and waning rhythm to events and to trust that good things can happen without our needing to control them. Acceptance is to simply see what is real without having to color it, or fix it, or soften it. It takes a certain kind of faith in ourselves and others not to make control the centerpiece of our transaction with the world. We have come to believe that control is essential to our survival and safety, and even our success. Everything around us reinforces this belief, as this book has tried to document. Stewardship is the choice to unravel this connection between control, safety, and success. The radical intent of stewardship is to be of service and to be accountable without having to be in charge. Unravelling control, safety, and success is essential to discovering what is possible for us and our workplace. It is not easy for those of us who have chosen safety all our lives to be shoved into such an adventure.

THE TRAIL IS INSIDE OUT

In any reform effort, the hardest change is the inside work, the emotional work. Creating partnership in a work setting is a shift in beliefs and a personal shift in the way we make contact with those in power. And with those we have power over. These are issues for the artist in us to revisit. Our first instinct is to want to engineer change. To focus on what is outside of us. It is easiest to change those things that are easiest to talk about. So we focus on structure, roles, responsibilities. We have intense discussions about innovative pay systems, self-management strategies, and the elements of total quality management. Discussion of what is concrete and visible and measurable is the engineer in us at work. The engineering work of reform is the actual redesign effort. It is essential, but it is not enough. Something more is required. There is artwork to be done, internal seeing and reevaluation of our own wants, longings, and expectations. If there is no transformation inside each of us, all the structural change in the world will have no impact on our institutions. The moment we think we get the point, and others don't, it is back to square one.

> *If* there is no transformation inside each of us, all the structural change in the world will have no impact on our institutions.

FACING THE WISH FOR DEPENDENCY AND DOMINANCE

The heart of the internal work is to sort through our way of relating to those people who have some power over us and those people whom we have power over. Stated more simply, how to resolve our wishes for dependency and for dominance. Dependency is the belief that my safety, my self-esteem, and my freedom are in the hands of other people. If we are children, safety, self-esteem, and freedom are realistically under our parents' control. When we reach the age of consent, responsibility for our well-being shifts into our own hands. This assumption of responsibility is ritualized by society in giving us the right to vote, the right to defend our country, the right to enter into legal contracts. On our eighteenth birthday, we become adults, and placing our safety, our self-esteem, and our freedom into the hands of others is no longer required or functional. Adults place their autonomy in the hands of others by choice.

THE WISH FOR DEPENDENCY

As a child, as a student, or as a partner in relationship, most of us at some point have given away to another the power to determine how valued we are, how happy we can be, and how much freedom we can have. When we go to work, no matter how tough we think we have become, we look to our bosses and others above us and hand to them the power to determine, once again, how valued we are, how secure we can be, how much freedom we have. It is this willingness to place our survival in others' hands that fuels the engine of patriarchy. We do it without others' having to ask. Our bosses do not wake up in the morning and decide to create doubt in our minds and rein us back under control. They come to work, see the longing in our eyes, and try to be the kind of boss we have been waiting for. This wish to be taken care of, including to be led, is a form of our own self-centeredness. Our own choice for self-interest over service.

If we can see clearly how the wish for dependency works within ourselves, we can then begin to see how it works in others. If we only focus on helping other people work through their desire to be taken care of, then we are engaging in simply a more subtle form of patriarchy...we have the answer and others are going to get that answer and we are going to call it help. Experiencing the depth of our own longing for others to provide us safety and freedom is the absolute first step in creating organizations that are based on partnership, empowerment, and responsibility. The wish for safety surfaces in our expectations and disappointments in people who have some power over us. Since we all have someone above us, we all are looking for a little bit of safety. Our willingness to reevaluate our expectations is the first step in implementing stewardship. Renegotiating this internal transaction, beginning with our own needs of those above us, is the artwork, the emotional work of stewardship. We cannot create partnership or foster empowerment within our own unit if we continue to relate to those above us as parents. Until we take back control from those above, we will not be able to extend it to those below.

> *There was this recurring sense that I could decide all that morality stuff later, that the expediency of making sure everyone liked me would carry me until I was old enough to determine a moral course. I allowed the merchants free reign of the temples, never realizing how at home they had become.*
>
> Donna Schaper,
> *A Book of Common Power*

THE WISH FOR DOMINANCE

The coin of dependency has an opposite side, and that is the wish for dominance. Claiming control over others who are adults is also a choice. We may think that they are not ready to exercise their freedom, but this is mostly our rationalization. Dominance fulfills the wish to be in control. It may take the softer guise of being the all-knowing, omniscient, loving parent. Or you may see it as being a strong leader, giving people structure, clarity, and something to lean on and react to. These are all indirect forms of staying on top.

A regional sales manager for a pharmaceutical company stated after the second day of an empowerment workshop, "I spent $2,000 to come to a workshop to learn something that I have been doing all along. I have always done what I want. I have always acted autonomously." We should have given him half his money back, because he got only half the point. He had claimed his freedom, but had not yet begun to offer it to those around him. The desire to be on top, to be right, to be invulnerable, to know what is best for other people, all are qualities of great parents and fertile territory to be explored. Unexamined dominance creates cosmetic empowerment and feeds continued patriarchy.

Dominance may take the form of seeing the world as a battleground, wanting to win, to be associated with winners, hard-nosed, bottom line, number one, best-in-class. We hear the wish for dominance come out in our language. "We want to surround the competition." "We take no prisoners." "We are engaged in an economic war." This kind of talk is the voice and lyrics of patriarchy. We create a battle code to explain and sustain our aggression. And it works. The kind of competitive spirit that keeps the world going round, and makes racquet ball and poker such fine games, expresses the part of us that wants control, loyalty, and gratitude.

Unfortunately, many of us are too sophisticated to come right out and say we want to control our people. We are schooled in the language of equality. We call subordinates "associates," "colleagues," or "people who work with us, not for us." One candy company calls employees "associates," then requires everyone to punch a time clock twice a day. No punch, no pay. Using soft language means we have simply found indirect ways to act on our desire for control. Our own wish for control, regardless of how it is expressed, has to be owned before we are ready to be serious about stewardship.

WHERE IS EVERYONE?

Given some attention to our own dependency and dominance, we need a way of responding to others. It is frustrating to send an invitation for partnership, and discover that there are supervisors and core workers who will not even send their regrets. We have taken a stand for empowerment, offered others their freedom, and yet they seem to sit in the cage with the door wide open. It can be disheartening. It seems that a certain percentage of people just do not want to claim their autonomy. The percentage varies with each of us. Some of us think 10 to 20 percent just want things the way they have always been, others think as many as 60 to 70 percent still want good parents for their leaders. The reality is that each one of us has deep ambivalence about how much freedom we want to claim for ourselves and how much control over others we want to surrender. If you think you have completely resolved these questions, you haven't looked deeply enough. Maya Angelou said in a recent talk that she is always struck when someone claims they are a Christian; her response invariably is, "So soon?"

> *So* long as man remains free he strives for nothing so incessantly and so painfully as to find someone to worship.
>
> Feodor Dostoevsky,
> *The Brothers Karamazov*

Identifying our wish for dependency and dominance is just a first step. The overarching intent of the discussion here is to offer a way of minimizing their interference. This brings us back to the idea of surrender. We need a deeper way of understanding our emotional investment in the patriarchal contract. If we stop at the level of stating that some people want their freedom and some people don't, or that some managers are willing to give up control and some are not, then we end up searching for the right people and becoming increasingly discouraged. The task is to renegotiate our contracts with those around us, from parenting to partnership agreements. The way into the center of renegotiating contracts is to accept the dominance and dependency that live deep within ourselves and others.

EVERYONE IS ON THE BUS

There are not dependent people and dominant people. There are not autonomous people and participative people. This is the psychologist's viewpoint, who then wants to create a personality test to identify empowered employees and empowering managers and use the results to select and develop the right people. Viewing the solution as a talent search so externalizes the problem that we stay immobile, stuck on that wooden horse where we began.

Instead, hold on to the idea that there is a dependent and autonomous part of each of us. There is also a dominant and yielding part of each of us. Accepting this thought does two things. First, it places the problem within our control, rather than projecting it onto others. To speak as if we are empowered and those people are not, as if we have claimed our freedom and they have not, is just a subtle form of some Darwinian wish to be further along than others. By acknowledging the struggle is ours, we keep ourselves humble and focused on the right spot. Second, it means there is hope for those who seem to resist the ideas of partnership and empowerment and the responsibility that goes along with them. If there is in each person a wish for more autonomy and a wish to give up control, then it gives us something in each person to speak to.

UNSTATED EMOTIONAL WANTS: BREAKING THE PATTERN

Dependency and dominance get lived out through the mechanism of unstated emotional wants. Parenting and patriarchy endure through the unstated and irrational expectations we have of those around us. The expectations of dependency are that others will provide safety, freedom, and self-esteem. The expectations we have of dominance are that we are entitled to compliance, loyalty, and gratitude. These expectations, called *unstated emotional wants* here, have been traditionally evoked and agreed to each time we joined an institution. It didn't matter whether the institution was our family, school, work, or church. The institution wanted compliance and loyalty, and in return we wanted them to provide us with safety and self-esteem. It was our wish for safety that led to our willingness to yield sovereignty. It was the institution's belief that it needs loyalty (the nobler word for compliance) that led it to make the promise of safety and protection. This exchange used to work. But it is exactly this contract that is no longer fulfillable. Our organizations are no longer able to offer the safety they once did. Conversely, marketplace demands require something more than compliance from our people. If you doubt the existence of this wish for safety, just look at the clothes we wear to work. Suits, ties, and pantyhose are not how you dress for adventure. When we see people not wanting to take responsibility, they are just continuing to live under the old social contract. It was a deal we used to agree to, so don't be too harsh on them.

It is hard to know who is the greater fool, the one who makes a promise of safety, or the one who believes it.

Successfully renegotiating the old contract is the early emotional work of political reform. The renegotiation begins by acknowledging and accepting the power of these unstated emotional wants. Once accepted, we can stop being controlled by them.

DOING SOMETHING ABOUT THE WANTS

We can use exaggeration to see even more clearly the part of us that wants others to provide us our safety, self-esteem, and freedom. Exaggeration is the antidote to our tendency to deny our more uncomfortable desires.

When people are asked to state their normally unstated wants from those around them, and to exaggerate, here is what they/we long for.

EXPECTATIONS OF A RELATIONSHIP
Place my needs above all others.

Provide me with safety at all times.

Include me in all decisions.

Never argue with me.

Want to be with me always.

Take care of me so I don't have to be responsible for myself.

Trust and agree with all my decisions.

Give me my freedom…all the space I need.

Never need anything I don't want to give.

WHICH GET EXPRESSED IN EXPECTATIONS OF A BOSS
I want to be your favorite.

Ask my advice before you do anything impacting me or my work.

Make me your confidante.

Make my advancement your personal responsibility.

See my weaknesses as charming.

Leave me alone…except when I am in trouble, then rescue me.

Protect me from powerful foes, run interference for me.

On the flip side, as bosses, we have our own emotional demands of our subordinates. The ones that meet these expectations affirm to us that we are good at what we do, and we tend to call them high performers.

A BOSS'S RECIPROCAL EXPECTATIONS OF A SUBORDINATE
Value me more than any boss you have ever had.

Know what I need and want without my having to ask.

Accept my controlling behavior as timely and helpful.

Don't bother me with problems.

Come to me only with solutions and successes.

Even though I occasionally embarrass you in front of peers, consider me your friend.

Be loyal to me, regardless of how I operate.

Be grateful for the opportunity to work for me and learn from me.

Finally, those in service/staff roles have their own desires of their "clients."

SERVICE/STAFF PERSON'S EXPECTATIONS OF A CLIENT

Don't act without asking my advice. Tell me you have learned
   more from me than anyone else.
Tell others how good I am, especially up the line.
Keep needing me, don't get too independent.
Teach me what I need to know, and be grateful for the opportunity.
Accept my desire to control you as an act of service.

None of us feels all of these, but if we identify with even one, we have a clearer idea about the way our dependency and dominance work. These are emotional wants. They are not rational wants. Rational wants *can* be fulfilled by others. Emotional wants, however strongly felt, represent questions and doubts about our life that other human beings cannot fully answer. They can try, and even succeed for a while, but anyone who acts as if they can provide us safety, self-esteem, and freedom does us a disservice. We have to provide these things for ourselves.

*E*motional wants represent questions and doubts about our life that other human beings cannot fully answer.

Sometimes people ask, "Isn't there anyone we can be dependent upon to fulfill our longings?" The answer is to look to God to answer these questions, but not to a second-level supervisor. Above all, we need to accept these wants and see them clearly. They are longings that may never fully disappear, but we do have a choice about how we act on them, and this is the key. Choosing stewardship is the choice to say no to others' desire for you to claim control and in exchange offer them protection. Choosing stewardship is our choice to be accountable while supporting freedom in ourselves and others. This is a risky choice and comes packaged in more anxiety than we had bargained for. This choice for accountability and freedom is the essence of the entrepreneurial spirit. It forms the basis for the social contract essential to ownership and responsibility at every level of our organization. It confronts self-interest and is the alternative to entitlement. It is the contract essential to a democratic society. Plus, with a little encouragement, this contract will also put out the cat, wash the dishes, and pick up your cleaning at the laundry.

Creating a social contract based on partnership and empowerment is the difficult emotional work of stewardship. This means saying no to others' wishes for protection and relinquishing our claims for control. What is so difficult to see and yet so powerful is that at the moment we look to others to protect and take care of us, we also hand over to them some semblance of sovereignty and control over what we do. This is where bosses get their hunting rights. We ask bosses to be our guardian. Guardianship under the law gives you legal rights to make decisions about another's life.

Similarly, when we decide to take care of and protect others who work for us or with us, we are claiming sovereignty, even in our generosity. That is why caretaking of adults is no gift. When we claim sovereignty, we release the other from any requirement of ownership, responsibility, and emotional accountability. If ownership and responsibility are what we want, and also what the business requires, then sovereignty, in the form of caretaking, needs to be extracted from our relationships. It is this yielding and claiming transaction that we spend our lives re-forming.

JUST SAY NO

Extracting sovereignty from our relationships often means we start saying no. Saying no to unfulfillable expectations is critical and difficult. If people have specific wishes of us—such as to support their effort, watch them less closely, give them advice—the answer can be yes. To the extent, though, that these specifics are symbolic of their wishes for security, self-esteem, and freedom, the answer must be no. Even though they may experience our response as an act of abandonment or betrayal. They may feel that since we once offered them that protection and self-esteem, how could we now withhold it? The reason we do not offer security, self-esteem, and freedom to others is because it is not ours to give. Theirs to claim, yes. Ours to give, no. The fact that we once made an unfulfillable offer, because we thought we needed their compliance and we thought it was an act of kindness, is no reason to maintain the illusion.

TAKE A LOAD OFF ANNE

Moving from parent to partner comes down to a series of conversations. Dialogue is the solution. The conversation is about purpose, ownership, and responsibility. Shifting these concerns from the exclusive province of the management class and distributing them among people doing the core work. We do this for the sake of the institution, not because the load is too heavy. The boss says in effect, "I want you to share in the felt ownership of this franchise. I plan to share with you the power and privilege of ownership, as long as it is used in service of the larger unit. This is the partnership agreement that I want to manage by." This conversation accompanies the definition of the stewardship contract discussed earlier, which defines the playing field.

An example of this renegotiation process took place recently in the marketing department of a utility company. The manager, Anne, wanted the department to become more entrepreneurial and take more initiative. The utility was facing competition for the first time and marketing was a part of the effort to bring a customer and marketplace focus to what was a bureaucratic environment. Early in the meeting, the conversation turned to the things Anne and her people wanted from each other to make this change work. The subordinates wanted assurances that Anne would take care of them. That she would continue to be responsible for their careers, look for their next move, counsel them on what they needed to do to move up and get ahead. Given the uncertainty of what the business was facing, they wanted a reaffirmation of a safe harbor.

Anne wanted from them their commitment to the new role in becoming a more aggressive department. She also wanted their loyalty and devotion and for them to take personal responsibility for the goals of the department.

I asked Anne what her response was to their wishes. Understanding the contract she used to have with them would not work, she was reluctant to agree to look after them in the way they wished. She said to them, "I am not responsible for your career. I am not busy looking for opportunities for my people. These jobs were not created as career opportunities, they were created to impact this business. The best I will offer is to give you absolutely honest information and encourage you in creating your own future." Renegotiating her contract about purpose and responsibility was underway. Their response was quick and clear, "If you do not take care of us, we will not give you the loyalty and devotion that you desire." This becomes a critical moment for Anne and the team. If she gets nervous and starts to bargain for their loyalty and devotion, she has lost it. She needs their commitment to the department and the utility, but she cannot purchase it through the caretaking promise. Commitment, ownership, and responsibility cannot be bargained for or bought. We cannot create an entrepreneurial future by offering safety. Anne understood this. Her response was, "Even though I want it, and I will miss it, I can get along without your loyalty and devotion. What you need to decide is whether you can commit to what this department needs to accomplish. Also you need to decide if you want to do this, given the uncertainty of the future."

Anne's response began a conversation among partners. The employees were not particularly happy about this conversation. Any time we set limits, we pay a price. Entitlement depends on the expectation that others should satisfy our wants for safety, self-esteem, and freedom. When we say no, there is a wave of blame and disappointment we need to ride out in the search for empowerment and partnership. Anne had the courage to place what was vital to her on the table. Placing the unstated emotional wants on the table exposed them, it did not create them. Expressing our wants gives us choice, denying them forces them to play themselves out in unconscious ways—they drive us in unseen ways. Of the eight members of Anne's team, three moved on, four stayed to fully engage in the redesign effort, and one is still thinking about it.

DON'T FEEL TOO GUILTY

When you hear the claim that employees have been betrayed when they are no longer offered long-term job security, remember that while it is a painful experience it is a questionable claim. The contract that I will be a loyal employee and in return you offer me a secure future is an unbalanced agreement. We want the institution to guarantee a future, but we want the right to leave any time we choose. What underlies our disappointment stems more from our expectations than from the inadequacy of another's response. This caretaking contract is very human but the antithesis of ownership and responsibility nevertheless. We are each in our own way afraid of the dark. Hidden bargains are destined to disappoint, and when they disappoint, it is so late and the feelings run so deep, that they make the relationship difficult to repair. They also make the illegitimacy of our own expectations difficult to own.

There is no easy way out of this. Allowing our dependency to continue is to forsake ourselves. We then have to endure the guilt of an unlived life. Yet claiming our freedom and making choices betrays others' wishes for us. Parents, teachers, bosses, friends, children—all have expectations of us that we do not meet. To claim stewardship, to claim our freedom even as an act of service, is a destabilizing act. This unsteadiness is in the nature of renegotiating social contracts, and it is going to happen because the safety-control-compliance compact doesn't work. To paraphrase Marion Woodman, the only question is whether we are going to work it out in this job or the next one.

As people go through the experience of exploring their unstated emotional wants, they begin to realize that, exaggerated as they might seem, they represent real desires. These expectations are the way that dependency and dominance get operationalized. Patriarchal contracts, parent-child contracts, feed on this kind of longing. They become the mechanisms by which we control each other and hold ourselves back from living out our own vision. It is because we want others to provide us safety and self-esteem that we are willing to live out the vision created by others and deny our own. Patriarchy becomes a refuge for our reluctance to choose adventure and pursue our own purpose.

When we give up the search for others to provide us safety and self-esteem, we need to replace it with something. In essence we are redefining our ambition. We are letting go of advancement and pleasing bosses as the measure of our success. Perhaps not voluntarily, but in most places, there is just no place to go. Our organizations are flattening as fast as they can. Also, the effort we make with advancement in mind is just not terribly functional. Our career progression is about as much in our own hands as our choice of parents and birth order. What has the potential to replace our desire to move ever upward is our desire to create an organization and culture we can believe in.

When we tell subordinates we can no longer take care of them and no longer choose to control them, we also need something positive to offer. What we are offering is real choice in defining and creating an organization that has purpose and meaning for them. This is the aim of political reform. A partnership in designing a governance system that fosters ownership and responsibility among those doing the core work. The basic exchange is to offer people more choice in return for a promise. Make sure that both a real choice and a real promise are in the equation. The choice is about having control over the way the work gets done and managed. The promise is about results.

When we tell subordinates we can no longer take care of them, we also need something to offer. What we are offering is real choice in defining an organization that has purpose and meaning for them.

There are many cases of management's requesting the promise without giving more choice. Whenever I hear someone say "I empower you to...," it is usually a demand without an offer. If the requirement is for more accountability, the offer in return that has the most currency is increased choice. The last thing to offer people for more effort is money.

I have also seen core workers offered more autonomy without being asked for a promise. A manufacturing plant decided to move toward empowerment and self-management. They created teams, eliminated supervisors, and had core workers plan, coordinate, and hire for themselves. They shared information, eliminated time clocks, gave extensive training. Performance stayed flat and in some cases got worse. What was missing was a commitment from the work teams to make the new structure work. The plant manager had not asked for a firm commitment about productivity and quality from each team until about six months into the process.

Choice in exchange for a promise. Both important, both offered up front. Stewardship chosen. Democracy rediscovered.

7

REDESIGNING MANAGEMENT PRACTICES AND STRUCTURES

Shifting the social contract from self-interest to service becomes concrete and enduring when traditional management practices and structures get redesigned and our lives are more and more congruent with our desires and intentions. What is important about these changes is that, in most cases, the redesign efforts, plus ongoing operational responsibilities, reside in the hands of the core work team, rather than with a expert staff group. The staff groups will help with the changes, but the power to choose is within the line organization and at the levels where the work gets done. The reintegration of the managing of the work with the doing of the work, the operational demise of the class system, the ideals of partnership and empowerment—all hinge on shifting practices in these new directions.

FULL DISCLOSURE

The starting point for the change effort is full disclosure. On the surface, giving people complete information sounds pretty straightforward. Not so. If knowledge is power, then patriarchal governance is very selective about what gets reported, when and to whom. Being careful about what we communicate probably stems as much from the wish to protect as the wish to control. What people don't know won't hurt them. No news is good news. The ancient habit of shooting the messenger is somewhere in the collective memory of each of us. All rationalizations.

> *Secrecy* cloaks the infectious madness that causes people to participate in their own destruction.
>
> Earl Shorris,
> *Scenes from*
> *Corporate Life*

Full disclosure is a critical dividing line between parenting and partnership. The things a parent would never tell a child have to be told to a partner. Children will never tell parents what they rejoice in telling their friends. Holding back information or shading reality from a parental boss...well, that goes with the territory. Truth untold to a partner is betrayal. Part of the argument for reducing the class system and moving toward more equal relationships in our organizations is that it creates the conditions for open and complete communication.

There are several particularly sensitive areas where complete information is difficult and vital.

DISHEARTENING PERFORMANCE

It is hard to admit mistakes. We use language to soften the admission. We never admit a new department was a mistake or that the performance of 90 percent of our acquisitions deteriorated after we bought them. We simply say something like, "In the process of repositioning ourselves for the challenges facing us in the coming millennium, we feel it is prudent to redeploy some of our resources and refocus our energies along the lines that are more consistent with what has proved successful in the past." That means we are eliminating the new department and dumping the acquisitions.

Stewardship means all employees need to know the truth about where we stand. They cannot contribute to what they cannot see. We need to give a complete picture about financial performance, good or bad. If we change our mind or just don't know what we are going to do, we have to get used to just saying so. Being indecisive at times, or confused, are human traits. Leadership, as we have created it, leaves little room for mistakes, ignorance, or confusion, which means it has little room for humanity. Let go of the mask of perfection. The desire to be perfect or look perfect is the wish to be God. And that is a sin.

> *L*ife is a form of not being sure. The moment you know how, you begin to die a little.
>
> Agnes DeMille

People in the public sector have a hard time with this. The public sector is just that, very public. Bad news in schools and government goes from someone's lips right into the newspaper, and this creates a great caution about what people inside those institutions are told. I was presenting some of these ideas to a group of public officials in Minneapolis, and one of them commented how difficult it was to disclose sensitive news to her own people, for fear the news media would get a hold of it and exaggerate the problem. A district attorney, though, disagreed. He said that the main thing the news and the public nail us for is lying. If public agencies make mistakes and own up to them the attention is manageable. Try to cover something up, and then the real problems begin.

Public or private sector, we do not need communication experts to coach us on how to tell the truth. Information, unlike a cue ball, needs no "positioning," requires no "spin." Positioning and spin stem from a deep cynicism about our constituents. Managing information like this builds distrust and treats our public as if they were fools. Sometimes they are fools, but that is still no reason to treat them that way.

UNSETTLING PLANS

One of the most difficult things to discuss openly are questions about when we are going to reorganize, or terminate a project, or reduce headcount. These sorts of actions destabilize our lives and create unanswerable anxiety. This is when our determination to stop caretaking gets tested. Despite the temptation, it is an act of betrayal to mask our intentions. When faced with the need to reduce labor costs and people, too many companies have hired outside consulting firms to come in and initiate a "Delta" project. The stated intention is to have the consultants "jointly with the employees" determine the value added by each department and to come up with recommendations to improve productivity and refocus energies. Despite the declared intention, reduced headcount is the inevitable outcome of these projects and, as a result, some level of integrity is sacrificed. If we cannot trust our own people to make the cuts necessary for the organization to survive, then we should confront that directly. Bringing in outsiders to do our dirty work is an absolute affirmation of patriarchy. And if, in the process, the consultants are espousing empowerment and partnership and stewardship, be doubly careful.

Genuine partnership means telling people about cutbacks, reorganizations, and the death of projects, almost as soon as we know about them. Whatever lost production results from a bout of free-floating anxiety or grieving after a grim announcement, it does not compare to the cost of the distrust born of withholding and deception. If we want people to be owners and responsible for the unit, they need to be part of these tough dialogues and learn to live with the anxiety that goes with them.

BUSINESS LITERACY

Business literacy includes all the things you would tell someone if you brought them in as a full partner. This covers the essential indicators of how this unit is doing and identifying those elements that need special watching. The Education Group in Union Carbide has developed an example of what constitutes business literacy. Here is a sample of what every employee should know.

CUSTOMER REQUIREMENTS

Who are the key customers, what are their critical desires, what is our history with them, how is the relationship going? It is always surprising to discover how many people have never really made contact with the external customers and often have never spent time with internal customers down the line from their own function.

COST STRUCTURE

What are key product/service costs? Cost of materials, administrative costs, operating margins? Overhead costs are an interesting one. We are very verbal about the costs of direct labor. There is much less information on the cost of field overhead or, especially, home office overhead charges and what they consist of. Making public the costs of planning and watching and controlling is a way of breaking down the class system between managers and workers. Volunteer agencies are required by law to share this information and it keeps them lean.

ORGANIZATION/DIVISION/UNIT FINANCIAL PERFORMANCE

Seems straightforward, but many places are still reluctant to disclose how they are doing. The argument is that they control the information for competitive reasons. It's a weak argument.

COMPARATIVE COMPETITIVE DATA

How we are doing against others who are in our business? There has been a recent surge in using competitors for benchmarking and setting a higher standard for our own practices.

INDIVIDUAL PERFORMANCE DATA

This is always controversial. It is clear you cannot tell third parties about an individual's performance ratings, but some places do not even tell the individual. They may tell the person how they were evaluated this year, but choose not to tell them overall where they rank. Regardless of the existence or absence of performance appraisals, partners have a right to know where they stand, if for no other reason than to make a good decision about their own future.

EXCEPTIONAL KNOWLEDGE

Core workers need to know how to make an exception to routine practices and procedures. One powerful role for supervision has been to control the information about when and how to grant exceptions to policy. To give a unique response to customers, we typically need a supervisor's signature. Try to get a refund when the item you are returning is well past the return date, and watch the salesperson disappear. Try to spend money in a crisis, without going through purchasing, and you need a special signature. Come in late, go home early, stay home Tuesday, schedule an extra class trip, offer special terms for a sale. Somebody makes these decisions and we have felt safer if it was a supervisor. The fear is that if we left the choice to workers they would take advantage of us. At what level moving up the organization do people suddenly become trustworthy? This is not arguing the case for people doing whatever they want. Let us give them the guidelines or thought process, then ask them to make good decisions about exceptions.

Sharing all this information sounds good, but we all have reservations about it. Situational communication, being careful to tell people what they are ready to hear, timing is everything, fears of the press or competitors getting hold of the data, not wanting productivity to drop because of the uncertainty of our future—all good reasons, but the reasoning of a patron, a parent, a patriarch. The histories of churches, governments, rulers are filled with the strategy of keeping a population uninformed as a means of staying in power. There was a time when you could be executed for reading the Bible aloud, in English, on a street corner in London. All because those in power felt that the citizenry was not emotionally prepared to hear the Bible other than from trained professionals, the clergy.

Obviously there are some restraints that must be exercised in reporting news to our own people. The point is that fuller disclosure is essential to break the caretaking contract. It removes a layer of protection from lower levels. Many of us do not want that much information, but that is the part of us that still wants to be taken care of, that wants to be a child. We hear the cry that all that "business literacy" stuff is for administrators and bureaucrats, leave us alone so we can just do our jobs. Don't nibble the bait off that hook. Customer, financial, and systems responsibility is essential

Learning what it takes to keep the ship afloat is the price we pay for our desire for more voice and more control.

to everybody's job. Anyone who does not want to learn these things cares little for the well-being of the larger organization. Another form of self-interest. Organizations that allow anybody to get too distant from either their bankers or their marketplace will not survive. Learning what it takes to keep the ship afloat is the price we pay for our desire for more voice and more control. There may be things we don't want to learn about budgeting and financial controls, but we cannot be accountable without knowing them.

MANAGEMENT PRACTICES

When the stewardship contract is clear and there is some agreement about it, and when there has been full disclosure about where things stand and some business literacy achieved, our attention turns to management practices. Practices are the day-to-day way service and stewardship get institutionalized. Here are very specific examples of how particular organizations have designed practices that reflect the stewardship principles listed in Chapter 5. These examples begin to define the agenda for changing practices. If you want more detail, the Lost and Found section, at the end of the book, has some places to look. What is offered here is a glimpse of what form the revolution is taking.

MANAGING THE CUSTOMER RELATIONSHIP

Most every change effort begins with finding out from the unit's customers what they value and how the unit is doing in living up to those values. Each person should be engaged in this discovery process. In a large retail chain, each employee stood outside the store for an hour every couple of weeks interviewing customers as they left the store, asking them what it was like shopping there. The key questions to customers are whether they feel understood by employees and whether they feel they have been given responses that are unique to their needs. Don't limit the questions to simply cost, schedule, and product quality.

Each person can also take on some ongoing contact with customers. Some core workers actually negotiate service agreements and make promises, where this was previously done only by supervisors. Others simply maintain some regular contact. Each top executive should also be responsible for some customer contact.

WORK FLOW AND JOB DESIGN

This is a whole world in and of itself, but the heart of it is that work is redesigned as "whole jobs," where all the elements of producing the product or service are bundled so that they can be done by one person or a single team. Division of labor into simple, repetitive tasks is eliminated. Each person learns all the tasks. The person or the team has broad powers and responsibility for satisfying a customer.

DISCIPLINE

Teams of peers define when discipline is required and how it will be enforced. Teams agree to live by the ground rules they create. Bosses are brought in as a last resort.

PURCHASING AND SUPPLIER RELATIONSHIPS

People doing the work decide on the equipment they need. They maintain relationships with suppliers and use purchasing professionals as a resource on how to do this well. There have been major innovations in reducing inventory by having materials arrive at a plant the moment they are needed. The cost of the purchase order process has been reduced drastically in some manufacturing operations. The innovations that have had the most success are the ones where operator choice is a key part of the action.

QUALITY CONTROL

Each team is responsible for monitoring its own quality and for creating the measurements and the tracking systems for maintaining control. Standards are set by those doing the work, in collaboration with customers, staying within the results defined by management.

PRODUCT AND SERVICE IMPROVEMENTS

Improvement is everyone's job, process improvement becomes the main purpose of meetings. Customers as partners get involved. Teams have the power to implement improvements in most cases, and when approval is needed, only one level has to be involved.

REPORTING RESULTS

Meetings to discuss results include core workers reporting jointly with bosses. Reporting systems are designed primarily for the use of core work teams so they know how they are doing all the time. The goal is a fully informed and business-literate work force. Meetings become multilevel and cross-functional. This delivers a common message, reinforces the idea that we are in this together, creating consciousness about our interdependency.

STRUCTURE AROUND CUSTOMERS

Organize groups according to customers, business units, or geography, rather than by function. A simple example is the insurance company that had six different functions dealing with agents. An agent called a different place for service on invoices, underwriting, policy information, claims data, and the like. Each function was easy to manage and had its own measurements on productivity. The problem was that agent calls felt like an interruption to getting the paperwork done that they were measured on. They restructured by assigning teams to groupings of agents. Each member agreed to learn all the jobs, and to get to know the agents. They got better results with fewer supervisors and more interesting jobs.

In addition to this list, there are major changes taking place in the areas of finance and personnel which are discussed later. All of these form much of what constitutes governance. They shape our day-to-day lives. They instruct us in what is required of a democracy. They are a major means of how we channel energy toward a customer and a marketplace. They are half the battle, not because they are the only right practices, but because being willing to significantly change them symbolizes the sincerity of our willingness to live according to our words. The tangible takes on meaning as a symbol of something deeper and more spiritual.

There is nothing inherently noble or right about any single practice. We will not earn a spot in heaven because of our ability to purchase our own equipment, contract with our own customers, and join in hiring our own peers. What is noble, however, is when core workers are given the right to redesign the way they live out their work lives in service of a larger purpose. This is where the perspectives of the journey and the destination converge. Practices that impact the business, redesigned by what were previously low-power people. If we do not appreciate the value of the symbolism that comes from the redesign effort, we will become exhausted by the magnitude of the practices that need to be changed.

We will never reform all our practices, even though they are important and need changing. There will always be requirements that are patriarchal and reinforce the world of consistency and control that we are moving away from. It does not matter. Once this redesign process has begun, the reform has taken place. Governance has shifted, even though the task is unfinished.

Changing Basic Architecture

There are more fundamental questions than management practices that also require our attention. These address the structure of the organization, the role of managers, the role of staff groups, and the reward system. These are more difficult to change, partly because they are complex and touch every corner of the institution, and partly because they touch upon sacred ground. Everyone has a vested interest in how roles, rewards, and structure are changed or maintained. Because of their complexity and volatility, it helps to treat them as separate categories within the landscape of our workplace. The rest of this chapter addresses the questions of structure and bosses. The subjects of staff groups and rewards get chapters all their own.

STRUCTURES THAT SUPPORT STEWARDSHIP

We are most familiar and comfortable with highly functional organizations. Manufacturing, marketing, research in business. In schools we divide by grade level and by subject matter: you do geography, I do mathematics; students progress through factory-like grade levels. Health care is organized by medical specialty; hospitals by departments devoted to nursing, lab work, admissions, and the like. My favorite functional organization is the state motor vehicle department. As a monopoly, they can organize any way they want. And it is all displayed in front of you in a large room filled with signs and lines. You want to drive a car, you want to register a car, you go through six lines each handling a different form and step in the process. My favorite is line number one, the longest line, which directs you to which of the other five lines you should stand in.

Functional organizations, with deep silos, are the ideal structure for command-and-control governance. They were born of the industrial revolution where economies of scale and specialization of labor became the religion. Functional organizations make administration easier. You can hire, train, monitor, corral expertise, and deploy people best when you have a pool of homogeneous resources to draw from.

As the marketplace places the premium on cycle time, adaptability, and giving a unique response to the customer, the advantages of the functional organization no longer hold. The alternative is to create multifunctional units organized around customers. You create teams responsible for doing the whole task, dedicated to certain customers. Customers with common requirements or in certain geographic areas are served by teams that contain all the expertise required to service them. What you lose in control and predictability, you make up in response time and a widespread intimacy with the customer. Also if we want to breed ownership and responsibility close to the work, teams being responsible for whole tasks is one way to do it.

Of course, every organization will have a mixture of both functional and customer teams, perhaps a matrix structure which tries to gain the benefits of both. A volatile environment, though, plus a desire to give priority to service, pushes in the direction of multi-skill teams responsible for the whole product or service aimed at a specific set of customers. One way of organizing around product or customer is to create business units, which has been a common practice for quite some time.

Changing structure is part of the school reform effort. Site-based management and the "Effective Schools" effort are restructuring strategies. The concept is that the school building is the basic unit of delivery. This means that a building team including students and parents begins to make decisions about budget, personnel, curriculum, and outcome goals. The superintendent's office, which used to make these decisions, becomes a support group serving the school teams. There are strong restructuring movements within government as well, often in the form of contracting services to private companies. The city of New Orleans and the state of Florida are on this path. These are all based on the belief that smaller, free-standing units can serve their marketplace more effectively. An interesting book by David Osborne and Ted Gaebler, *Reinventing Government*, documents these efforts.

The more common change in structure is simply to shrink and flatten the hierarchy. Much of this is done to save money. We call it "right-sizing," as if it were not our choice, but a mandate from nature to reduce labor costs. A side benefit from flattening is that there are fewer supervisors and therefore fewer people watching, which means core workers can exercise more choice. If flatter is not better, maybe smaller is better. Dana Corporation for years has kept subdividing units whenever they got to about four hundred people, letting these units pretty much decide for themselves how to govern themselves.

An interesting feature of all the flattening is that much of the attention is still on the lower levels of the organization.

An interesting feature of all the flattening is that much of the attention is still on the lower levels of the organization. The discussion about self-management is usually about how non-supervisory core work teams can operate with little supervision. Often there are forty subordinates to one supervisor. There is little talk of self-management at the top levels of organization. This became clear when I saw the organization chart of a field sales group. There were fourteen sales people reporting to a district manager, eight district managers reporting to an area manager, six district managers reporting to a regional manager, and four regional managers reporting to a vice-president. The span of control at the top was one manager to four subordinates, the span of control at the bottom was one manager to fourteen subordinates. The question I asked was, "Why do people at the top need more supervision than those at the bottom?"

BEYOND HIERARCHY

A common belief is that a change in structure is a means for changing culture or changing behavior. Changing structure alone is never enough. If the structure changes but the belief system about maintaining control and consistency and predictability remains untouched, nothing fundamental changes. We have been swinging between centralization and decentralization for decades, with our patriarchal method of governance remaining unscathed. Decentralization usually means that instead of one patriarch at the top, we now have seven patriarchs running seven decentralized divisions. All we do is push patriarchy down a level. Decentralization is a change in structure, yes. But it is not a change in governance, except for those top seven people. In fact, decentralization often has the opposite effect of its intention. Each new autonomous division starts recreating within itself the empire we thought we were breaking up. Ask the core workers of the decentralized units whether their lives have changed at all. If the answer is no, then the benefits of the new structure were never realized. The same caution holds for creating any smaller operating groups or

> *Decentralization usually means that instead of one patriarch at the top, we now have seven patriarchs running seven decentralized divisions. All we do is push patriarchy down a level.*

business units. If the beliefs about governance do not change with the new structure, then the benefits of restructuring will be marginal.

There are a number of people attempting to think of structure in more dramatically different ways in a desire to find an alternative to hierarchy. These ideas are useful in illustrating the intent of becoming as congruent as possible in affirming partnership and keeping an organization's attention on service rather than on command and control. One such idea is networking, where groups exist in parallel with each other and connect with other functions as the task requires. Structure is formed around the flow of the work process rather by administrative levels. Another example is the way Frances Hesselbein has conceptualized the structure of the Girl Scouts of America as a series of concentric circles. Information and ideas begin with the local units and pass through the circles toward the central executive group in the middle circle. The circles were to give emphasis to dialogue and exchange and the idea that everyone was equally important in the operation of the whole system.

THE DISAPPEARING BOSS

The second element of architecture, after structure, is how we define the role of bosses. When the day-to-day practices begin to change, middle managers and supervisors begin to get the feeling that they are not needed. Every discussion of partnership and self-management seems to lead to the question, "What is the new role of the supervisor or manager?" What *do* supervisors do in this empowered organization?

The intense interest in the question is itself an expression of our reluctance to redistribute privilege. When we centralize and tighten control, there are no long discussions, books, and training courses on the new and changing role of subordinates. We have less interest in protecting core workers from the tightening of power than we have energy for protecting managers from the loss of power.

THE COACH DISGUISE

The most common answer to the question of the new role for supervisors plays around the theme of coaching. Bosses no longer plan, organize, delegate, and control, they act as coaches, trainers, resources, consultants. The boss's job is to build effective work teams. The boss's job is to secure funding, get support from other departments, keep top management informed and on our side. Positive image, this role of coach.

It is an attractive thought, but not an adequate answer. We cannot justify a layer of supervision whose primary job is to facilitate any more than we can support a layer of supervision whose primary job is to watch and monitor. The function of coaching and facilitation is needed, but should not be sanctified as a separate organizational level.

Embracing the role of coaching as a supervisory task masks our reluctance to really integrate the managing with the doing of the work. The role of coach has a benevolent face, but it carries the same business limitations as the harsher look of patriarchy. Coaches maintain power and privilege, they just use it in a more nurturing way. If you want to see this most clearly, just take a look at our favorite source of analogies, the world of athletics. Basketball, baseball, football, tennis. The coach has all the power and privilege. In basketball, the coach wears the coat and tie, the players wear short pants. People in power positions do not wear short pants. They just don't. Coaches have offices, players have lockers. In some cases the players may have the cash, but the coaches have the marbles. Coach directs, players follow. The coach is a parenting role. Using parenting language…"Finest bunch of kids ever had play for me."

Turning supervisors into coaches keeps the managing and the doing of the work separate. Perhaps a coach is needed for a transitional stage. Keeping coaches for the first phase of the transition makes sense if you can afford it. The core workers will need to learn the management functions. They will need help learning to self-regulate, deal with customers, plan and budget, discipline and appraise. Let current managers play that role for a while, six months or a year. But in the longer run, the coaching function needs to come from somewhere other than above us in the hierarchy. Otherwise coaching will become simply a revitalized form of patriarchy. Remember, caretaking is the form of control that is hardest to give up. The basic point is that coaching is a human function, not a management function.

So, the answer to the question "What is the new role of managers?" is that supervisory and management positions will survive to the extent that they provide value added to the core work teams, who are their customers. Remembering that value added needs to be defined by the customer, it is through a dialogue with the work team that supervisors will discover what they have to offer that the team cannot or will not do for itself.

If we buy this concept, we do our supervisors an injustice by telling them that coach and facilitator is their new role. Something more than coaching is required to justify a value-added position. The management class was once justified on the basis of the need for more control, consistency, and predictability. As we move toward service, ownership, and responsibility, we no longer need this class of jobs. Let alone the fact we can no longer afford the luxury of this class system. Promising anxious supervisors a full-time permanent job as coach/facilitator, when in reality it is a transitional role, is a form of manipulation. When a level of management has to look up in the organization like chicks in a nest, and ask, "If I don't control, what's my new role? What's my new role?" the tough, honest answer is "If you are looking for us to answer the question for you, you may not have a new role." The fact that middle managers keep asking others to define their jobs is their recognition that they are an endangered species. If they have the courage, they have the capability to answer the question themselves, through dialogue and negotiation with those that report to them.

BOSS AS BANKER AND BROKER

There is no question that there is a place for bosses, just not so many of them and not operating as before. The task, then, is to define the unique value added by the position. When we say that the subordinate is the customer of the boss, we look for what service the boss has to offer. Banker is one answer. The boss secures funds for the unit operation and, like any banker, communicates the results and requirements for continued financial support. Morley Winograd, an AT&T executive who is committed to creating partnership in his sales organization, suggested to me that bosses are also brokers for their subordinates. Through their position and experience, they can obtain support, services, and customers from the rest of the organization. A clean and powerful concept. The team in effect contracts with a broker for resources they have trouble getting on their own. This is something a work team will be willing to pay for. Banker and broker works as a concept because even though they are vital to our business they do not govern it. Or at least not unless it is falling apart.

Even though our need for bosses is shrinking, we do have a job and role for the individuals who are now supervisors and managers. They are valuable people. They have specialized knowledge, longer experience, we chose them because we thought they were the best we had. We need these individuals, but not so many in positions of power and privilege. Let them coach and teach and communicate, but from a staff position, in service of those doing the work. And let the teams of people doing the work have choice over the kind of service they receive. Service providers, in this case "coaches," should not have direct authority over those receiving their service. Customer-driven organizations place those in charge of receiving the service in charge of the relationship, or at least make it a fifty-fifty partnership. Coach as boss will not wear well, coach as staff person or support function maintains the integrity of keeping ownership in the hands of the touch labor.

▼▼▼

THE PHONE CENTER STORY

What follows is a snapshot of a place where many of these redesign ideas were implemented. For seven years, from 1985 to 1992, Bob Martin was a vice president of AT&T and responsible for the 425 AT&T Phone Centers. The stores in 1985 were on the path to extinction when Bob took them over.

There are few other places where a more comprehensive effort to reform a business governance system has occurred. The ideas of empowerment and partnership along with a refocusing on customers were the centerpiece of the reform efforts. Here are some of the highlights of this grand experiment. It has meaning not only for the innovativeness of the effort, but that it took place within a large bureaucratic organization, which many say is impossible. It is a tribute to the phone store people who gave this business new life, and to the larger organization that allowed it.

These highlights come from a presentation Bob and I made to 175 Japanese executives in Tokyo. They represent some of the key elements of the effort to make the phone stores competitive. The odds were against the Phone Centers' even surviving. The retail business was not an AT&T strength. The stores were in weak locations; they sold AT&T products at a premium price over what the customer would pay for the same product in a discount or department store.

In 1985, the stores were managed in a highly centralized way. Hiring, merchandising, pricing, layout, forecasting were all done by the central corporate group. This changed dramatically and the decision was made to ask each store to operate as its own business, making decisions that were good for their customers and their people. This was a big shift for what had been one of the country's largest private bureaucracies.

Here are some of the key elements in the shift, described with Bob's own comments.

VISION

Early on, 150 employees who volunteered to come to a two-day meeting created a vision for the Phone Center organization. This was displayed and communicated widely.

Bob's comments on vision: "Raising the question of the vision leads to discussions about how you and your boss are going to partner on the day-to-day business.

"Renegotiation takes place slowly over time. Living out the new contract is life work, and not resolved by one dialogue, or one piece of paper, or one team building session or one workshop."

PHONE CENTER PRINCIPLES

If each store were to operate as its own business, there was a need for some ground rules, limits, and guidelines for people to exercise their autonomy. Bob comments about what were to become the Phone Center Principles: "The store managers wanted individualized store design. We would have had a different look in different markets. This was not possible, outside the limits. We needed a consistent identity for customers shopping market-to-market to know they are in a AT&T store."

This meant that the first task was to identify the restraints to the individual store. A playing field for the expression of empowerment. These became the Phone Center Principles, which evolved over a three-year period.

The principles were

1. Customers. Customers are always right, and always come first.

2. Integrity. We do not cheat on our results, manipulate numbers, ignore policies on special programs, or find ways to bend rules or seek advantage to serve our personal interests ahead of those of our business.

3. Product Assortment. We carry all of the products in the AT&T line authorized for Phone Centers, we display all of these products, and we carry no products that are non-AT&T branded.

4. Pricing. We maintain the AT&T retail price in the marketplace, discounting that price only for national or approved area plans or promotions, or when appropriate and usually as a last resort to please a customer who otherwise would be dissatisfied with AT&T.

5. Store Presentation. Our store presentation upholds the highest quality image of AT&T brand, and produces a uniform national look designed to attract customers and maximize profitable sales.

6. Advertising. We advertise nationally, as a part of approved area advertising campaigns, and locally when approved by headquarters. This approval process is in place to ensure that the AT&T brand quality is upheld in our advertising at the local level.

7. Asset Management. We protect our cash, our products, our credit offerings, and other AT&T assets as if they were our own.

8. Internal AT&T Partnerships. We uphold our partnership agreements with other internal AT&T organizations and with our two unions.

9. The Family. We respect all members of this family, and offer support to each other in owning our collective greatness.

10. Ownership. We take a stand for these principles, own them personally, and disclose violations with a strong heart and a gentle voice.

Bob felt that "creating these limits forces you to choose what you think is important. Too many restraints will result in business as usual. Keeping them few in number prevents people from hiding behind the rules. The principles evolve out of a dialogue so that all can own them. It is up to all of us to insure that all members of the family live the principles.

"Eliminating the rule book means that each person has to struggle with the right action for their situation.

"The process may seem slow, but it moves as fast as we are willing to let go of control and our need for approval. The organization moves no faster than its slowest member, which most often is us."

THE MEASUREMENT SYSTEM

After the principles, the Phone Centers began to look at the system used to measure the stores. In the past they had measured

▼   How much a store sold.

▼   How much a store spent.

"We were good at measuring whether the store met its sales target and its cost budget," Bob observed. "Sales quotas and budgets were created outside the store. External measurements and external goal setting feeds patriarchy. So we evolved two concepts.

▼   The measurement system for each store should be the same as for the whole business.

▼   Each store gets its own profit-and-loss statement.

"This was a radical move, creating 425 profit centers in a bureaucracy. Up to then there were only twenty executives in all of AT&T with profit-and-loss responsibility.

"Shifting the measurement system was huge task. The information systems group was its own power base and they were reluctant to redo the whole data management system. It took one and one-half years even after we decided what we wanted. This change signaled to our own people that we were taking this empowerment business seriously.

"The intent was to give to people the information they needed to make the trade off between the customer and the organization, on the street and in the presence of the customer.

"The measurement system is an expression of the contract you want with your people. Systems are usually designed to control people, not to give those close to the customer information to make good decisions for the business.

"The answer to business improvement exists in the minds of your people and is awaiting your call to make it real. A small change in the measurement system can bring large impact in support of the kind of business you are creating."

HUMAN RESOURCE PRACTICES

The recruitment question was framed as who owns the hiring decision. The sales associates in the store agreed that the new hire would be someone they wanted to work with or they would not hire. All applicants began visiting the store instead of an AT&T employment office. This change resulted in the elimination of over one hundred employment office jobs.

Each person became responsible for their own performance appraisal once a year. The emphasis was on their assessment of how they had contributed to the business. They presented their assessment to their boss and to a group of peers and subordinates whom they had chosen.

For career development the emphasis was on staying in a job long enough to master it. Very ambitious people who wanted to move up quickly were encouraged find some other place to progress.

Communications to staff had been filled with positioning. Telling half-truths for attitude reasons. Under partnership, people were told

▼ Strategic future of the business.

▼ New product plans.

▼ Financial condition and how to assess it.

People want to know the good news, but they are desperate to know the bad news. Four times a year Bob wrote a fifteen-page report giving the good and bad news about the business. This included Bob's personal feelings about the business.

FINANCIAL MANAGEMENT AND CONTROLS

Partnership gets expressed by the way you plan your business. Is planning done by a central staff group or people in the field? Sales forecasting for the phone stores was a difficult issue. It had traditionally been done by a central group three times a year, based on past-period data. Bob felt this delivered a message that they did not trust the field people to know their business. The process was changed so that each store manager created an annual business plan which included the products needed every three months. After a learning period, this worked as well or better than the central planning. Field people consistently committed to higher sales and lower expenses than management would have assigned.

STRUCTURE

In 1985 there were five levels between Bob and the sales associates. Five regional vice presidents, ten area managers. There were 150 people on the corporate staff. There were another 300 people supporting the stores in the field. Bob noticed that they spent 75 percent of their time talking to each other.

By 1989 there were five area managers. No regional vice presidents or staff. There were thirty people in staff functions. Total overhead labor reduced by 50 percent. The staff that remained were in areas such as data systems and real estate/store maintenance.

Initially each store paid one thousand dollars per month for the staff functions; in year two it was down to four hundred dollars per month. Middle mangers began to take on the tasks of the staff groups in addition to their regular jobs. There was a yearly conference to address staff issues on a national level. They took on the top twenty-five projects, each headed by a zone manager who implemented the ideas in their own zone and reported back on what worked.

The flatter structure made the stores more flexible in the marketplace and quicker in their decisions.

RESULTS

In 1985 the stores were six months from being closed. In 1992 they were still open, and contributing profit to the business. Customer complaints went down by two-thirds over the six-year period. Despite this, there was no guarantee about the future of the Phone Centers. Many inside the corporation had doubts about the viability of these outlets. Early in 1992 Bob took on different responsibilities.

▼▼▼

8

RETHINKING THE ROLE OF STAFF FUNCTIONS

Given all the attention to leadership, quality improvement, and participation over the last ten years, the staff function is one area of organizational life that has received too little attention. We have flattened ourselves, created self-managed units, organized around customers and businesses, and identified more people as our customers than we have named families to be dysfunctional. Despite this, the roles of our legal, finance, human resources, and other staff departments have remained relatively untouched. They have grown a little thinner, been forced to justify their costs, been persuaded to emotionally connect with the operations a little more, but the fundamental way they are used, namely as an arm and extension of top management, persists. The issue to be raised here about staff groups is not their cost, or the value of their expertise, rather it is how they get used. Political reform means raising the same questions about the role of staff groups as we have raised about the role of supervisors.

Staff groups such as finance, personnel, information systems, planning, centralized technical groups, and legal departments have specialized expertise; the functions they perform are referred to as support activities. They do not get directly involved in actually delivering the product or service that is the primary purpose of the organization. Groups that invent, design, produce, market, sell, and deliver the product or service are the line functions. The line functions are what are referred to in this book as the core work teams or core workers. The distinction between line and staff is not always that clean, but no need to get fussy at this point.

People who work in a central or corporate office also qualify for the "staff" designation. In education, the state education departments and the workers in each superintendent's office would be what we are calling a staff function. In a hospital, the administrative staff fall into this category. In the government there are whole agencies doing budget and finance and oversight work that are staff functions. The term *staff* does not mean that they have no direct power, because many staff groups have great power indeed. It is just that these groups do not directly create the product or service that touches a customer. That is why they are often accounted for as overhead, a term which turns out to be particularly well-chosen.

Strong, top-focused staff functions and the principles of stewardship are incompatible when we are serious about political reform. Stewardship is accountability combined with the belief in widely dispersed power and a reliance on self-control to keep the ship afloat. In contrast, staff groups have been set up to concentrate power and build a reliance on controls determined by people outside a core work unit. Staff functions as we know them are a co-creation of line managers who want control and protection and staff managers who are happy to provide it. The ground rules most staff groups still operate under interfere with partnership, empowerment, and stewardship in several ways.

Staff groups have been set up to concentrate power and build a reliance on controls determined by people outside a core work unit.

IN THE SERVICE OF TOP MANAGEMENT

Staff groups affirm patriarchy by whom they define as their primary client. When you ask most vice-presidents of legal, finance, and personnel what their number one concern is, they answer that it is the relationship with the top of the house. They want a seat at the table when the future of the enterprise is discussed, and much of their time is spent keeping that seat secure. Most every professional conference I have been to has had a major segment on how to have more influence with top management. Personnel leaders seek with great intensity an advisory and intimate relationship with the top executive.

The same in finance organizations. The chief financial officer usually defines the task for their function as being part of the implementation arm for the economic goals set by top management. Many financial officers also have a loud voice in setting those goals. This direct line to the top has been institutionalized in the audit function in publicly-held corporations. The board of directors has an audit committee and the audit function in finance reports directly to that committee. So you have a unit in finance evaluating the operating controls of line departments and reporting directly to the board of directors. Very muscular.

The audit is only one example of high-order parenting. Most other staff functions hold the same intentions, they just have not been as successful. Giving such attention to those at the top creates a controlling and compliance-creating attitude that determines how services are offered down through each staff organization.

Treating top management as the primary client is understandable, very human, and a desire that will never disappear entirely. The question is whether this is the best way to be of service. For all the reasons outlined already in this book, the task of staff is to serve the people who serve customers and touch the product. If staff become the eyes and ears and even voice of top management, which is what results from treating them as our main client, we reinforce the separation between those who do the work and those who manage the work. Too often the people down the line do not feel staff groups are on their side and in fact they are right. If we want the top line people to treat their subordinates as their primary customers, then the staff functions need to also treat the middle and bottom as their primary customers. We cannot position ourselves as agents of the top and still call the bottom our customer. Stewardship would have top management be one client of the staff function, but only one, and not the primary one.

DECENTRALIZING DOES NOT HELP

The role and focus of staff services is not an issue of centralized or decentralized functions. Staff people will sometimes say that they treat people close to the work as customers because they have a controller or employee relations person in each location, each plant, each clinic, each department. Not necessarily so. If that local staff person treats the local executive as their main client, nothing has changed. This is, once again, decentralized patriarchy. Now we have someone in each location treating the top as number one. In some ways we exercise more control by having our staff people at each location than if we kept them at home. Something more fundamental needs to change than taking a central office activity and placing it in a field location. It is a change in mindset and definition of service that we are after.

Stewardship thrives on the question, "Who are we here to serve?" Our history has us primarily in service of the management class. As we reintegrate the managing and the doing of the work, our future has us defining those close to customers as primary clients. It makes a difference.

POLICE AND CONSCIENCE TO THE LINE

Given top management as their client, staff groups have drawn their strength from their role in policing, auditing, and acting as a conscience. Top management creates policy and the staff groups are responsible for seeing to its implementation. A key financial person is called the controller. Not exactly a subtle or ambiguous job title. A staff unit responsible for controlling expenditures of operating groups is parenting in action. Human resources has managers of affirmative action and managers of compensation. Affirmative action units are designed to insure that the organization's intentions about fair treatment of women and minorities are carried out. The compensation unit is designed to make sure line people stay within compensation policy guidelines. Both are reasonable goals, but the staff groups become the parenting and patriarchal conscience of the institution. They are held responsible for seeing that others do their jobs. This is the command-and-control mentality. We are busy reforming it within the line organization but keep it intact almost as an insurance policy within our staff groups.

SOME EXAMPLES

To see the police and conscience role at work on a grander scale, watch the federal government's use of oversight committees, the General Accounting Office, and the Office of Management and Budget. These are prime examples of policing in the name of help. All-powerful groups, performing policing functions, often used as political instruments in the partisan world of public service. We begin to talk about total quality and customer service in government, but live with a police-and-defend mentality that permeates each contract for the delivery of those services.

Another example. School systems initiate site-based management within individual school buildings. On the one hand this gives teachers, parents, and principals much more ownership of the classroom, yet curriculum specialists work with the board of education on setting standards and determining how subject matter should be positioned. This has a staff person, the curriculum specialist, in ways having more power in the school system than the classroom teacher, who personifies the delivery system in each building.

John McKnight, who lives in the world of community organizing and social policy, writes

The President's Council on Integrity and Efficiency: They will develop a policy and procedures manual for the audits of federal entities' financial statements and define the appropriate level of auditor assistance to management in the preparation of financial statements.

From a talk by the Deputy Director for Management at the U.S. Office of Management and Budget about the patriarchal ways the service role is enacted. He explores the self-serving nature of human services and states that whenever the server has power over the "client," whom he pointedly refers to as a citizen, the interests of the citizen are betrayed. "The ultimate sign of the 'serviced society,'" McKnight says, "is a professional saying, 'I'm so pleased by what you've done.' The demise of citizenship is to respond, 'Thank you.'" A good example of service for the sake of the servers is the school system, where grades have such currency. "Unlike most servicing systems, the school is transparent in its institutional definition of the client's role," according to McKnight. "The school client is evaluated in terms of ability to satisfy the professional. The explicit outcome of the system is professional approval of behavior and performance."

Staff functions inside organizations are in the same relationship to their "customers" as the human service professionals McKnight writes about. He focuses in even more pointedly. "It is clear that 'care' is a potent political symbol. What is not so clear is that its use masks the political interests of the servicers. This fact is further obscured by the symbolic link between care and love. The result is that the political-economic issues of service are hidden behind the mask of love.... Behind that mask are servicers, their systems, techniques, and technologies—a business in need of markets, an economy seeking new growth potential, professionals in need of an income." The accuracy of this for the staff functions gets expressed in our cynicism when people from the home office, finance, or personnel reassure us that they are only here to be helpful. While their intentions may be sincere, there is a dimension of power and control that goes unspoken in the reassurance. One more quote from McKnight: "It is clear that the disabling function of unilateral professional help is the hidden assumption, 'You will be better because I know better.'"

Pick your institution and you will find staff groups established to maintain consistency, control, and predictability. As soon as they do this, they join the parenting contingent. The irony is that sometimes in the name of quality, organization improvement, and customer service we set up specialized groups to make sure that the programs get implemented.

Staff responsibility for insuring consistency and control becomes a policing and parenting activity, no matter how gently or collaboratively carried out. The staff person who asks a client to brainstorm ways to bring travel costs under control, or prescribes training to reduce accidents and worker's compensation costs, is still performing a policing role, they are just doing it with listening and understanding. They have learned how to be good police, how to be good parents. Another way to frame the issue is to ask whether people go to the staff groups for permission or for help. Units that give permission have claimed for themselves power that partners do not require.

The other side of the policing role has staff groups act as institutional caretakers. The line organization uses the staff people to keep them out of trouble. When managers want to fire someone, they call employee relations and tell them to either do it, or to prepare the case and the paperwork. There are employee conflicts or trouble with the union and the personnel department gets brought in to smooth over the waters. Many staff people are actually told that their job is to keep the line managers out of trouble. These are overt acts of taking ownership and responsibility away from the core work process and placing them in the hands of the staff function.

Quality control departments have been the classic example of the caretaker role. Until the mid-1980s, the dominant belief was that those who produced a product could not inspect it. Quality control was a separate department responsible for product quality. A whole profession emerged dedicated to methodologies for assuring quality performance from those who manufacture a product. The American Society for Quality Control has over one hundred thousand members. They have traditionally defined their role as helping some unit, other than their own, improve their performance, and most often through audit, inspection, rule making, and training. Their philosophy has recently started to shift more toward self-inspection and the prevention of defects, but the

M o n o p o l y

mindset that separate units are needed to take personal responsibility for the output of the core work process remains.

The fact that the line organization has asked a staff group to protect it does not dissolve the control inherent in that protection. When you ask someone to take care of you, you give them at that moment the right to make claims on you. If your staff groups seem at times to restrain your freedom to run your unit, this is because you gave them that power when you asked them to take care of you. Do not blame the staff group, they have only taken what you have given them.

TAKING CREDIT IS A FORM OF INTRUSION

Another telltale sign that the relationship is out of balance is when a staff group lists in their accomplishments the fact that they made recommendations to the operating people that saved the organization money or improved output. Something more than partnership has taken place here. Parents take credit for the accomplishments of those they watch. Partners do not take credit for one another's actions.

Consistency and control have been the way we rationalize the need for policing and auditing. When we give up consistency and control as the core beliefs for governance, the need for third parties to watch, police, and audit disappears as well. In stewardship, the staff functions are still needed, but for purposes other than enforcement. We need the expertise of the staff functions, but we need them packaged as authentic service units.

MANDATED SUPPLIER

Most staff groups would characterize themselves as a service function. They would call the whole organization their customer, even though they may have a sweet spot for the top. Many staff groups are engaged in their own internal quality improvement effort which identifies customer requirements and they take pride in meeting or exceeding those requirements. What interferes with partnership, though, is the fact that their customers generally have no choice about the service they receive.

Staff functions within organizations are most often monopolies. If someone in the core work group wants help on an employee relations matter or a financial matter or has questions about an information system, they are required to use the internal group. This is why government agencies and internal staff groups have never really had to be too worried about how they are managed or how their customers feel about the nature and quality of the service rendered. As long as they keep their bosses happy, it is business as usual.

If we wanted to create staff groups who lived partnership, we would set them up so that their customers had a choice about how and where they get their service.

If we wanted to create staff groups who lived partnership, we would set them up so that their customers had a choice about how and where they get their service. In a patriarchal structure, customers now have the choice to either use the internal group or receive no help at all. Too many choose to receive no help at all. Some managers have the budget or the willfulness to still go outside the organization to buy services that are available from internal groups, but since they have usually prepaid for the internal group through an overhead charge, they are doubling the cost of the services.

MANDATED SERVICES

Another element of choice that is taken away from core work units is whether they have a right to determine exactly what services they receive. This is a separate issue from whether they can choose their own supplier. The question here is whether people can really choose or amend the services being offered. Every staff group has procedures, training courses, and approval protocols that are required of each "customer." Management development has its core curriculum, purchasing has its requisition form, some information systems groups will only support systems and hardware that they have installed. All of these mandated services are based on a fundamental distrust of the line organization. It is based on the belief that left unexamined, and unpoliced and unprescribed by an outside group, employees will engage in illegal or incompetent acts which will dissipate the assets of the institution. There is no debate about the existence of mistaken and questionable decisions. The choice is about who is to control them, the work unit itself, or a third party.

SOME EXAMPLES

▼ A plant manager is told to attend a one-week course on diversity. He asks why he is going. The answer is that everyone at his level is attending the course.

▼ A safety manager has determined all salaried people in his plant need twenty hours of training on federal and state environmental and safety regulations.

▼ A "results management" unit requires each department to submit three stretch goals for the coming year, and to define the milestones for measurement along the way.

▼ Department heads are told to work with an internal consultant in developing a unit vision and values statement that supports the corporate vision and values statement.

▼ The head of nursing in a hospital has been told her unit has been targeted for an operations review. When would she like to schedule it?

▼ There is a new performance appraisal process tied to a change in the merit pay system. An afternoon meeting has been scheduled to explain it. Plan on the whole afternoon.

▼ Finance is beginning a review of its financial operations manual. A sales manager has been selected to sit on the committee charged with the review.

And so it goes. All business-oriented, reasonable requests. All integral elements of each staff unit's efforts to maximize its own contribution to the business. What these requests all have in common, though, is that if the line people had been given a choice, they would have said no to most of them. They would not have argued with the intentions of these activities, but they would have taken exception to the form and the timing of the service to be delivered.

DON'T CALL THEM A CUSTOMER
IF THEY HAVE NO CHOICE

When staff groups take the initiative to gain top management commitment and provide consistency down through the organization, they bring into play the limitations of what we call leadership. What gets inverted is the question of who is the customer and who is deciding on the nature of the service. Staff groups deciding what is good for their customers is not stewardship, it is paternalism. It is control disguised as service. If you have the right to dictate service to others, you cannot call them a customer. Calling people you can demand a response from a "customer" is manipulation...using the language of consideration to soften the coercion in the relationship.

> *If you have the right to dictate service to others, you cannot call them a customer.*

BUREAUCRACY BY ANY OTHER NAME

The enveloping arms of staff groups is what we commonly think of when we complain about bureaucracy. The problem with complaining about bureaucracy is that it is always someone else's regulations that we want suspended. Just like we all want to cut back on the federal deficit by reducing expenditures in congressional districts other than our own. Simply eliminating a list of regulations will have only a marginal benefit. Stating that we need to cut back on bureaucracy is a solution with no substance, too cheaply bought. We could easily go to each staff group and reduce its demands, item by item. Eliminate the training, the reviews, the audits, the task forces, the visioning process and you buy some short-term benefit. But soon these activities will be replaced by others. An accident will happen, money will be lost, a project will come in late and over budget, noise over the new pay system will intensify and, in response, top management will demonstrate leadership, and the rule making and legislation cycle will begin again.

If we want political reform, something more fundamental needs to change than restraining staff requests. As stated throughout this book, our belief in consistency and control as the cornerstone of governance needs to be abandoned. As long as we believe that consistency and control are the basis for creating productive communities, we will have leadership from the top and muscular staff groups, no matter how self-managing and customer-focused the core work process may be.

OFFERING CHOICE AND BUILDING CAPABILITY

The stewardship alternative is to require staff groups to operate as authentic service units. The core work units become their primary customers. As customers, line groups gain more control over the relationship and can obtain a unique response from the staff groups. Staff groups give up power in this process in exchange for the possibility of serving the organization in a more important way. Instead of maintaining consistency and control, their contribution is that of building capability. This needs to happen not out of altruism, but in order to survive. In the longer run, it is the core work customers, not top management, who will keep staff groups alive and well. In flattening organizations under heavy cost pressure, even those protected by the power of the presidency will come under scrutiny. It has not happened yet, but when it does, only those who have won the support of middle managers will survive. The survival question will be, "What value have you added to the process of delivering our product or service to our customers?" Work teams responsible for managing the core work process will be the ones whose answer counts. When given a choice, and it is coming, the line organization will not continue to buy policing, inspection, and caretaking services. If staff groups do not face this turning point themselves, someone else will do it for them, and not so gently.

No one has an easy time giving up power, especially after only recently acquiring it. We cannot, however, speak the language of employee involvement and empowerment without asking the staff groups to follow suit in giving more choice to lower levels of the line organization. Here are some of the elements required to make this work.

▼ **Staff groups are no longer held responsible for implementing top management policy and strategy.** Line management is responsible for implementing strategy, not staff groups. Staff groups implement strategy in the governance of their own affairs, but not in the governance of others' affairs.

▼ **Staff groups define teams involved in the core work process as their primary customers.** Staff units commit themselves to meeting the requirements of people close to the customer and close to the product or service. This means that each staff activity must say how it has direct impact on quality delivered to the institution's customers or on the people serving those customers. Top management becomes a secondary client. Top management needs support to deal with constituencies outside and above in their own organization. There are reporting requirements concerning finance, environmental protection, health and safety, and the like that staff groups are well-equipped to handle. The key is to keep the staff groups out of the internal control and consistency business. If staff groups focus their service toward the lower levels, the demand for control and consistency will dry up. When top management needs control and consistency, let them ask it of their subordinate organizations instead of seeking it through the staff functions.

▼ **The staff group's primary role is to transfer their expertise to the line units.** Education, support, and consultation is what replaces policing and granting permission. If it is a finance group, their task may be to teach core work teams how to set up control systems, how to make good capital investment decisions, how to manage a budget. If it is a human resources group, they teach line people how to design a pay system, how to redesign their work teams, how to make good hiring decisions.

ROLE RENEGOTIATION
FOR THE STAFF FUNCTION

When staff groups operate as authentic service units, they then need to contract for the delivery of their services at various levels of the organization. They already have good experience contracting for services at the top, but have typically done less and less contracting as you go down the organization. Let work units of a certain size, say fifty or a hundred people, contract for the services they require. Such a contract negotiation would have the client groups defining three areas of service.

▼ **What the staff function currently does that the client wants them to continue doing.** These services may be such that scarce, highly specialized knowledge is required, or genuine economies of scale warrant centralization. Legal knowledge, accounting practices, or very technical business and scientific expertise fall into this category. Highly repetitive activities may also fall in this area. Meeting payroll requirements, handling accounts payable and receivable, the operations component of systems departments.

▼ **What the staff function does now that should be stopped altogether.** These are often inspection, oversight, review, measurement, and approval functions.

▼ **What the staff does now that the client group should do for itself.** Self-management means self-monitoring. Measuring, inspection, and review moves to the core work teams.

Both the staff and the line have a voice in this dialogue. Both sides have a right to say no. If, however, the two sides cannot reach agreement, the client group has the right to seek the service they want outside the organization. Do not take the dispute to a higher level. Let the line organization have the final word. This is how a free market operates. And this is how accountability is built within the line organization. If the line group has to pay more, or gets poor service elsewhere, so be it. Let them answer to their own management.

Rest assured, there are certain things the staff groups do now that they will continue to do. There are certain functions simply better done in a centralized way. Some purchasing still benefits from an economy of scale. The general ledger activities of finance and the benefits, training, and personnel record-keeping functions of human resources will usually stay as they are. Systems groups will remain the home base for programmers and systems analysts. The point is not to eliminate staff functions altogether. The point is that people close to the work have choice in the services they receive.

DIRECT BILLING

In their revised roles, staff groups bill their services to the line units on a project basis, not as an annual overhead charge. In most organizations where staff groups are driving toward a purely support role, they begin billing their services to lower-level groups. In the past staff groups have always billed their services, but only to the top. This cost is then passed on down the line as an overhead charge. If staff groups begin to define core work units as their prime customers, then to make it real, the core work units need an economic voice. One advantage to billing the line directly is that the staff groups develop more confidence that their services are seen as value added to the basic organization's purpose. People only value what they have chosen to pay for. If core work units choose to budget for your services, it gives you more leverage over them than if they have prepaid for you as an overhead item.

Another advantage to staff groups of direct service billing is that you find out who your good people are. It is difficult in a staff service operation to evaluate people because you generally are not in the room when they are with their clients. When clients have to keep redeciding to pay for services, they get picky and staff people find out where they stand quickly. This is also a source of anxiety for every staff group...if the line people had more choice, they might choose elsewhere. However, if we are advocating accountability at every level of the organization, then we have to live it. Most staff groups who have had the courage to go to direct billing have been surprised and reassured by the demand for their services. The services demanded may change in nature, but the demand is there.

RECONTRACTING

There are limitations to keep in mind about the direct billing process. Most groups that have done it began slowly and billed, say, 30 percent the first year and added another 30 percent the second year. The goal for direct billing will always be something less than 100 percent. There will likely be some portion of the staff's work still dedicated to the organization at large and this will continue to be covered through an overhead charge.

SOMETIMES THE MAGIC WORKS

An interesting arena where many of these changes are happening is in management information systems (MIS) groups. Until the late 1970s, MIS held a monopoly over their users. When systems were driven by large, expensive mainframe computers, the systems groups, in control of this technology, were very much in control of their relationship with their customers. Users knew it, complained about it, and were helpless to do anything about it. Systems groups tended to be managed in very traditional top-down ways, and systems departments were fundamentally at war with their customers.

Then technology changed everything. The personal computer dramatically changed the relationship between systems groups and their customers. Systems groups lost much of their monopoly, users could afford to satisfy many of their own information needs. As a result systems groups had to rethink the way they worked with their customers. There now came to be more balance in the customer relationship and systems groups became more collaborative and user friendly. Changes in the customer relationship also caused changes in the way systems groups were internally managed. What was previously a quite traditional, high-control management style has now changed in many places. Many systems groups are at the front of the movement toward partnership and empowerment. Some of this innovation is due to the difficulty in finding and keeping good systems people, but it is also a case where new technology changed the fundamental relationship with the customer, which in turn created pressure to search for new ways to govern.

When systems groups lost their monopoly, they were forced to give their customers more control over the relationship. All because the advent of the personal computer meant the customer could do for themselves what they had previously been dependent on a centralized service group to deliver. Systems groups now had real business reasons to engage in partnerships.

PRIVATIZING AND VENDORIZING

Somebody save us from the language of institutions. The next time someone tries to privatize or vendorize you, call security. Despite the jargony labels, the ideas need attention. An interesting variation on how to govern support services can be seen in the recent movement for city and state governments to contract out services they used to manage directly themselves. Sanitation, roads, and parks maintenance are examples. They are creating competition for services that were once a monopoly.

Our loss of faith in some of our institutions stems as much from the fact that they are the only game in town as it does from the way they are managed. This is not to say that public agencies do not care about their customers, many of them have mounted enormous quality improvement efforts. They realize that in the long run the quality of their service determines their survival through the political process. But, because they are monopolies, they can maintain sovereignty over their customers and employees for long periods of time. These agencies are in much the same place as many staff groups inside private organizations.

Despite some of the real fears we may have about contracting out services, this strategy is a vote for better service. The belief is that we will get better service if the providers have to compete to get the work. This gets controversial because government workers feel it is costing them jobs and is a way to get around the public employees' union. So, if competition is being fostered in the public service arena, then public employees should also have the right to compete. Let them bid for the jobs that are being contracted to outsiders. Also, let them sell their services to the private sector.

Let the marketplace work in both directions.

Similarly, let internal staff groups can also sell their services outside the organization. If the line organization is free to purchase elsewhere, let the staff be free to sell elsewhere. We do not really understand accountability and ownership until we have direct experience in a free market environment. Few things will raise the competency of our staff functions more quickly than their having to sell their services to strangers. Standing alone in a marketplace is a first order wake-up call and we all need that experience. We know that the organization we work for can no longer provide us the safety we long for, so let us provide the means for people to provide that safety for themselves.

There must be a few restraints on staff groups selling services to other organizations, however. They can't sell to the competition. They shouldn't sell more than a certain percentage of their services outside so they do not lose focus on their main customer inside. Limit outside sales to 25 percent of the total budget. Limit the nature of the services staff groups offer to outside customers to the same thing being offered inside the organization, so there is no deflection from their basic mission. The sooner "private" service agencies (staff groups) and public service agencies choose on their own initiative to give more choice to their customers, the better chance they will have to withstand some more drastic measures imposed by others.

Service Guarantee

There is one other element of strategy to underline the authentic service role of staff groups. This has to do with the service guarantee they would be willing to offer their customers. Christopher Hart has explored the impact that service guarantees can have on the governance of a service—or in this case, of the staff organization. He found that if the service guarantee has real bite to it, it can force-feed a strong service mentality into all aspects of the operation. For a service guarantee to have power it must meet certain criteria.

▼ The guarantee must be absolutely clear and concrete. It must be stated so that it is either fulfilled or not. No ambiguity allowed.

▼ It must be easy for the customer to make a claim against the guarantee. No negotiations or hurdles in the way of the customer claim. The process must be painless for the customer.

▼ The service organization must pay a serious price, suffer some pain for not having fulfilled the guarantee.

A good example would be a systems group promising to design a way to track the sales to certain key customers on a monthly basis. The systems group commits to a schedule for the new report, commits to train the sales staff in how to operate the system, and commits to the quality of output of the system. With a real service guarantee, the systems group needs to be very specific about their promises. They need to define exactly what the new system will deliver, to spell out what constitutes a fully trained sales staff, and to pick a delivery date that is fail-safe. Up to this point, this is nothing that unique. Most groups work hard at defining the expectations on their projects and take their promises seriously. What is unique about a service guarantee are the last two covenants—how can we make it easy for the customer to invoke the guarantee and what penalty does the service organization pay for not fulfilling promises? If our systems group is serious about their guarantee, they might say that anyone at any level of the sales organization can invoke the guarantee, and all they have to do is make one phone call. If any customer states that they were not adequately trained, that the schedule was missed, that the report did not meet specifications, the systems group must deliver on the guarantee. Taken literally, this means no arguing about perceptions, no defending by producing data on how 90 percent of the promise was fulfilled. If only one person representing the customer produces one piece of proof that the promise was not fulfilled, the guarantee is invoked.

The guarantee might read something like this: "If we do not fulfill any part of our promise, we will refund all of the money we charged you for the project. We will then fix the system to your satisfaction. If you do not want us to complete the job or fix the system, we, the staff group, will pay out of our budget the money for you, the customer, to find the supplier of your choice to complete the job. You pick them, we pay." This is a strong guarantee, incurring real pain to the supplier of staff services.

There are two points to notice about a guarantee like this. One is that it forces enormous attention on the promise made to internal customers. This attention ultimately will underscore how critical core workers are to the unit and will support the idea that they need to have the power to do what is best for the customer. It will also lead to the core workers' having a voice in the promises being made by the staff service unit. So often the boss in staff groups makes promises to customers with no input from the person having to deliver on the promise. A service guarantee will force a dialogue between the people making promises and the one fulfilling them. These are key elements of the partnership we are striving for.

A service guarantee will force a dialogue between the people making promises and the one fulfilling them.

The second consequence of a strong guarantee is that it equalizes the power between staff groups and their line organization clients. Staff groups will have a hard time mandating services and acting as a conscience when a dissatisfied line unit can have such an immediate impact on their budget. Strong guarantees force parity in the dialogue between supplier and consumer, which is what stewardship and partnership look like.

Recreating organizational governance in line with stewardship structures and practices produces substantial and striking shifts in the role of staff groups and forever changes the way the staff works with the line. The next two chapters get more specific about what these changes would entail in our financial management and human resource practices.

9

FINANCIAL PRACTICES: CREATING ACCOUNTABILITY WITH SELF-CONTROL

Years ago at Exxon they had a philosophy of decentralization. The corporate executives would give autonomy to their operating companies in all areas of operation but two—the control of people and the control of money. They understood that how you control money and how you control personnel practices are the keys to the kingdom. This chapter is about the money, the next one is about the people.

Money is vital to how we govern because it is the universal measuring device. It does not measure everything we care about, but it is the common language we use to measure the health of the institution, as well as our promises to each other and how well we have delivered on those promises. We have created the financial function to help us become fully informed and communicate about performance. Financial functions also help people, through budgets, to document and keep track of their promises. These intentions are service-oriented and a critical means for people at all levels to fulfill their stewardship responsibility.

What has happened in many organizations, however, is that the service intentions of the financial function have been pressed into becoming an arm of patriarchy and have become a powerful control center in their own right. The legitimate need for consistency in measuring and reporting across the organization has become a lever to exercise control. What began as a partnership function designed to offer line people the methodology to maintain control over their own affairs has evolved into a parenting function that top management uses to hold their own subordinate units accountable. The financial profession, of its own accord and eagerness, has been in most cases a willing participant in taking on the parenting role.

Reforming the distribution of power and privilege means reassessing financial practices that are deeply ingrained in our way of thinking about organization. Too many managers are eager to embrace the concept of self-managing work teams, but have made minimal efforts to release to those teams greater control over money.

Our attitudes about money, which get expressed in the way we charter our finance departments, continue to be healthy remnants of the direct command-and-control governance strategy. This is very visible in the arena of public service. At every level of government, there are watchdog and review units. Their intent is to control fraud and costs. They are given license to dictate controls and exercise oversight. Little happens without passing through their screens. Every organization has its counterparts. In many financial departments, as mentioned earlier, one of the top jobs is often called controller. This is not what you would call a customer-oriented job title.

Managers are eager to embrace the concept of self-managing work teams, but have made minimal efforts to release to those teams greater control over money.

When you control something, backed by charter, guided by generally accepted accounting principles, watched yourself by external auditors and supported by top management, the extent of the parenting role is evident.

To put stewardship into practice and to support widespread accountability, there has to be a way of thinking about how to control money that does not institutionalize controlling and caretaking functions within one department, namely finance. A reminder...all this discussion is not so much a commentary about the finance function, it is about our attitudes about controlling money. The financial function is simply performing the function that we have asked it to do. If our financial staff represent the implementation arm of patriarchy, which I think they do, it is because we have collectively decided that patriarchy is how we wish to govern.

THE MONEY IS THE MESSAGE

Financial planning and controls are a major device for living out our intentions. Few things symbolize our beliefs, philosophy, and fears more vividly than the systems and procedures we establish to control money. Financial procedures determine the way we talk about our plans, our performance, our history. Economics has become such a central theme in our lives that we even give money the power to determine our self-esteem. If we want to know where we stand at work, our budget and our spending authority are the most trustworthy, unambiguous indication of how the organization feels about us. Value and trust are measured by the amount of money we are paid and the amount of money we are free to spend.

The extent of the financial controls tells us whether we are an insider or an outsider, whether our star is rising or falling, whether we are accepted for who we are, or whether there is still much to prove. The size of our budget and our approval authority is tightly interwoven with our system of privilege and prerogative. The amount of dollars at our disposal is the badge of initiation and the larger the number, the deeper into the ruling class we have entered. Controlling dollars, in and of itself, has become the trophy, whether or not it is good for the business.

We too easily claim sovereignty by the way we control money. If you doubt this, try to remember an unemotional discussion you have had about allowances with your parents or your children. Redistributing ownership and responsibility will be credible only when we are willing to redesign our financial controls and practices to give more choice to people close to the customer. You cannot have participation and self-management at the bottom of the organization and maintain highly centralized financial practices sitting unchanged at the top.

The right to manage the money of others is in some ways more powerful than the right to fire somebody. Firing happens so infrequently that it lacks day-to-day currency. Controlling dollars, because of the frequency and immediacy of the act, is the operational definition of power in our institutions. As a result, the redistribution of decision making goes hand in hand with reevaluating the systems and procedures used to spend and control money. Approval levels, the budgeting process, the disclosure of economic information, the ability to purchase and spend money at the point of making the product, selling the product, and servicing customers are all at the center of empowerment and widely felt partnership.

> **The redistribution of decision making goes hand in hand with reevaluating the systems and procedures used to spend and control money.**

BUILDING WIDESPREAD FINANCIAL STEWARDSHIP

If we wanted the way we approached money to reflect our commitment to stewardship, here is our agenda.

FULL DISCLOSURE AND ECONOMIC LITERACY

For all the reasons discussed earlier in the context of renegotiating the contract toward stewardship, full information also holds here. Whomever we wish to be accountable for outcomes needs to understand the economic realities of the organization and they also need to understand how you go about getting money and spending money. Being fully informed means we understand the economic consequences of the choices we make.

One concern about full disclosure is that there is information that we do not want competitors to know—some of our cost structure, our plans for getting in or out of new products or businesses.

It comes down to how much we can trust the people in our unit and how vulnerable we think we are to betrayal. The bias should be toward disclosing what we know. Much of what we think is so confidential the world already knows about or will read in the papers in the morning.

Controlling financial information is also a way of maintaining power. We have the technology for widespread economic knowledge about the organization. What is required is the will and the trust to spread it. When people are fully informed, power gets balanced.

BUDGET ACCOUNTABILITY

There is a need for each person or team to be responsible for the budget that covers their activities. This is especially difficult because most of us are not spending our own money. It is not only someone else's money, but most of us never write a check or see a bank balance. Budgets are funny money that we do not naturally come to own. Emotionally, ownership and responsibility come from the act of creation and the state of full knowledge. One key question is, where is the budget initiated? A budget is a promise. It is the commitment to meet a set of objectives, to deliver a set of products or services for a predetermined and fixed level of expenditure. The most primitive question is whether core workers create and commit to their own budgets, or is a budget handed to them, either by supervision or a staff group? Choosing the restraints and ground rules by which we live is what creates accountability. Being handed the budget promise in the form of a menu of acceptable expenditures robs those doing the work of accountability. If we are reluctant to fully involve people in the budgeting process it often means that we do not want to make visible to them the ways we have made decisions that impact them and their work.

Another symptom of the patriarchy in many budgeting processes is the padding that goes on. The belief is that I have to ask for more money than I need so that there will be a surplus for someone else to take away. An expression of a low-trust, high-control environment.

MONITORING

The monitoring process names the people that we want to be responsible for economic stewardship. One of the financial function's primary contribution is to provide a common way of tracking and communicating the economic performance of the organization. This information is needed to decide where to allocate resources and to know when units are in trouble. How the measurements are chosen and how the reporting is done make all the difference. When line organizations fight against common measuring and common reporting processes, it is because they do not trust how the centralized financial group and their own management will use the information. It is a delicate balance between being the agency that collects the performance information and still staying in the service and partnership role with the line organization. When the finance group gets too active with top management in pinpointing problems and offering prescriptions, they let the line organization off the hook for taking responsibility for our economic future. Partnership means that each party has a hand in choosing which dollars are to be watched most closely, the way of communicating the results of the watching, and especially the actions that follow. Part of the problem is that we have the technology for wide numbers of people to easily get lots of information on every operation. A simple example is that managers can effortlessly get detailed travel expense and phone bill data for subordinates several levels down. Just because the technology can get us the information, it does not mean we have to use it. Stewardship will become a reality when teams of core workers have the tools in their own hands to analyze their own economic well-being and retain the choice of how to act on the data.

*P*artnership means that each party has a hand in choosing which dollars are to be watched most closely, the way of communicating the results of the watching.

SPENDING AUTHORITY

Spending authority is the quickest measure of privilege available. Setting spending authority by level is the vehicle by which the class system gets established. The notion of having people at higher levels able to make larger dollar decisions makes some sense, since they have a wider view of the organization. The disparity in spending authority between levels, though, is worth looking at. Often we have people who are responsible for a three-million-dollar budget unable to spend five hundred dollars without permission. What is critical is that there is a good business justification for expenditures. Core workers need to learn how to calculate rates of return and they need to know what rate of return is required by the bankers. Given this literacy, they have the resources to own the decision.

Approval authority has to do with how many signatures are needed before money is spent. Why more than two signatures? The only justification for three or four levels to sign off on an expenditure is to reinforce sovereignty, not to add to the wisdom of the decision. At the China Lakes Naval Weapons Center the signature process was causing costly delays. To solve this, they gave credit cards to four hundred employees, who can now go to town to buy what is needed to get the job done. They are told to use normal channels for purchasing first, but if that does not get them what they need soon enough, go to town. They create the paper trail after the decision is made and the problem is solved. There is a message of trust in this innovative procedure that probably has benefits equal to the value of speeding up purchases. Two years into the procedure, the trust had not been betrayed.

CENTRALIZED PURCHASING

A major justification for centralizing spending authority has been the economies of scale gained by a purchasing department. Purchasing people are skilled in vendor negotiations and can get better terms with a quantity buy. In many instances this represents a real advantage, but what does not get measured is the cost of the people who are doing the work having to wait for what they need. If speed of response to a marketplace or customer is critical, the total cost of a slow purchase may far outweigh the price advantages of a more skilled or controlled purchase. The alternative is to have the amount of controls and the location of the purchase decision be defined primarily by the requirements of the line organization. Let the level of spending authority and the flexibility to spend money be determined by the nature of the task and the need for short-cycle decisions.

Reassessing the cost of our control systems will also serve to save money in the purchasing process itself. There are too many stories of spending four dollars to purchase a six-dollar item. This may seem humorous, but I know of one company that, when they looked at the cost of their own purchasing practices, discovered they were spending four million dollars to control the purchase of six-million-dollars worth of raw materials.

When purchasing and financial control groups decide to define their role as teaching the line organization how to design their own controls, rather than to enforce control and consistency, then they will have begun to treat the core work teams as customers. They will negotiate a range of different services and levels of involvement depending on the group. We may not all get credit cards, but maybe a charge account at the local deli.

THE AUDIT FUNCTION

Auditing units have the most difficult role in choosing how to serve the institution. They are required by regulation in many cases to perform a policing function in service of top management. At the same time they want to support line managers in performing better. Auditing always has a choice, though. They can give emphasis to policing and protection or they can give emphasis to learning and consultation. Auditing was born of police-and-protect parents and giving this heritage up is not easy and to some extent not advisable. There is a need to guard against fraud and you need arms-length third parties to do that.

Audit crosses over the line, though, when it becomes a surrogate manager and takes responsibility for eliminating ineffective practices. A federal oversight agency discovered that a waste management contractor had spent $150 for a reindeer suit for a Christmas party and charged it against the contract as part of their general and administrative expense. There was nothing illegal about doing this. The auditors just thought it was stupid. Otherwise, the contractor was doing a good job on the project. The $150 made it into the news anyway as an example of waste. The real waste was that it probably cost the government $500 to find that reindeer suit, plus ten times that amount from the disruption of the working relationship and the point-and-defend gyrations that always follow this kind of finding.

Auditing's deeper purpose is to support stewardship responsibilities at every level. In a stewardship environment, middle managers and core workers would be prime customers, top management and audit committees would get secondary attention.

In general, the finance function supports patriarchy when it chooses to

▼ Take sole responsibility to write policy and procedures to control expenditures and conform to the law.

▼ Be responsible for compliance with those procedures and policies.

▼ Conduct studies to assess compliance with those policies and procedures.

▼ Report to the top on the outcome of those studies.

Deeper accountability from the line organization would result from having finance do the following:

▼ Teach line people how to create their own policies and procedures. Write policies only as requested by operating units.

▼ Jointly sponsor studies, at the invitation of line units where possible. Have the line units determine how the findings will be acted upon. Let the outcome of the studies be the property of the requesting line unit. Have reporting up the line done by line managers, with the audit group in attendance, not leading. Fraud and safety issues would be the only exceptions. No policing on simply ineffective practices.

▼ Identify the absolute minimum of standard practices that need to be done consistently across operating groups. Have minimal formats for reporting results. Require the financial group to justify consistency, rather than asking line units to justify exceptions.

The principle is that people are responsible for creating the standards against which they choose to be measured. Also that individuals and teams are capable of self-monitoring their own performance against those measures. The role of the staff group is to consult and to teach the tools, skills, and ways of thinking about how to create effective controls and measures. Maybe 20 percent of the time the requirements and controls are so technical that it does not pay for the line to learn how to design them. But let staff-driven controls and staff-driven watching be the exception. The staff role is then an educational function performed in service to self-management.

> *The role of the staff group is to consult and to teach the tools, skills, and ways of thinking about how to create effective controls and measures.*

LIVING WITHIN THE LAW

One of the difficulties of changing the way the financial groups relate to the line organization is the existence of regulations and the world of generally accepted accounting principles. Any time you loosen central controls and more widely distribute financial decisions you are taking some risk. The task of the financial profession is not to be responsible for eliminating risks, but to clarify what the risks are and what the consequences of failure are. The desire to create a risk-free environment is exactly what bureaucracy is about. Every policy and regulation on the books exists because someone in the past, through ignorance or irresponsibility, made a mistake. The bigger the mistake, the bigger and more pervasive the regulation. The belief, especially in public service, is that we can legislate errors, loss, and embarrassment out of our institutions. Each act of control, inspection, and regulation reduces responsibility and ownership from those living under its rule.

For stewardship to be widespread, controls should be designed for others with great caution and dialogue. The act of faith is that with good information and good will, people can make responsible decisions about what controls they require and whom they want to implement them. This makes it possible for financial people to stay primarily in the service business. They have unique skills in understanding control systems, in knowing effective accounting practices, and in processing financial information and presenting it in useful ways. They can earn their seat at the table by their ability to understand the economics of the organization rather than by their ability to control it. In fact, this is the relationship financial people already have with people at the top of the organizations they serve. The shift then is to relate in the same way to people at the middle and lower levels.

10

HUMAN RESOURCES: ENDING THE PRACTICE OF PATERNALISM

The process of managing people, just like managing money, is everybody's job. The human resource function, as a staff group, is a focal point for defining practices and policies that embody our intentions about how to govern. Our belief that consistency and control are the cornerstones for running productive organizations is visibly reflected in our human resource policies and in the way we expect this staff function to operate. Human resources (HR) has evolved into a caretaking and enabling function whose assignment is to take responsibility for the morale and emotional well-being of employees.

The traditional role of line management is to be in charge of patriarchy, their primitive statement to employees being, "We own you." To balance this, human resources has been put in charge of paternalism. Their primitive statement to employees is, "Don't worry so much about the fact that they own you, because we will take care of you." This combination creates the golden handcuffs that make living in a world of dominance and dependency so tolerable. As subordinates, we yield sovereignty with the expectation that those in charge of us will care for us in a reasonable and compassionate way. As leaders, as opposed to stewards, we think that if we have protective and

*L*eadership does not question its own desire for dominance, it asks only that the dominance be implemented humanely.

caring human resource policies, we have ruled with grace and kindness. Leadership does not question its own desire for dominance, it asks only that the dominance be implemented humanely. The handcuffs of control become golden when they are fitted with the promise of protection and satisfaction.

INSTITUTIONAL CARETAKER

We have designed human resource policies and used the human resource function to deliver on this promise of protection and satisfaction. As mentioned so many times in this book, caretaking and protection feeds self-interest and undermines ownership and responsibility. The entrepreneurial mindset is incompatible with handcuffs for bracelets, no matter how valuable their metal.

Choosing stewardship, therefore, means fundamentally rethinking our human resource policies and the role of the human resource function. Stated most simply, it is a move from parent to partner in how we hire, fire, pay, appraise, train, promote, transfer, provide benefits, and improve the organization. HR has the task of creating policies in these areas and assuring their implementation. Muscle, in the form of approval authority, has been given to the function to insure compliance and consistency. In most organizations, if you want to do training, adjust your pay system, add a new job or a new level, hire someone, redo any people-related process, you go to human resources for their formal or informal approval. The fact that your HR department may be supportive and sensitive to your requirements, and more often than not give you what you ask for, does not change the approval-seeking nature of the relationship.

A NEW PURPOSE AND ROLE

Stewardship for human resources requires renegotiating their role away from the policy-selling, policy-implementing business. No more personnel policies centrally defined and implemented across the board. No more approval authority residing in a staff function. HR can live out its own stewardship more cleanly by defining core work teams as their primary client, rather than top management. HR can see its task to provide the tools and skills and process for people close to the work to develop their own personnel practices and procedures. Let a plant, a department, a sales region design its own hiring, pay, appraisal, training practices. If there is a genuine need for consistency across units, let the plant or department or region know that, and they can accommodate the need for, say, consistent reporting in their redesign effort. Human resources has special expertise in the people area and in the realm of creating culture, so let them teach that expertise, and let go the role of creator and compliance officer. The teaching role is much better aligned with partnership and distributing ownership and responsibility.

HR can live out its own stewardship more cleanly by defining core work teams as their primary client, rather than top management.

In some cases, staff people rightly claim that the line organization does not want to create their own personnel practices. That the line likes having the HR function to send people to when problems occur. The line gets a payoff from the parenting role of the staff groups…they have someone outside the intimacy of their own family group to hold responsible for unpopular decisions. All this may be true. But any staff group, like HR, usually has a choice about the nature of the services they want to offer, just as the line groups need to have a choice about the services they want to receive. If top management commands the staff group to act in a policing way, there may be no choice…we all work for a living. In most cases, though, it is the staff group like HR that has sought a more muscular role, feeling that policing powers would enhance their contribution. What we have sought and received, we can give back. When HR sees its primary contribution as creating a governance system of partnership and self-management, it will start to happen.

As with most other staff functions, top management has been HR's primary customer, especially for the top human resource executive. As HR groups have defined their role as implementing top management's strategic intentions, they have become an agent of top management. The HR executive becomes the counselor to the top executive. In and of itself there is no problem with this, everyone needs an advisor. It becomes a problem when attention to the top becomes a primary focus, when it becomes a statement of purpose.

HR's frequent dialogue with executives on how to handle "those people," patronizing as it is, will continue if we think our most critical relationship is with the top of the house. This is our collusion with patriarchy. As soon as HR defines its purpose as supporting partnership among those in the line organization, however, it must change its relationship with the top. We then stop being the agent of the top, and work with them in discovering ways they can better support core workers. In stewardship, core workers are the customers of top management and it is no easy task to learn how to live that out. No longer will we use our influence with the top to help them better control and shape core workers.

To make these ideas more concrete, there are two aspects of the HR function that are worth exploring. One is the way the function is structured and works with its customers. The other is the set of beliefs underlying the human resource policies and practices. Most of our widely-accepted personnel practices are deeply parenting and paternalistic.

THE STRUCTURE OF HUMAN RESOURCES

As part of its legacy of defining and implementing policy, HR is organized according to professional specialty. There are separate sections on compensation, executive compensation, management development, skills training, recruiting, benefits, affirmative action, organization development, total quality management, labor or industrial relations, and employee relations. As with every functional structure, organizing this way makes it easier to train people, to control the operation, and to focus energy, plus it allows you to support more in-depth, specialized knowledge. The main limitation of a functional structure is that it does not react well to the customer's need for quick and whole-system oriented solutions. The different functions in HR are so interrelated, you cannot really solve a problem in one area without touching many of the others. When a supervisor comes to the compensation person and says, "I need an exception to keep one of my best people," you are most likely treating a symptom. The underlying problem could be a recruiting issue, where a promise was made upon hiring that was unfulfillable; it could be a problem with how a team is working together, which would involve the organizational development group. Or this request for exceptional pay treatment could involve a performance appraisal or career development problem. A functional organization has trouble bringing to bear five different viewpoints on a customer

If **human resources intends to be a model of a customer-oriented service function, it argues for a structure organized around customers.**

problem. If human resources intends to be a model of a customer-oriented service function, it argues for a structure organized around customers. We would create teams serving client groups with the intent that all of the team members would learn all of the disciplines of human resources. This is where the line organization is headed. They are organizing into teams responsible for a whole work process or teams organized around customers.

How we are structured also affects how we make the transition from a policing and conscience role to one of service to a customer who has a choice of suppliers. Helping departments redesign their own practices requires one or two internal HR consultants working with the line group on the total redesign, rather than five or six individuals consulting with the group on each of their specialties. The task becomes to help the line group redesign a pay system rather than be in the expert role of doing the redesign for the line client. Organizing teams of staff people with good consulting skills around customer groups provides structural support to a service and stewardship orientation.

HUMAN RESOURCE PRACTICES THAT SUPPORT STEWARDSHIP

In addition to rethinking the structure of the human resource group, the actual substance of human resource practices needs to be placed on the table. Here is a brief helicopter survey of how conventional personnel practices embody patriarchy, caretaking, and compliance, plus some thoughts on the stewardship option.

BURYING PERFORMANCE APPRAISAL

Performance appraisals are an instrument for social control. They are annual discussions, avoided more often than held, in which one adult identifies for another adult three improvement areas they should work on over the next twelve months. You can soften them all you want, call them development discussions, have them on a regular basis, have the subordinate identify the improvement areas instead of the boss, and discuss values. None of this changes the basic transaction. Bosses evaluating subordinates, with the outcome determining pay treatment. As a boss you can conduct the appraisal in as loving way as possible. Most supervisors have been trained in listening skills, making good eye contact, asking open-ended questions, checking for agreement, making support statements, and identifying strengths so we do not become obsessed with weaknesses. All of this helps, none of it heals. The transaction has a element of sovereignty to it that will not go away. If the intent of the appraisal is learning, it is not going to happen when the context of the dialogue is evaluation and judgment.

Besides not being conducive to learning, performance appraisals as we know them are a mistake from the viewpoint of accountability. We should be appraised by those to whom we are accountable. Stewardship means accountability to those we have power over. If you insist on having an appraisal process, let people be appraised by their customers. This means bosses will be appraised by their subordinates, each person is appraised by the people they define as their customers/suppliers. When we have people appraised by their bosses, what we are creating is trained followership. If we want stewardship, turn it around. One way is to let each person be responsible for one appraisal per year...their own. This gives them a choice about whether they want to use this method to learn, it

If **you insist on having an appraisal process, let people be appraised by their customers.**

gives them choice over the people they learn from, and it puts the responsibility for learning with each individual, where it belongs.

Self-directed appraisal will work only if we unhinge the learning process from the pay system. If you must rate people to pay them, then have the discussion, tell each person where they stand, ask for questions, and end the conversation. Don't call it a learning experience. Save your skills for a time when they have a chance to work. Call it a meeting, not a performance appraisal or a developmental experience. No learning can take place when we are being told by powerful people how much we are loved and how much we are going to get paid for that love.

The appraisal process is a tough one to let go. I was talking about all this with a group of school superintendents, and one of them stated that he did two hundred teacher evaluations each year. He had developed a rating scale of effective teaching behaviors, and he showed us numbers to demonstrate that each year teachers were improving on his scale as a result of his evaluations. He also was confident the teachers appreciated his evaluations. The point he missed is the dependency that his practice creates. Here is a superintendent, going around the building principal, taking responsibility for teacher improvement, measuring dimensions he alone has chosen, deciding when and where the teachers' learning should take place. And then feeling useful when the teachers tell him they appreciate being watched. It is so deeply ingrained in us to expect an evaluation from people we report to, and to give an evaluation to those that report to us, that we feel a little lost when it does not happen. This is the child in us, equating people's opinion of us with their protection. If I please them, they will provide for me. This is the parent in us, believing that the way I show concern for those I manage is by evaluating them and helping them grow.

Let our desire for feedback and learning come out of conversations with our customers and peers. However deep and human the longing for praise from powerful people, keep it out of the means we use to govern. We do not want to institutionalize dominance and we do not want to institutionalize compliance, so we search for ways to get feedback and ways to find out where we stand that encourage us to live as partners.

If you are a boss and your people want to know where they stand, tell them, but do not formalize it, document it, and file it. If at some point you have to fire someone, you will have time to create the documentation. It is so rare that we fire someone, why drag everyone through the knothole of appraisals to be legally safe for the 1 or 2 percent we eventually let go? What we seek in each practice we design is a way to answer a business requirement—in this case, learning how to improve—with each person taking responsibility for meeting the requirement.

HIRING

This one is fairly simple. The intent of community is to have all of us committed to each other's success. We commit ourselves to those we have chosen. If bosses choose subordinates, as tradition dictates, then it is the boss who is committed to make that choice work. Team members may choose to support a new member, as they most often do, but peers are not accountable to one another unless they have in some way selected one another. So, have teams hire new members. If consensus is too hard to achieve, give each member of the team veto power, so at least they will not have to live with someone they have strong objections to. Treat the boss as a full member of the team; bosses should not have to live with someone they do not want either.

ENDING THE CAREER PROMISE

Our practices in career development are the seedbed of institutionalized caretaking. In our recruiting efforts, at the point of hire and often on an annual basis, we promise people we will take responsibility for their careers. The purpose of a career development discussion is to help people think about where they are headed and determine what training and work experience they need to get there. In the more sophisticated organizations, bosses place emphasis on the employee's taking initiative in defining their own future. We help them clarify their values, we help them identify their strengths and their desires.

No matter how human and helpful the dialogue, its structure and implied promise make it a vehicle of parenting. The elements of parenting are

▼ The boss calls the meeting.

▼ The focus is exclusively on the subordinate.

▼ The boss has private information about the subordinate's future that is rarely shared. And for good reason. If the boss discusses a future move, it had better be a done deal. We pay dearly for creating expectations for others that we cannot fulfill...100 percent of the time.

▼ The discussion in places is a requirement. The boss and the subordinate must talk about the employee's future. You even hear some employees complain because they have not had their career development discussion. Is there any doubt about who the child is and who the parent is at this moment?

Leadership as we have known it takes a proprietary interest in the future and the well-being of those being led. One of the hallmarks of autocratic leaders is the pride they take in providing for the future well-being of those who have been loyal to them. When people become our possessions, we feel responsible for their well-being and their future, as we do so deeply about our children. This caretaking inevitably has an element of control in it. The career development process is one of the key moments at work where the vow of caretaking in exchange for compliance gets consummated.

One of the hallmarks of autocratic leaders is the pride they take in providing for the future well-being of those who have been loyal to them. When people become our possessions, we feel responsible for their well-being and their future.

Partners care about each other's plans and future, but take no responsibility making it happen for the other person. Stewardship honors people's career aspirations but keeps responsibility for a career within the individual. There is no need to institutionalize the process of helping people with their future. The way to decrease someone's dependency on us is to keep clear that their future is in their own hands. They do not have to please us to get what they want. If someone wants a discussion about their future, let them ask for it. They are not limited to asking their boss, let them ask anyone they think can give them good information. If they want to write down their aspirations and have us keep that list in their file, let them write them down, and we will file it for them.

Management may want to do its own planning of personnel moves to make sure they have good people ready for key jobs when they are needed. Succession planning makes sense. Management does this for its own sake, though, not for the sake of the employee. We should not imply that any human resource planning system is designed to provide a structured career path with the employee's interests primarily in mind. The reason we do not want to make the promise is that when we tell people we will provide a career for them, we can deliver on the promise for only about the top 10 percent of them. The rest are essentially on their own. Better, for reasons of partnership and practicality, to keep career development completely in the hands of the individual. We will support people in their aspirations when we can and when we choose to. But no annual discussions, no formal procedure, no hiring sealed with a promise. No recruiting brochures showing employees with two years of service making presentations to attentive executives in paneled offices. These practices conspire to make an unfulfillable promise in addition to feeding the self-interest of people who would join us for the sake of a fast-track career, rather than joining us to be part of this entrepreneurial experiment. Our intent is to pay well and promote as best we can, we just cannot promise any of it.

REFORMING MANAGEMENT DEVELOPMENT AND TRAINING

Another area of human resources that needs attention is how we go about training and development. If our intent is to invest in the skills and capabilities of people in a way that keeps ownership and responsibility in their hands, the strategy hinges on who chooses the training and what form it takes.

STOP REINFORCING THE CLASS SYSTEM

We frequently organize training events by the organizational level of the participants. Many places have a person in charge of executive development, another in charge of middle manager development, a supervisory training person, a skills training person, and finally an organization development person who consults more than trains but stands with the others under the same umbrella. Needless to say, the executive development training is done in a quite different style from the supervisory and skills training. For executive training, the higher the cost of the instructor, the more elegant the learning space, and the more special the meals, the more attractive the package looks. In contrast, for supervisory training, heaven is when we have a low-cost instructor, inexpensive learning space, and the group is on its own for lunch. All this is done to align the training with the status expectations of the students, it has little to do with their learning requirements. Each executive session conducted in an exclusive resort, in this way, reinforces patriarchy. Each two-hour-a-week session, taught after hours on people's own time, reinforces patriarchy from the other direction. The solution is not to send everyone to the resort or to the basement, just send them to the same space.

MIX LEVELS IN THE CLASSROOM

Composition is another training question. When we segregate participants by job level, we perpetuate their isolation from each other. There may be some genuine differences in the requirements between levels, but not to the extent that we consistently separate

TRAINING

When we segregate participants by job level, we perpetuate their isolation from each other.

them. Plus, what better place for people to cross the boundaries that separate levels than in a learning environment? Let them cross the boundaries as students in training together. Stop having an executive come in for a short presentation and a half-hour of question and answer. In the training business I am part of, we still get calls from people who like our course content, but ask whether we will have any vice-presidents in an upcoming class, because a certain executive insists on attending courses with other executives with "similar problems." Makes sense on the surface, but it is code for the class system.

When constructing any training on quality, changing culture, fostering high-performing and self-managing teams, set the rule that each class needs three or four levels in it. Make classes for separate levels the exception. As far as the structure of the management development unit, let a team of training people serve the training needs of all levels. This breaks down the elitism within the staff functions as well.

CHOICE IN LEARNING

The third training and development strategy that would support stewardship is to give people real choice in the matter of their own learning, especially at the lower levels. Consider the principle discussed earlier that people need to choose the services they receive. People at the lower levels of most organizations are nominated or sent to training, they do not really choose it. Typically, managers are informed of training opportunities by a training department and they then fit the person or the team to the course. This means that the manager's choice is limited to the menu offered by the training function, and the core worker's and supervisor's only choice is to say yes or no to what is offered. Saying that we do not force people to go, that we only "nominate" them, is fancy footwork. Even when high-quality training is offered and participants learn, the intention of supporting ownership and responsibility is undermined.

The matter of choice also brings into question the use of across-the-board, common learning experiences. The usual argument is that by having everybody go through the same course they gain a common language and common tools, which eases a culture change effort. Most of the time this wish is not fulfilled. Everyone likes the program, but few own the outcome. One division of AT&T sent all employees through a five-day training program every year for four years. Each year the program changed, each year the ratings were high, each year business was conducted much as the year before. So much training for so many people, with so little impact on people's fundamental experience at work. It was a high-control, caretaking system at the start and still is today.

If you want to create a common language, hold a meeting. Even a long meeting. Make clear your intentions for the business. Then let teams or small units decide on their training and their own path.

Train Teams

We know that personal skills and management training for individuals has little impact on changing organizations. It becomes difficult for an individual to sustain new behaviors in an old environment. Yet we still send individuals to training programs. If our intent is to create community, and teams are a vehicle for doing that, we should offer training that is attended primarily by teams. No team, no training. Or at least we could say that unless three people from a unit attend a program, no one should come. Technical training may be an exception, but when we offer training for people one at a time, we are supporting individualism and missing an opportunity to be a force for political reform. Even the stance of saying that our management development strategy is to train teams is a political stance in and of itself.

You can look at each and every practice in the realm of human resources and easily imagine what the application of stewardship would look like. The above are just some examples that everyone is touched by. Human resource practices do not impact the culture of an institution, they *are* the culture. And most of our common practices reflect our consistency and control legacy. When we seek to find great leaders, we will create congruent practices in an effort to create great followers. Human resources along with financial practices are the primary messengers for communicating the kind of relationship an institution wishes to have with its members and, through them, with its customers. Whatever the name of your change effort—total quality, self-management, entrepreneurial government, school-based education—nothing will get institutionalized until practices in these arenas are redesigned.

When we seek to find great leaders, we will create congruent practices in an effort to create great followers.

11

COMPENSATION AND PERFORMANCE EVALUATION: OVERTURNING THE CLASS SYSTEM

Two elderly ladies leaving a restaurant:
Alice: The food in that restaurant is terrible!
Ruth: I know, and the portions are so small!

The movie *Hannah and Her Sisters*

Compensation systems are like a bad marriage. Not happy, but if we get out of it and look for something better, we fear we might end up worse off than before. So it is with the sacred ground of how we pay people. We have energy about pay that far transcends what you would expect from an economic transaction between employee and employer. Our feelings about it rank right up there with births, weddings, and the big bang theory.

Looking at our paycheck, we draw conclusions about self-worth, justice in the world, our political and economic system, and our personal security. This is all based on whether our supervisor has given us a 4.56 percent or a 6.93 percent salary increase. Keep in mind that this is a supervisor whom I may not want as a neighbor, doesn't really know how complex my job is, and

doesn't really understand the depth of my real contribution to this zoo I call my workplace. Whether they rate me large, colossal, or mammoth, though, affects my pay, and pay is what it is all about. This is the mindset for beginning any discussion of rewards.

THE DIVINE RIGHT OF KINGS

The reward systems that most of us live under are a reflection of our enduring class system and our love affair with leadership. The challenge is to create pay practices that support the heart of stewardship, which is accountability and commitment to the well-being of the whole. Here is an executive summary of five ways our pay practices are incongruent with creating a service- and market-driven institution.

If you are one of the beneficiaries of our current pay practices, don't get defensive. We have all created this system together and we are all trying our best to take advantage of it. Just because we are not winners does not mean we don't believe in it.

THE CLASS SYSTEM

Our compensation practices reinforce the belief in separating the managing from the doing of the work. This is the basis of the class system. Often there is one pay system for executives, the intent of which is to pay them as much as possible. There are other pay systems for managers and core workers. The intent of these is to keep labor costs as low as possible. If we want to reintegrate the managing and the doing of the work, then all levels work under the same pay system. Let the philosophy at every level be to pay people as much as we can. Not that everyone makes the same amount of money, we just play by similar rules.

PAY AND PERFORMANCE

Pay practices are based on the belief that you can buy behavior. We have bought the notion that one of the tasks of leadership is to define the desired behaviors of subordinates and then induce those behaviors by offering money for compliance. We think pay, motivation, and performance are related, despite the absence of any consistent evidence that the more you pay people, the higher their motivation or performance. The effect of this is that when we want to change the behavior of others, we start tinkering with how to pay for the new behavior. Always a mistake. The belief in the purchasability of behavior is the ultimate act of sovereignty. Stewardship has pay be a question of equity and common purpose, not a driver of behavior.

THE BEST AND THE BRIGHTEST

Our pay systems are aimed at rewarding individual behavior. We are preoccupied with nurturing the top 10 percent of our workforce and are fearful of rewarding teams. This communicates low esteem for interdependence, teams, and community. Paying primarily for individual effort is rewarding self-interest. Stewardship pays primarily for team and departmental effort.

WE OWN YOU

We magnify the power of the supervisor through our pay practices in two ways. First we establish pay grades on the basis of the size of a person's empire. Empire is measured by budget responsibility, direct reports, and breadth of responsibility. Second, we equate performance with supervisory evaluations. We call you a good performer if your supervisor gives you a high rating. These both act as the glue to a command-and-compliance form of governance.

PRIVATE AND CONFIDENTIAL

We maintain secrecy about how the pay systems work. If we are fortunate, we know the pay system and pay package that applies to our own job. Unless we work for the government, we most often do not know how other

Curiously, the secrets of corporations are seldom active secrets, and often not even a means to hide unfairness. Men may be paid similar salaries for similar work, but when their salaries are not made public, the unknown works against employees, eliciting the bad dreams of envy.

Earl Shorris,
Scenes from Corporate Life

people are paid, especially those at higher levels. This is not referring to what specific individuals get paid, this is about the system itself.

To better see the incongruencies between our pay practices and stewardship, read on.

PAY REINFORCES CLASS DISTINCTIONS

The problem with special pay practices for executives is not so much that people at the top make too much money. If our top executives' pay is out of line, which makes for interesting press, it is that they are good at playing a game that we have all created. If we are tempted to blame them for their salaries, we should ask ourselves when was the last time we turned down a salary increase or a bonus? Plus, if we are going to continue to worship our leaders and expect them to save us, then they are going to continue to make those salaries. The longer-term problem is not excessive executive salaries. The marketplace and public consciousness will correct that over time. The problem is that we have such different rules for paying our leaders than we do for paying everyone else.

The pay strategy for those at the top is to find a way to pay them as much as possible. In larger organizations there is a special section or person in charge of executive compensation. Their task is to design pay packages that will retain top executives. They work with the full menu of pay options. Special tax-deferred retirement plans, stock options, corporate living arrangements, low-interest loans, termination guarantees, plus bonus plans where 30 to 50 percent bonuses are feasible. In contrast, there is a separate compensation unit that is responsible for non-executive pay practices. Their focus is on pay strategies for the people at the middle and bottom. The goal there is to attract and retain good people, but to do it by paying them as little as possible. The common way of talking about it is to say that we need to work hard at controlling labor costs. When we say that, though, we are only thinking of low-power people.

It is this class distinction that results in the incongruence of massive layoffs and record profits and executive bonuses all in the same year. Our beliefs about pay systems reinforce the inequitable distribution of

The pay strategy for those at the top is to find a way to pay them as much as possible.

wealth and sanction the belief that Wall Street is our primary customer and it is fine with us if our leaders are more interested in building a career and personal wealth than in building a human organization.

Don't let this emphasis on for-profit companies imply that not-for-profit and government agencies are free from elitist pay practices. The mindset for designing special pay for executives exists in whatever segment of society we look. Superintendents have sweeter pay packages than teachers, the head of a major volunteer agency made the news by riding too often in the back seat of a long black automobile, and our elected officials don't ride the bus either. We have all become accustomed to extending wealth and privilege to the top levels.

Taken seriously, stewardship requires the redistribution of wealth. It becomes difficult to espouse partnership, empowerment, and a service orientation while those at the top enhance their wealth at the expense of those at lower levels. Part of the justification for extreme pay treatment for those at the top is that they are required to make choices that place the weight of the entire institution on their shoulders and place their own jobs at risk. This is true and they should be paid more for the weight of that responsibility—and they are. Carrying the weight of an organization, though, is not something unique to those at the top. People at the middle and at the bottom also carry their load.

THE BELL CURVE

Middle managers and non-union salaried workers are usually paid on the basis of a normal distribution curve. Without getting into graphs, it works out that the people rated in the bottom 10 percent are given minimal or zero increases, the people rated in the top 10 percent are given maximum increases, usually about 4 percent higher than inflation, and everyone else is placed somewhere in the middle. Everyone has to be force-fitted onto this bell-shaped curve. In other words, only 10 percent can be called top performers, and 10 percent must be called poor performers. If you are a manager and you think 20 percent of your people are top performers, you have an olympic-sized battle on your hands. This restraint, though, does not apply for people at the top three levels. They have a different system, reinforcing the belief that we are dealing with two different classes of people.

CLASS DIFFERENCES IN WHAT WE MEASURE

Even the measurement system perpetuates the idea of class differences. People paid on a hourly basis, who generally live under as restrictive a pay system as the salaried people, are called "direct labor." The direct labor cost of a product is a number carefully computed and widely known. Ask most any executive or manager and they can tell you the direct labor cost of the product or service they offer. It is this number that is the basis for sending jobs to other countries due to their low direct labor costs. For example, in my business, a training business, the direct labor cost for a consulting day is about 35 percent of the price to the client. Another example: a pair of jeans has about $2.70 worth of direct labor in it. These are well-measured, well-controlled costs. Now, ask the same executive or manager what the labor cost of the top three levels of the organization is, and most would have no idea. Compensation costs at the top are not measured; overhead costs for centralized groups are not widely shared and are not known in the same way as costs for lower levels. The economics of patriarchy is having $3.50 in salaried overhead cost busy controlling, planning, and watching $2.50 of direct labor engaged in making the product. When we then export the direct labor to a third world country, the $2.50 cost goes to $.90 and the $3.50 remains untouched. Another expression of the class bias inherent in our two pay systems.

Performance Not for Sale

Pay also institutionalizes our belief in patriarchy by the connection we make between money and behavior. Even though we know that pay is not a "motivator," we still believe that we can barter for behavior and that managers can evoke the actions they desire by manipulating pay to subordinates. The conventional wisdom is that by specifying the desired behavior and outcomes and then connecting them to the appraisal and pay system, we can create a culture that will give us the behavior that we want. In simple terms, what gets rewarded is what gets done. It is the marriage of economics and engineering. It is through this basic belief that we rationalize our current pay systems. Change this belief, which is where we are headed, and the way we currently pay people makes little sense.

We still believe that we can barter for behavior and that managers can evoke the actions they desire by manipulating pay to subordinates.

Why is it so hard to accept is that pay and productivity are strangers to each other? There is just no evidence that giving people more money creates better outcomes. We have to repeat the studies to prove it to every generation in every sector of society. A recent example: public school teachers' pay rose sharply between 1985 and 1990, yet classroom outcomes remained flat. This does not mean that teachers should not have gotten those pay increases. It means that we should not have raised their pay with the expectation that the money would buy better outcomes. It is important to understand that improving our pay system, or even increasing an individual's pay, will not result in higher performance, nor will it produce a deeper sense of ownership or responsibility. Productivity and feelings of ownership and responsibility cannot be purchased.

This does not mean that everyone should make the same amount of money. This is the reptilian outcry that usually arises at this point in a workshop discussion. As if the Equal Rights Amendment were a mandate for unisex bathrooms. There are good reasons that better performers should make more money, that people at higher levels with broader responsibility should make more money, that organizations that better serve customers should prosper. But it is not the pay system that drives their behavior and the end results. Pay is not the driver, not the creator, not the fuel, not the determinant of high performance. It is true that we all work for money, but it ain't true that we are going to work harder or smarter or sweeter if they just give us more.

The reasons this simple idea is so controversial are very complicated. One reason is that we relate the purchase of things with the purchase of motivation or energy. We know that by manipulating the price of goods, we can have an impact on how much people will buy. We know that the more we are willing to spend for something, the more likely someone will sell it to us. We know that if we pay a salesperson a 20 percent commission for selling item A and a 5 percent commission for selling item B, the salesperson will lean toward item A. But it is a mistake to leap from these observations to the belief that organizational performance or emotional ownership will operate with the same buy-and-sell dynamic. Just because people will act in their self-interest, it does not mean that economics will drive their choice.

We need to let go of this economic-engineering model. Pay practices have meanings that far overshadow the actual amount of money involved. And other forces in the workplace are so powerful in guiding our behavior that they almost completely sever the relationship between pay and performance. Simply put, even though it is just and useful to pay more when high performance occurs, the act of paying more does not create high performance.

THE RISK OF PROMISING PAY FOR PERFORMANCE

Using money to manipulate behavior gets us in all kinds of trouble. We dig a hole for ourselves when we promise what may not come true. Helen, an experienced, high-performing machine operator, was a recent reminder of this point. Her manufacturing plant manager had decided to move toward empowerment and self-management.

He created teams to coordinate the work, flat-tened the organization, and changed the pay sys-tem. He eliminated individual incentive pay, raised the base hourly rate of everyone to a liv-ing wage, and set team targets, so that if a team met its targets, they could all make two dollars an hour more than the highest performer had earned previously. Sounds reasonable. Well, in the early days, the teams were not making their goals, so everyone was stuck at the base hourly rate of $6.23 an hour, which was lower than the

Generally speaking, the relation between work done and money earned is so hard to grasp that it appears almost accidental, so that labor takes on the aspect of servitude, money that of favor.

Simone Weil

top performers used to make. At that point Joel Henning and I were running a workshop for these operators, and Joel had just given a stirring lecture to about a hundred machine operators on how under the old patriarchal system, you brought your body to work and left your mind and your heart at home. Now, with the team concept, you could bring all of yourself, your mind and your heart, into the facto-ry. During a pause in Joel's speech, Helen stood up and said, "Joel, I used to bring just my body to work and I made $8.75 an hour. Now I bring my mind and my heart to work and I make $6.23 an hour." Wild applause from the operators, nervous laughter from Joel and me....

The new pay structure had been initiated with a sincere and even generous intent. The big error was in thinking that the new pay structure would induce or facilitate the new culture and way of doing business. The new pay structure made a promise to Helen it could not fulfill. The plant manager thought the new pay system would motivate the teams so that everyone's pay would benefit.

When we try to use money to induce behavior, it backfires. We all like the money, but we won't be bought. There may be some higher economic threshold, where a large enough pay increase might result in more productive actions, but the day-to-day reality is that we do not have enough money to actually purchase behav-ior from people inside an organization.

Sometimes we change pay systems first, under pressure from employees or a union. If employees want to be paid more before they invest in a redesign effort, be wary. It usually means they do not want to do the redesign. Changing the pay system or sweetening the pot will not change their minds. Every time management thinks it will facilitate a change process by going from individual incentive pay to hourly pay, or from hourly to salary, or by raising the hourly pay, it usually leads to disappointment. The idea that everyone shares in the wealth *after* organizational performance improves is a different story and a fair request.

What we must confront in our current thinking about compensation is that we treat pay more as a means to control and restrain behavior than as a means of building an organization.

What we must confront in our current thinking about compensation is that we treat pay more as a means to control and restrain behavior than as a means of building an organization that serves its marketplace. Pay becomes a tool for communicating and enabling patriarchy, dominance, and dependency. The possibility of withholding pay has a punitive effect. Being generous with pay is a way of bestowing a blessing. Control over another's income demonstrates power and creates compliance. If we are serious about stewardship, then we need a philosophy and system of compensation that does not feed dominance and submission, does not deliver punishment and blessing, and does not create isolation and distrust.

RANK INDIVIDUALISM

Ranking individuals and paying them according to their ranking also needs questioning. The theory is that this will motivate people to want to be at the top. It is also a value statement that high performance comes from outstanding individual performance. The conventional wisdom is that if we do not nurture those outstanding individuals, they will not stay with us for long and performance overall will suffer. This faith in individualism is so deeply ingrained in the American culture, it seems that no amount of experience to the contrary can challenge it.

A more reasoned stance would be that the importance of individuals versus teams will vary with the nature of the task and the organization. Some tasks are individualistic by nature. Elements of scientific or technical invention, writing, some selling jobs. Many more jobs, though, require much more interdependence than our pay practices would indicate. We cannot create community by ranking individuals against each other and paying them accordingly.

The impact of rank-and-pay schemes is that the top 15 percent or so like the system, the other 85 percent feel like they have lost. Every ranking system creates more losers than winners. That is why we have always been reluctant to tell those in the middle where they stand. This pay system not only creates a feeling of losing among the majority, but it also pits people on the same team against each other. We communicate that if they compete against each other it is fine with us, in fact we have designed the system to encourage that. In my first job years ago in what was then Esso Engineering, they used to rank order fifteen hundred engineers from top to bottom. It took the managers the better part of two weeks to fight for their people and rank order them all, one to fifteen hundred. (I am afraid to ask if they still do this.) The strain among the managers alone was enough to call the practice into question, never mind the ill will from placing the engineers in a zero-sum competition for being valued.

Rank ordering is literally a means for keeping people in line. Patriarchy is designed to keep people in isolation from each other as a means of maintaining social control. Individualistic pay systems are elegant in their ability to do that.

> *B*ig systems enjoy big success by destroying communities. They trick us into thinking that we must fight them as individuals. They trick us into thinking there is nothing but ourselves. As individuals we haven't a prayer against big systems.
>
> Donna Schaper,
> *A Book of Common Power*

Confusing Supervisory Evaluations with Performance

Everyone likes the idea of pay for performance, but most of us have rarely experienced it. We most often get paid on the basis of how our boss evaluates us. This is more accurately called "pay for compliance." One human being's evaluation of another is fundamentally subjective. We try to overcome subjectivity by using numbers to rate each other. We try to be objective in what we look at and pick hard-nosed business objectives to evaluate. Still, it is very difficult to directly attribute real organizational outcomes to the actions of a single individual. Even when we think we can measure a job, like with the dollar volume produced by a salesperson, we can see that sales productivity is a much more complicated equation. A salesperson is so dependent on their service unit, on the product getting to the customer on time, on having the right product to sell, and especially on the quality of their territory that any assessment attributing one sale to one person describes only a partial reality.

Given the subjective nature of evaluations, we are as likely to be rating and paying people for compliance as we are for performance. Small wonder that when I ask groups to raise their hands if they feel they are paid for performance, 90 percent of them miss out on the chance for exercise.

When we promise a pay-for-performance system we will be greeted with cynicism. The solution is to stop making the promise. Then we need to create pay systems at every level that are tied to real organizational outcomes, not supervisory perceptions. Pay for the product created and sold, service delivered, the customer satisfied and returning. What we have now are pay systems based on a parent-child model and they invite disillusionment. We cannot create a feeling of ownership and responsibility with pay systems that depend on someone else's generosity.

Given the subjective nature of evaluations, we are as likely to be rating and paying people for compliance as we are for performance.

PAY FOR EMPIRE

Another type of pay structure that interferes with stewardship is commonly called the "Hay system." It is a widely accepted method of using job descriptions—including the number of direct reports, type of budget responsibility, and levels of responsibility and decision-making authority—to make rational the different pay levels within an organization. For what it was asked to accomplish, this system has done an elegant and durable job. But we must question exactly what it was we asked the Hay system to do—to pay people based on the size of their territory, number of subordinates, budget size, level of authority....

Soften it if you like, but these are measures of empire, not contribution to the organization. The effect is to reward and value territorial expansion, and keeping the lines between the silos, or functions, clean and separate. Today, we call for teamwork. We have renewed interest in cross-functional dialogue, we ask people to act in the best interest of the whole organization. Yet, when we put money on the line, as in the Hay-type pay system, it is the large, powerful, clearly defined department or territory that is valued above all else.

REWARD SYSTEMS THAT SUPPORT STEWARDSHIP

We need a reward system that gives preference to service over self-interest. One that values accountability for the success of the enterprise. This means we all get paid for outcomes of concrete value to the organization. It also means there needs to be an equitable distribution of wealth. One test of equity is whether how well we pay can withstand the light of day. One intent of a pay practice is to affirm the fact that the success of the institution is in the hands of people at each level. An institution's wealth and value, in the broadest sense, is then a community creation. These three elements—to affirm purpose, to share wealth, to end secrecy—are central to a pay strategy that helps institutionalize stewardship.

PAY GROUPS FOR REAL OUTCOMES

Rather than seeing pay as a determinant of behavior, think of pay as a way of communicating and affirming purpose. The way we design our pay system communicates in concrete ways the kind of organization we want to create. So, design pay systems that value interdependence, teamwork, success in the creation of products, customer satisfaction.... The process starts when we begin to pay teams or units for real outcomes delivered, primarily in the form of variable pay, namely, salary increases and bonuses.

Every unit has a boss/banker, someone who puts up money in the form of a budget in return for a set of results. Achieving those results with fewer people, or faster, or with higher quality, or even exceeding those results, in each case returns a dollar value to the larger institution. It does not matter whether you are for or against profit, what your unit does has a measurable value, so let that be translated into dollars for team incentives. How does that work? How do you measure, for example, the value of a staff communications unit? Let the staff group bill their services and then they will find out their value. If billings and demand go up within the organization, then let a percentage of the increased billings go for pay bonuses. If demand decreases, no bonus. The principle is for variable pay to rise and fall on team outcomes. If the work is so interdependent that team results are hard to define, then let the bonus ride with the larger unit, say, a whole production line, a whole mental health department, a whole school building, even an entire branch of the Division of Motor Vehicles.

An example of this principle at work recently took place in a French class in a high school in Texas. In school, of course, grades are the equivalent of cash. The French teacher took seriously the goal of learning for all and was discouraged and disturbed by the wide variability of performance in the class. He told the class that each student bore some responsibility for the learning of the total class, so 40 percent of their grade would be determined by overall class performance on tests. Talk about radical acts. After each test, he would post the class average, including the range of scores. He would then give them time to help each other. Best performing class he ever taught, plus it renewed his desire to keep on teaching.

Our emphasis on the team does not exclude recognizing individuals. If an individual does something outstanding and easily identifiable, give them some money. This should be the exception, however. Also, notice that we have eliminated supervisory evaluations as the basis for determining pay. The moment the judgment of the boss dictates pay for the subordinate, the intent of the organization has been deflected from rewarding outcomes to paying for approval and compliance. If people want to know where they stand with their boss, let them ask their boss for feedback. If subordinates are not getting it done, let bosses express their disappointment. We do not need money on the table to give meaning to these conversations.

BALANCE THE WEALTH

In addition to valuing communal outcomes, reward systems need take a stand on the issue of equity.

Partnership and empowerment cannot be built or coexist in the long run by separating the managing and the doing of the work. The search is for systems that express the idea that wealth is created at every level of the organization and that we should pay people as much as possible rather than as little as possible. These ideas argue for one pay system for all levels of the organization. This sort of system exists now in many government agencies. That is the good news. What is missing in public service is an element of variable pay related to outcomes. Want a simple way to implement this? Take the compensation structure that exists for your organization's top two levels, whatever it might be, and roll it down through the organization.

> *The* search is for systems that express the idea that wealth is created at every level of the organization and that we should pay people as much as possible rather than as little as possible.

High levels will still have higher earnings, but the system is the same for all. Let each level work under a system that

▼ Connects earnings to real outcomes of a unit or larger divisions.

▼ Pays higher percentage bonuses if the money is there.

▼ Offers tax advantages or special earnings possibilities.

▼ Has the objective of paying as much as possible.

▼ Provides a soft landing in case of termination, acquisition, or contraction.

▼ Offers some equity in the institution.

Some of this is already beginning to happen. Here are some of the easier steps to take.

GAINSHARING

Gainsharing has individuals and teams benefit directly from economic improvements they deliver. One small company will pay a team 25 percent of every real dollar saved over and above a budgeted set of goals. Real dollars means that the costs of achieving the savings must be deducted from the savings before the team gets their 25 percent. Fair enough, that is how the marketplace works. Pretty generous.

At the other extreme, I have seen a simple suggestion system that pays for good ideas touted as gainsharing and a means of culture change. A well-paying suggestion system, no matter what you call it, does not represent an equitable pay system or mean there has been a shift in governance. If our day-to-day experience does not move toward giving us more control over what we do, it is patriarchy as usual. In most places, gainsharing plans are tied to meaningful economic results, a genuine attempt to distribute wealth more equitably and to base it on real outcomes.

PAY FOR SKILLS

Pay for skills is a system where you get salary increases or a higher hourly wage the more different tasks or jobs you can do in a unit. Valuable concept: the more jobs we can do and the more of the organization we understand, the more valuable we are. Pay for skills is a worthwhile step to take, but if taking this step does not shift the mindset about individual pay or the belief that you can buy behavior, then it will not create equity and the mindset of partnership at the lower levels.

STOCK OPTIONS AND OWNERSHIP

Stock options are a pay vehicle that has traditionally been reserved for the management class. Really for the executive class. Stock options represent the purest relationship between individual wealth and that aspect of organizational performance that is measured by stock price. A stock option means you are given a guaranteed purchase price for a share of stock. The benefit is that you do not have to buy the stock to guarantee that price. You are then given a period of time, say five years, to exercise the option. Which means that if the price of the stock goes up, you can sell it at that higher price and make money without ever putting any of your own money at risk. It is a fail-safe opportunity to benefit from improved performance. What is important to our discussion is that the stance on stock options is a powerful statement about who we believe truly delivers the profit. Restricting stock options as a compensation tool for the executive class is an expression of our belief in patriarchy, the belief that those at the top are most critical in creating the wealth.

The stance on stock options is a powerful statement about who we believe truly delivers the profit.

A belief in partnership would extend to people at each level the privilege of no-risk earnings from the growth of stock price. Some companies are beginning to offer such incentives to those at lower levels. A large pharmaceutical company recently gave all employees a certain number of stock options. It was an effort to make them all owners and to express appreciation for the success of the business. A step forward. Their ambivalence about reducing the class differences was evident, though, in the fact that executives and managers were given a much lower option price than people at the bottom. The management class will profit from increased stock price much sooner than the core workers. Still, take the steps when they come.

The idea that employees should own part of a business has been around for a long time. Employee Stock Ownership Plans (ESOPs) have made it easier for employees to purchase stock and made it more attractive for owners to sell. There is no question that economic ownership facilitates emotional ownership. But stock ownership alone does not change the fundamentals of governance and, too often, employees may own some stock, but they do not own much more of what makes the business function. At worst, employee stock ownership carries the illusion of partnership with no substance; at best, stock ownership underscores the organization's intent to treat employees as owners in a thousand other ways.

END SECRECY

The final covenant for stewardship pay practices is to let all employees know what pay systems exist for different levels of the organization. Secrecy about pay systems is a sure sign that there are inequities that cannot be justified, even perhaps to those who benefit from them. Public and non-profit agencies live with a fresh air policy about pay. If you work for the Parks and Recreation Department of the city of Boston, you know how much money every one makes, including the commissioner. This doesn't mean their pay system is perfect, but they pass the secrecy test.

MAKING THE CHANGE: THE PHONE CENTERS

The AT&T Phone Centers described earlier are a place where many of these ideas have been put into place. The head of the Phone Centers, Bob Martin, did all he could to put choice and control of the business close to the customer. One of his adventures was with the pay system for store managers. He said that never had he experienced so much heat and so little light as when he started changing the pay system. He had over four hundred Phone Centers with standard job descriptions for the jobs of store manager and salesperson. Each job

The Gods only laugh when men pray to them for wealth.

Japanese proverb

had a pay scale, and store managers and salespeople were evaluated by their bosses and got raises accordingly. The average pay for a store manager was about $35,000.

Wanting to foster the attitude that each store operated as its own business, Bob sought a pay system that captured this entrepreneurial spirit. He decided to restructure the pay for the store manager so that the manager could make two to three times their current pay if the store did well, but the manager would get no increase if the store did not meet its targets. The store manager would also have to take a cut in pay to get on this system. If any store manager did not want to live under this system, they were encouraged and supported to pursue jobs elsewhere in the AT&T system, which is what many did. The key measurement for pay increases was also changed from store sales to store profitability.

Two years later, over 60 percent of the store managers decided they did not want to live under the uncertainty of an entrepreneurial system, even though some of the store managers made close to $100,000. The new pay system was just one factor in their decision, but it had certainly added to the volatility of the world they decided to leave. Creating a pay system aligned with the intent of having people at all levels be responsible for the success of the organization may not be a welcome or popular strategy, even though it may be the right thing to do. The benefit of what Bob did with the pay system in the phone stores was that it reinforced the message he was sending about the change required to save that business. Everyone got the point that safety first was not going to be a winning strategy. The downside of what Bob did was that it was Bob's new pay system and no one else owned it. After a year or so of wrestling with the situation, they created a team of store managers to come up with a pay system that fit an entrepreneurial business strategy. He did not pick compensation consultants or the internal specialists to design the system. They were available to help, but not held responsible for the new system. Ownership of the pay system was the central issue, and a team of people redesigning their own pay system was the right response.

The store managers made a few changes to Bob's original system, reaffirmed its basic fit to their situation, and the new structure settled into place and served them well.

This story vividly demonstrates the difficulty in changing pay systems. It is clear that we need those who will live under a new system to struggle with the complexity of changing it. On the other hand, we are all so anxious about pay in general that most of us would rather make the system we have be more generous than search for outcome-based but higher-risk alternatives.

It seems best to have people redesign their own pay systems, using clear guidelines that require the new system to honor the well-being of the whole organization and to bring equity and an end to the class system. One of the problems the Phone Centers faced was that the store managers had been a protected class of managers. They got their pay regardless of how the business performed. Ruling classes do not give up privilege easily, unless they make the choice to do so. It is also clear that changing the pay system is not done to raise morale, for as many people will be unhappy with the new system as the old one. This will be especially true in changing the pay systems in education and government. There is always discussion of paying teachers and government workers along the lines of the incentive systems common in private industry. This strategy ignores the fact that pay systems in industry do not work very well, other than to breed caution and self-interest. Plus the faith that a pay system change will result in more citizens being better served or students better educated is ill-placed. Government and education need to stop focusing on pay, and the unions that protect pay. Whatever system that exists now is not the problem and changing it right away will not be the solution.

It seems best to have people redesign their own pay systems, using clear guidelines that require the new system to honor the well-being of the whole organization and to bring equity and an end to the class system.

At some point, however, changing the pay system becomes a requirement of political reform. I recommend postponing dealing with pay until successes have come from other aspects of the change. And get people who are affected involved in the redesign, and let go of the one-size-fits-all mentality. Allow the pay system to fit the situation, with different units having different plans. The only restraints are that the new plan must move in the direction of stewardship, and the dollars have to stay within what the unit can afford.

THE END OF CARETAKING

There is a price to be paid for more equitable and less oppressive and more outcome-based pay systems. The protection of the old systems disappear. Many of us believe that our organization should guarantee that our pay keeps even with inflation, and that we should make as much or more next year as we did this year. This is our wish to be taken care of, regardless of what we deliver or the organization's ability to pay. If we choose partnership, we have to live with the risks of being an owner. The price we pay for claiming ownership is we lose the safety and reassurance that tomorrow will be provided for us. Guaranteed annual increases is one of the provisions that does not fit with this revolution. You cannot eliminate them, however, unless the social contract is really changing and the day-to-day existence of core workers changes. Eliminating annual increases as a way of saving money is exploitation.

When money is used to insure compliance, which is its dominant use, it more often than not has the opposite effect. For one thing it puts a lot of energy into the pay system. It becomes a source of resistance to other things we want to do. It is difficult to use money to purchase loyalty. The people who join us, or stay with us, primarily for the money will leave us for the same reason. Unless the economy is on its back, some other organization can always afford to recruit our people for more money that we can afford to pay them.

Anyone who says they work just for the money has given up the hope that anything more is possible.

Anyone who says they work just for the money has given up the hope that anything more is possible. When money becomes the noisy issue, it is a sure sign of despair. Our organizations do not have the money to really make sure someone will stay, and they usually do not pay so little that someone has to leave. When there is shouting about pay, something else is wrong. Buying silence is no solution. Granted when people leave, they always say it is because they will be getting more money, but don't ever believe that was the reason. Coming or going for money is the one reason we can give where no one is at fault—no bridges are burned, no difficult issues have to be confronted or responsibility taken. Money as the reason for people's emotional response to the organization is a convenient, no-fault form of our denial. The goal of our reform is to make the pay system basically fair, connected to how the organization is doing, to keep it simple and, after the dust has subsided, rather dull.

PART III

THE TRIUMPH OF HOPE OVER EXPERIENCE

We have few flesh and blood role models for stewardship. Most of our experience is with leadership, in either its harsher or kindlier forms. Our institutional models are basically patriarchal; it is hard to find partnership on a large scale. Choosing to create our own experiment is walking into a room unlit.

For these reasons and more, the choice for service begins with an act of faith.

12

COSMETIC REFORM: WHEN THE DISEASE BECOMES THE CURE

The task for each of us is to define a future we choose to create, using the workplace as the medium. As we turn our attention to finding the process through which to live out our intentions, we are faced with a paradox: how does patriarchy go about the task of changing or healing itself? This chapter is about how the means chosen often become the source of our interference.

Even with the consciousness that top-down, parenting management strategies will not win, many efforts to change will inevitably reenact the very same set of beliefs that created the need for change in the first place. Patriarchy will use a mixture of leadership, consistency, control, and predictability to try to implement the ideas of empowerment, partnership, and self-management. Patriarchy will reinvent itself in living out the promise of its own demise. This reality is a major source of the cynicism about whether cultural change is at all possible or lasting. If the experience of moving from leadership to stewardship does not in itself incorporate choice and local autonomy, then it has no credibility and will forever remain a program requiring constant infusions.

The symptom of our doubt is the question that keeps coming up, "What is next...after empowerment, after continuous improvement? We are into

*M*an can only create himself through his freedom; otherwise, he is created, an object, without dignity. Yet those who would aid him in his life and his productivity are often willing to sacrifice his autonomy, which is his essential well-being, on behalf of his physical or social well-being.

Earl Shorris,
*Scenes from
Corporate Life*

total quality, moving toward the learning organization, how do we stay in front?" This is a teflon question. It is based on the experience that nothing ever really sticks or makes a fundamental difference. All of these ideas for cultural change are useful, but the need for a new fix every couple of years means our experience with them has no depth. They each give our organizations a new look, but the features and the mindset and living style stay the same. These efforts then are simply cosmetic. And we switch quickly from one to the next. Like restlessly changing channels, never questioning that it is the act of watching television that is the source of our discontent. The answer to the question of what is next is, "Nothing is next. Nothing that will be any more helpful than what is on our plate now." Any of these ideas, committed to over time, will give us what we need. It is our willingness to engage in cosmetic strategies that keeps us looking elsewhere and feeds our cynicism.

To be even more blunt, it is the colonial tactics we use to initiate change that interferes with our desire to create ownership and responsibility close to the work and those we wish to serve. Too often we put patriarchal methods in camouflage and use them to implement partnership. What we have come to know as "strong leadership" too easily operates to unintentionally sustain patriarchy and prevent its healing.

THE OPEN OFFICE

Here is an example that has the key elements of how patriarchy re-creates itself, even as it attempts to be an advocate for participation.

A sales office of a large U.S. computer company in Europe decided to run their business along the principles of stewardship.

One of the strategies that Brent, the vice president, was pursuing was to give the sales and support people more ownership for the business. They were moving into new office space, so the decision was made to have responsibility for designing the new space rest with those who would be using it. Teams of sales people, support people, and supervisors met with interior designers and office suppliers to explore what kind of office would balance their needs for workspace, meetings, privacy, social contact, community, and storage. What they finally came up with was essentially a large living room. There would be tables where they could work alone or meet in small groups. There would be lounge chairs where they could sit back and read or relax. Computer terminals would be on small carts, connected by spring cables to the ceiling, so they could be moved anywhere someone was working. Supervisors would join with everyone else in selecting each day what desk-chair-sitting work arrangement was right for them that particular day. The teams also selected the lighting, decor, colors, and textures they wanted for their environment.

The office designed by the teams was built and worked well. The space was functional. The cost of the new office was about 20 percent less than usual for that number of people in that location. The environment also supported the aim of creating community among the different functions and made a strong statement in support of partnership. The office soon began to attract some very positive publicity. It began to be touted as a shining example of the office of the future. It even won an award from an American university

> [There are] three principles in man's being and life, the principle of thought, the principle of speech and the principle of action. The origin of all conflict between me and my fellow-men is that I do not say what I mean, and that I do not do what I say. For this confuses and poisons, again and again and in increasing measure, the situation between myself and the other man, and I, in my internal disintegration, am no longer able to master it but, contrary to all my illusions, have become its slave.
>
> Martin Buber,
> *The Way of Man,*
> *According to the*
> *Teaching of Hasidism*

for innovation in office design. Up to this point, an encouraging but not so unusual story of innovation and empowerment in action.

The edge to the story comes when we see how the corporate mind in the European regional office responded to this success in one of its locations. They rightfully raised the question of how to bring this success to other parts of the business. This regional management group defined their role as bringing leadership, consistency, and control to the company's European operations. So, through the eyes of this parent, the innovation that mattered was the office design itself, not the way it was created. The office design got the award, costs were lower, flexibility was higher, performance equal or better, so management's strategy was to export the design to other locations. They then began the process of persuading other sales organizations to copy the office, acting as if the innovation of value was the design of the office, instead of the redistribution of power and privilege it symbolized.

The originator, Brent, had consciously chosen to place power and privilege in the hands of those closest to the customer and the work. The redesign of the office was to him only one means for expressing his intention to redesign the governance strategy for the business. He had also initiated parallel changes in other areas. He was neutral to the office design per se, he was an advocate of political reform.

His bosses, though, saw his success as a triumph of office design, choosing not to recognize the more radical process of reformed governance. What they saw fit to disseminate across Europe was a program of redesigning offices. They set standards and requirements for the new office plans. They wanted timetables and the reassurance that this innovative office design would be the standard within a certain time frame. Business as usual. The demand to institute the new design got compliance in some places, resistance in others, and rarely delivered the outcomes of the original site. In time the idea got to corporate headquarters in the United States. It was by then sold to the field on the basis that the shared, open space would not only save money, but would in effect force salespeople out of the office and into the field. This met strong resistance and eventually fell of its own weight.

What had begun as an act to give people more control over their own jobs was warped, through the process of dissemination, into a coercive strategy to standardize offices, save money, and exert more control over salespeople, namely, to force them out into the field. The office of the future became the office of the past. Partnership was co-opted by patriarchy. Patriarchy won. The business lost.

The act of implementing stewardship principles through leadership based on consistency, control, and predictability is what keeps patriarchy from helping itself. Well-meaning people in power (all of us) repeatedly take ideas like service, quality, and partnership and thwart them by our strategies of how to make changes. We make the false connection that if we want consistency and control in the quality of product or service we deliver to a customer, we must have consistency and control in the way we govern the people creating the product or service. So cosmetic change results. In a shifting, customer-driven environment, improvement efforts that produce no redistribution of power, purpose, or privilege will produce no real improvement. This is why most large organizations in the 1990s are still unable to make widespread use of knowledge about organizational innovation that they have had since the 1970s.

> *The act of implementing stewardship principles through leadership based on consistency, control, and predictability is what keeps patriarchy from helping itself.*

Another simple example is the Malcolm Baldrige Quality Award given by the President of the United States. Its intent was to acknowledge and encourage quality consciousness. It began by recognizing companies that have given high attention to quality, have articulated clear values about quality, and have engaged in training, work process analysis, participative management, and a whole host of activities to meet customer requirements. Sounds reasonable and was for the first couple of years. The irony develops when a manager decides he or she is going to reward and punish according to the Baldrige criteria. Some organizations have created internal Baldrige examiners as a means of assuring quality. The Baldrige criteria thus move from serving as the framework for an award and recognition effort to being an instrument of coercion and compliance. The spirit of the Baldrige criteria is to place ownership and pride at the point where the work is actually done. Attempting to induce Baldrige criteria through means of control and command does just the opposite. It resurrects the mid-century belief that quality is achieved by having third parties watch and check your performance. A once noble intent undermined by the method of implementation.

Patriarchy Recreating Itself

Without an understanding of how the methods of change we choose can undermine our intentions, partnership and stewardship will occur as mere isolated, short-term events. To enable our seeing more clearly how popular strategies of improvement so frequently reinforce patriarchy, here is an inventory of actions that typically feed rather than confront our belief in consistency and control. It illustrates how, time and again, patriarchy interferes with its own healing.

TOP CREATES VISION

Since the mid-1980s, every top management team has created its vision statement and worked hard on communicating it.

We have bought the notion that vision must come from the top. What this means in practical terms is that a consultant or staff person has spent a lot of time interviewing executives and writing vision paragraphs. A half- or full-day retreat is then convened so the top group can wordsmith the statement and plan for its distribution. The intent is sincere and the content is always appealing. Each management team affirms its uniqueness by declaring that it

Is committed to being world class.

Will be number one in its markets.

Believes in its people.

Stands firm for quality.

Cares for customers.

Affirms honesty and integrity.

Supports teams.

Is going to make a lot of money for shareholders

   (or, will be fiscally responsible to its stakeholders).

Sincere intentions. Appealing statements. What's the problem? Only two...ownership and implementation. Ownership resides with those who craft and create a vision, and with them alone. A statement created for a team to endorse is not owned by the team. An even more fundamental defect is that, in most cases, the vision statement is created for the rest of the organization to live out. Notice that the vision here is used to define a culture or a set of values to be lived. This is different from top management's rightful task to define business mission and set business goals. A vision created for others to live out is patriarchy in action. There is no ownership in endorsement or enrollment.

The belief that crafting the vision is primarily a leadership-at-the-top function defeats, right at the beginning, the intent of driving ownership and responsibility toward those close to the work and the customer. Creating vision is in fact an ownership function, and if we want ownership widely dispersed, then each person needs to struggle with articulating their own, personal vision for their function or unit.

Top management surely needs a vision statement, but for themselves alone to live out and be accountable for. As soon as top management creates a vision statement for the rest of the organization to embrace, the parenting relationship has begun again, only this time cloaked in the robe of partnership.

There is something so deep in each of us that wants a common vision articulated by those in power—to suggest otherwise is almost heresy. This longing for a common vision is the wish for someone

else to create the unity we seek. Someone else above to create community, rallying cries, common purpose. We continue to want strong leadership from above even though it steals accountability from those below. Ownership comes from an investment, and the investment required from each of us is to define purpose for ourselves. Each person defining vision for their area of responsibility is how partnership is created. Why do we have such doubts about purposes or visions not defined by those at the top of the organization? There is ample evidence that the people at the top of our organizations are at least as capable of self-centeredness as those in the middle or

If **this were our own business, it is unlikely we would allow someone else to define values for us.**

bottom. If we fear conflict at our own level, why are we not capable of resolving it? The desire for vision from the top is a subtle way of disclaiming ownership and responsibility. If this were our own business, it is unlikely we would allow someone else to define values for us.

OPEN ENROLLMENT

In addition to over-valuing vision at the top, patriarchy has its leaders enroll others in their vision. *Enrollment* is a seductive term. Sounds harmless enough, like an invitation or the signing-up process for an educational event. In reality, enrollment is a soft-core act of colonialism. It creates compliance. Owners create. Owners choose. Enrollment has us sign up for something that others have created for us. Partners do not enroll each other in programs and efforts they have created independently. Enrollment as enacted by most large organizations is a selling and enlistment process that chokes the spirit of stewardship and service.

Enrollment has a cousin called "managing perceptions." Staff and consultant language for ways of selling a strategy. Selling is a noble activity. Marketing to our own people is fine. Persuasion and even direct orders are clean, straightforward ways to get action. Using words that promise people more choice than they actually have, though, becomes manipulation. If the vision has to do with participation, don't sell it with wall plaques and executive videos.

TOP DRIVES THE EFFORT

Conventional wisdom says that change has to happen from the top down. This belief, that if top management doesn't support the move toward partnership nothing important will happen, is another expression of our dependency. This simplistic belief does have a certain appeal.

▼ Top management likes it because it keeps them feeling that they are in charge. That they are managing the change process.

▼ Staff groups and consultants like it because it puts them in intimate contact with those who have power, privilege, and wealth. It also makes their selling job a lot easier.

▼ Middle management and below like it because it lets them off the hook. Getting sponsorship from the top provides safety.

In reality, change in the direction of high control, centralization, and economic constraints is the only change that can be implemented successfully from the top. People at the top have the power to legislate. Changes that are amenable to legislation can work well coming from the top. Layoffs, plant closings, cost restraints are nicely legislated. Changes focusing on customer service, quality, or cycle time do not fall into this category. They require ownership and responsibility...changes in mindset and beliefs, not changes in practice and procedure.

Social change does not cascade down through the organization, any more than it cascades down through society. If you look closely at successful change efforts in American industry, like Ford's employee involvement effort, you will see that the innovation started from the middle and spread outward. Taking the Ford example, a group of middle managers were placed on a blue ribbon committee and given a black ribbon assignment—to decide how to reduce the workforce by several thousand employees. After completing this assignment, they continued to meet on their own, to combat their frustration with what was happening to the company they cared so much about. Out of this committee experience, they initiated several employee involvement experiments. As these took hold, they met with staff people and eventually with Philip

Caldwell, Ford's president at the time, who had the good sense to take the idea and make it a core business strategy for the company. His successor, Donald Petersen, really supported the effort and made it his personal legacy.

This is how successful change most often works in reality. The top picks up on and supports efforts after they are underway and showing promise. It is only in retrospect, wanting to confirm our belief in patriarchy, that we resurrect the myth that change begins at the top. A change effort predicated on the belief that strategy comes from the top, tactics from the middle, and the bottom is left to implement, is no change at all.

KEEP MEASURES QUANTITATIVE AND SHORT TERM

A demand for measurement is an expression of doubt and lack of faith. The deeper our doubt, the greater the emphasis on hard measures and short time frames. When participation is advocated, we want tight measures and quick results. Consider these changes:

Employee involvement
Strong decentralized units
Self-inspecting quality efforts
Liberalized bonus systems for the bottom three levels
Self-managing teams

The first line of questions always seems to focus on how we are going to measure the effectiveness of these efforts. How many employee involvement teams do we have? What is the economic value of their suggestions? How many people have we trained in the quality process? These are, of course, fair questions, but when they are the first questions, they deflect our purpose. They lead us to implement strategies that give good answers to the questions— we tend to train across the board, go for quick gains, the "low hanging fruit." Distracted by short-term reporting of activity levels and other easy-to-quantify features, we postpone the more in-depth and fundamental changes that are required.

Conversely, when we make changes that feed patriarchy, we hear very few measurement demands. Think of these programs:

Management by objectives
Zero-based budgeting
Stronger centralized staff groups
Liberalized bonus systems for the top three levels

Each of these efforts serves to strengthen predictability, consistency, and control, the pillars of patriarchy. There is rarely a call for measuring the short-term, quantitative results when we institute these kinds of changes. In fact, their effectiveness has hardly been measured at all. They are rarely reviewed quarterly or monthly to assess their impact on performance. The demand for quantitative, short-term measures does not occur when we make high-control changes.

Patriarchy's stance on measurement is part of the reason our change efforts are so often short-lived. Genuine reform produces long-term, qualitative changes. Differences in our sense of ownership, acceptance of responsibility, commitment to the business. So hold off and measure the impact of social change by the real, long-term outcomes to the organization. Real quality measures like customer satisfaction, literacy scores, and reduced cycle time will change somewhat slowly over time. By responding to the demand for short-term, quantifiable results, we funnel and constrain our efforts in our aim to satisfy the scorekeepers. The question "What is next?" follows soon after.

CREATE A NEW DEPARTMENT

The creation of staff groups to carry out work that rightfully belongs to the line organization is the most common form of infection that patriarchy spreads. It is such a paradox, a sign of our

deep and irrational belief in control, that our efforts to fight bureaucracy are institutionalized in the form of additional levels, titles, and departments.

The ruler in us holds on to the belief that unless someone with power and privilege has sole responsibility for an effort, nothing will happen. So for each change we desire, we create a new department. You can now make a living as

Director of Total Quality Management
Director of Diversity
Director of Results Management
Director of Productivity
Director of School Improvement
Director of Committee on Oversight
Director of Continuous Improvement
Director of Corporate Values and Vision

Patrick Dolan reminds people that the classic example of creating a new department, or silo, occurred in the thirteenth century. The Catholic church, concerned about a growing lack of faith, decided to mobilize a staff function to manage the problem. They called it the Inquisition. The assignment of the Inquisition was to support, communicate, and teach the core values of the church by punishing heresy. Granted, the punishment of death for non-compliance is heavy-handed by any standard, but the church's basic strategy for implementing its intentions was no different in kind from our current practice of creating new departments to bring about change.

No matter how supportable its original purpose, a specially created staff function will inevitably breathe with the power of those at the top. It will begin a measurement, reporting, and enforcement process, and it will use the argument of consistency, control, and predictability to live out a sovereign relationship with those it calls customers. As a result, ownership and accountability are removed from the line organization and the core work process, which retards reform every time.

CONDUCT A COMMON TRAINING PROGRAM

We know that change is a learning process, so what could make more sense than training? You can make a good living these days training people in leadership, empowerment, continuous improvement, managing change, accelerated improvement (advanced continuous improvement), total quality, coaching skills, and on and on.

It is so tempting to provide everyone a common learning experience. To mandate "workouts" for each department to engage in self-examination. To use training to create a common language. If you work for a company of more than three hundred employees, you have been to one of these courses. If you have not, you are either very new or are in trouble.

No **matter how supportable its original purpose, a specially created staff function will inevitably breathe with the power of those at the top.**

These courses are generally high-quality learning experiences. Quality is not the problem. The problem is in their mandatory nature; the traditional governance system stays strong and in place. Real responsibility for outcomes, direction, and recreating culture stays centralized. Line managers and people doing the work are told one more time the kind of learning they require. Training is prescribed, and consistency and control are reaffirmed by the act of prescription.

Advocates of these training programs are usually a combination of staff people and consultants. They operate on the belief that managers in the middle want to know what is expected of them, and that it is top management's job, with technical support from staff and consultants, to act to meet that need. Training is such a good way to let people know what is expected of them and to give them the tools to meet those expectations. This makes such common sense that it can be hard to see how the process simply reinforces the whole parenting regimen.

Prescribing training, defining how the middle and bottom should operate, listing competencies for others to live out are caretaking, a kindly variation of patriarchy. People at or near the top taking responsibility for others' actions and others' outcomes. If we want people serving customers and making product to take ownership and responsibility, they will have to define and create the means for successfully living out those responsibilities on their own. There is much the top and the bottom need from each other to live out partnership, but top- and staff-defined competencies and training prescriptions only reinforce dependency and the bureaucratic mindset. If training is needed, and it will be, let those who require it define it, choose it, and manage it. And let different units find different paths.

COERCE THROUGH REWARDS

We find it so hard to reject the economists' viewpoint that institutional rewards and punishments drive behavior that when we begin to implement change directed toward stewardship, we cannot wait to get our hands on the performance appraisal system.

A major consumer goods company recently decided that customers, empowerment, and shared values such as integrity, honesty, diversity, and teamwork were the keys to their continued success. A strong, meaningful stance. As hopeful and supportable a vision statement as you could hope to find. No greed. No arrogance. A commitment to service to its customers and to its own people. Then the discussion of implementation, of living out the vision, began. One of the first things they reached for was the performance appraisal form. To launch the effort a staff group was assigned to insert customers, empowerment, integrity, honesty, diversity, and teamwork into the appraisal process.

There is not a customer in the world who would submit to a performance appraisal by a supplier. Yet we are so ready to implement partnership, a process of treating our people as vital customers, via the process of appraising, judging, and evaluating them.

The ingrained belief is that if we want to move in new directions, we have to amend the performance appraisal process to reflect the dimensions of the change. This is one of the most vivid ways in which the very intent to implement empowerment, to treat our people as customers, and to value teamwork is subverted. There is not a customer in the world who would submit to a performance appraisal by a supplier. Yet we are so ready to implement partnership, a process of treating our people as vital customers, via the process of appraising, judging, and evaluating them.

Appraisal is a process of coercion. We also call it a reward system. Yet if it is a reward system, it is a punishment system too. There are ways to communicate what we value and what we require that are not punitive. Including reward and punishment mechanisms in an implementation strategy foils the creation of ownership and accountability at the bottom. If we want to create a credible system of appraisal and accountability in a partnership environment, then each person needs a voice in deciding what they will be judged on and by whom. Top-down appraising, no matter how generous or noble the criteria, is the wrong way to begin the redistribution of power, privilege, and purpose. We need equitable rewards for contributions at every level, it is true, but appraisals and the money attached to them buy us little but caution. It is deeply self-defeating to use appraisal as an instrument of change.

IMPLEMENTATION ACROSS THE BOARD

Finally, patriarchy produces cosmetic change, and prevents its own healing, through efforts to implement change simultaneously across the organization. Executives and consultants talk about large-system change. Writers and reporters document organization-wide changes. No one in the middle or the bottom, however, experiences change that way. Different departments and divisions and units within divisions, different buildings within a school district, will change at a pace and in a form that they determine themselves.

Authentic change in governance systems is idiosyncratic; it is not amenable to consistency and predictability. If our intent is to build an institution based on partnership and service, each unit needs to be in charge of its own transition. Some units will say no—if not in words, then through compliance and passivity.

Creating the demand or the expectation that we will all move together, along a common path, drives doubt and resistance underground. Organizations are too complex to engineer their complete transformation. If we begin the dialogue with the promise we will act in concert, then what you will get is a lot of acting and a short concert. Doubt, caution, and reservation need to be honored for a change process to have real effect. Efforts that are built on the expectation that the whole system is going to change will create the mere illusion of change and only slow down the process.

Selling and promoting a change is no substitute for redesigning a governance process. Talking about across-the-board change does not make it so. Organizational reform is a learning process, not an installation process. Different units will learn different things at different rates. Let the strategy acknowledge that and not pressure units to move in unison or before they are ready. There are certain things, of course, that all units have in common. Common customers, common goals, products and services, owners and boundaries. These are what form community. But the intention to move the whole organization at one time, toward one culture, by one means, is destined to evoke compliance, not commitment. It becomes high persuasion, not high performance.

The **intention to move the whole organization at one time, toward one culture, by one means, is destined to evoke compliance, not commitment. It becomes high persuasion, not high performance.**

What makes political reform so difficult is that we try to achieve it with methods springing from the very same belief system that we intend to reform. Reform efforts fail because the process of reform is not congruent with the intent. If our intention is to create ownership and responsibility at the point of contact with product, service, and customer, we need to give people at the bottom more control over how the change happens. To achieve this demands that we yield on consistency.

Patriarchal strategies producing cosmetic change can work in the short run, but they culminate in a process of waiting for the next infusion, anxious about the next regime. They have little lasting power because they too often address problems of service, quality, and ownership as problems in communication, skill development, and the like, rather than as problems in governance. They treat symptoms, without reforming the distribution of power and purpose and ownership that created in the first place the situation we aim to change.

The price we pay for employing cosmetic change strategies is that we have fooled ourselves into counting on a false promise. We have treated ourselves as children, leaned on strategies that will collapse from the lack of proper foundation, and sown the seeds of our own cynicism and despair toward whatever is next.

Enough about what not to do. Hope is next.

13

RECREATING OUR ORGANIZATION THROUGH STEWARDSHIP

If we want to create an organization that is service driven, we need a strategy for getting there that is consistent with that intent. Stewardship gives us the alternative to the patriarchal strategies that attempt to drive change down from the top. By now, each of our organizations has probably already conducted at least one successful experiment in participation and self-management, and these experiences are a fitting foundation for building our strategy. One of our goals, then, is to put into widespread practice the innovations that we know have worked well in other organizations, and the key to doing this successfully is to honor the management process that created those particular successes.

We do not want to replicate the open office story, exporting the design for the new office while ignoring the way in which the design was created. This instinct to widely implement the tangible end result of social innovations, without also instituting the participative process that created the innovation, is what makes it so difficult to successfully make use of what we already know.

It like reading only the last chapter of a mystery story. We know who did it, but the answer has no meaning and no lasting impression.

STEWARDSHIP STRATEGY FOR POLITICAL REFORM

Since the intent of our political reform is to widely distribute accountability for the success of the organization, each step needs to foster ownership and responsibility with all who touch it. Here is what such a reform process would look like. Think of these segments as items on a menu, rather than step-by-step instructions.

COMMUNICATE THE STEWARDSHIP CONTRACT

People need a good business reason to participate in a redesign effort. They also need to know what the ground rules are. Get good at telling this story and tell it often. Don't put it on video tape, because that interferes with conversation and is too filled with self-importance. Stewardship has us as trustee for the larger institution's well-being. Be about clear about mission, know unequivocally the customers we serve and what is unique about the product or service we offer. Be clear and specific about the results we require, and the constraints we live within. Finally, state that the changes we make will be in the direction of greater empowerment, partnership, and service—these are the principles of stewardship on which we will create our future.

These are the givens. If there are people who cannot commit to this basic contract, confront it in the beginning. An act of willfulness, not participation, is what is required here. If some ask how we can initiate partnership with a willful act, tell them that it is easy. Been doing it all our lives. More on dealing with cynics later.

EACH OWNS A VISION

Vision and culture are personal values put into action. So an early step is to have individuals define their own intentions and values. Culture is defined collectively by all members of a community. So work units meet to define the vision they have about how they want to work with their customers and each other. (For more specifics on the process, you can see *The Empowered Manager,* Chapter 4.) What matters here is that each person is responsible for articulating their vision. We come together to support each other in living out our values. We do not need common vision, least of all one articulated by a small group at the top. We need common mission, a common membership contract, but not a process to induce common values.

Encourage each unit to begin a dialogue about what values are important to each person at this stage of their life and how they can live them out more deeply in this workplace. The dialogue is key. The hallmark of stewardship in action here is to ask people to talk about what matters to them, not to ask people to support what matters to us. Discuss common values if you must, but do not institutionalize them. Once they appear on a wall plaque they become dogma and lose their meaning. If we need to write them everywhere to remember them, then how important were they? We only make lists of things we would just as soon forget.

START WHERE THERE IS DESIRE

Political reform comes from wherever there is motivation and commitment. If those at the top see the need to redo their governance process, all the better. The redesign will happen a little faster by virtue of having more power and resources behind it. If those closest to customers and product have the juice, it will take a little longer because they are a little more cautious and poorer. The change can start from wherever we happen to be. The reason we are doubtful about reform is the common belief that we need those in power on our side. Not true. And besides, the wait will kill you. When we change our own unit, the whole system of governance begins to shift.

Even when people running organizations initiate today's reforms, the frustrating thing for them is that that is all they can do initiate. The real work, the substantive work of redesign, has to be done by teams of core workers. Each designing what is right for

DESIRE

their own unit. Each self-managing team, for example, has to struggle with how much of the traditional supervisor's tasks they want to take on themselves. Does the team do discipline, schedule work, hire, coach and train new members, monitor outcomes, manage suppliers, reassign roles…all for itself? There is no one answer.

Let go of the notion that people at the top and in staff functions are responsible for accomplishing reform, that they should try to answer the bagful of questions about what the new governance will look like. The fundamental reason patriarchy cannot heal itself is its desire to determine and prescribe a way of living and working for others. When we offer detailed expert answers as either a boss or a staff person/consultant, we are at that moment voting for the status quo. Stewardship defines a structure for others to make their own choices, it does not make the choices for them.

The stewardship contract is the playing field that stewardship defines for others. On that field, teams of core workers then choose a series of paths and vehicles that others in the organization are there to support.

There are two major implications of supporting the idea of individualized paths to reform.

Each Major Unit Makes
Its Own Decision How to Proceed

When a boss decides that partnership and empowerment are required for a business to survive, each department is going to have to respond. The contract for stewardship has been redefined and the expectation is that most will support it. How to support the change can be a local decision. Let units move at different paces and develop their own framework for reform. We can live with different paths and different paces. What we cannot live with is poor outcomes. If a unit does not deliver results, then some action is demanded.

The New Role of Middle Managers

We do not have to define for middle managers what their new role will be. For one thing, we are not sure. Telling them that they are boundary managers, facilitators, and coaches is not giving them much to hold on to. The better response is that they are going to have to determine where and for what they are needed. We know that they exist to serve the people that report to them. They need to ask their "customers," their subordinates, what is needed from them, and this will vary from unit to unit and team to team. Middle managers who made a living planning, organizing, and controlling are no longer needed and, in fact, get in the way. If they cannot now answer the question of what real value they add to their unit, then perhaps they are no longer needed. Better to face this now and find a compassionate resolution than to smooth over the pain by having them wear the temporary hat of a facilitator.

CORE WORKERS CHOOSE MEASURES
WITH CUSTOMERS IN MIND

There are two basic reasons we measure. One is to get the information we need to improve. Each individual, each team, each unit has to know the results it is achieving in order to fulfill its contract with the larger institution. Services rendered, units produced, quality achieved, inventory reduced, waiting time per customer, retention rate in schools, jobs obtained by graduates, survivor rates of open heart surgery—measurements like these are a way of making accountability visible. First order measurement is about value received by customers and this data needs to be assembled to present a true picture, not an attractive picture.

> *E*ach individual, each team, each unit has to know the results it is achieving in order to fulfill its contract with the larger institution.

The second basic reason we measure is to control and direct the actions of others. In this case, measurement easily shifts from being a primary instrument of improvement to becoming a primary means of parenting.

MEASURING TO STIMULATE AND CONTROL

When we have a problem with education in the United States, our first act is to define and enforce national standards for school performance. As if drop outs and reading and math illiteracy were caused by a lack of clear standards and consistent measures. The

The belief that performance can be induced through coercion in the form of measurement is one of the roots of the problem we are trying to solve, and using tighter controls in the name of improvement is trying to cure ourselves by injecting larger doses of the virus causing the disease.

belief that performance can be induced through coercion in the form of measurement is one of the roots of the problem we are trying to solve, and using tighter controls in the name of improvement is trying to cure ourselves by injecting larger doses of the virus causing the disease.

When we try to initiate reform by measuring each of the steps along the way, we are in effect trying to control the means of performance instead of the results. We are measuring the means when our data is about things like

▼ Attendance.

▼ Classroom utilization for training programs.

▼ Number of quality improvement teams.

▼ Number of suggestions, number acted upon, their dollar value.

▼ Attitude surveys—asking people how they rate empowerment, employee involvement, supervisor behavior, and the like.

▼ Hours of training attended.

These measures have a certain face validity and seem innocent enough. Yet they are of a questionable nature. The test for useful measures is whether partners would choose these measures for each other, if the business were their own. Measuring the activities or methods used by others is a throwback to the class system we aim to reform. The managing class measuring the working class. It is hard to imagine measuring top executives on

▼ Their attendance at work.

▼ How well they utilize their work space.

▼ The number of teams they are a part of and the number of meetings they go to.

▼ The number of suggestions they make, how many are acted upon and their dollar value.

▼ An attitude survey of how executives feel about middle managers and core workers.

▼ The number of training days they attended over the last twelve months.

Our desire for a long list of short-term measures expresses our bias that the middle and bottom of the organization may be less committed, less responsible, and less accountable than those at the top. The consequence is, what you see is what you get. If we have the belief that people will not take responsibility, they will prove us right. Measurements are the carrier fluid of this belief. When we put stewardship into practice, we want to measure the results of our efforts and do it equally at each level. So let our concern about ongoing progress be a part of our continuing conversation with each other, but not institutionalized and measured through a system for tracking activities.

This means that we would account for ourselves during the reform process in these ways:

▼ **Hold firm on the results defined in the stewardship contract.** Even though there is usually a dip in performance during a learning process, the organization still has to be self-sustaining even as it changes.

▼ **Value qualitative measures of progress.** We know we are trying to change attitudes about commitment, ownership, and culture, dimensions of life that cannot be captured by the quantitative longings of the engineer and the economist.

What truly matters in our lives is measured through conversation. Our dialogue with customers, employees, peers, and our own hearts is the most powerful source of data about where we stand. Using a survey to ask employees to rate their feelings on a scale from one to ten does not make their answer hard data. We fool ourselves with most of the numbers that we read. Trusting the value of the personal connections we make with those we are there to serve is real accountability. One lunch room conversation is worth a hundred surveys.

What truly matters in our lives is measured through conversation. Our dialogue with customers, employees, peers, and our own hearts is the most powerful source of data about where we stand.

▼ **Early in the process, have individuals and teams define for themselves the measures for their account.** Partnership acknowledges that we are capable of defining for ourselves the rules and yardsticks by which we live and work. Asking people what information they need to learn and perform is how we diffuse and institutionalize ownership and responsibility.

▼ **Keep measurement in perspective.** It is a second- or third order concern. We are in business to deliver service, not to measure it. Alan Watts once said, "You do not go to a restaurant to eat the menu." We go for the meal or the quality of the experience. The menu is only a clue. The description or measurement of a service is not the service itself. When measurement becomes a top priority, it is for the sake of control, not learning.

Partnership acknowledges that we are capable of defining for ourselves the rules and yardsticks by which we live and work.

OUTCOMES WIDELY SHARED

A final thought on measures. Accountability rests on full disclosure. We have to be willing to widely publish the data we have about our performance. Any reports on reform efforts need to tell the truth, not simply put a positive face on the effort for the sake of persuasion and motivation. If you believe in accountability, let your customers know how you are doing. Here are some examples of difficult data that, when published to customers and constituents, drive reform:

▼ On-time arrivals for airlines.

▼ Hospital death rates for open heart surgery.

▼ Surgery mortality rates for individual physicians.

▼ Measures of reading and math and science mastery published by gender, race, and the wealth of the school.

▼ Drop-out rates, graduation rates, and college admission rates calculated on the basis of the total number of students who entered the school.

▼ Average waiting time for the motor vehicle agency, unemployment department, and the Amtrack railroad reservation number.

▼ Return rates for new cars, fat content of fast foods, number of VCRs that still flash 12:00 because fools like me cannot read instructions. Or cannot remember them when the power goes off.

Making this kind of information public will keep us awake and connected to our marketplace.

Stewardship is served when core work teams develop work process measures for themselves and do their own monitoring. Teams with peer accountability will handle those individuals who choose to avoid responsibility. Bosses will track real business outcomes and act clearly when they are not satisfactory. Stewardship trusts that each of us wants to know, and by and large does know, how we are doing. And that each of us wants to get better.

NO NEW DEPARTMENTS

Redesigning the workplace is not an added task for managers, it is their only task. Call it quality, customer service, partnership, empowerment—what else is there that is more critical to survival? There are staff and consulting specialists who may know more about specific tools and techniques, but if we want the middle and the core workers to treat this institution as their own, then they have to steer the reform efforts with their own hands. Some examples of these steering functions are:

▼ Determining how we are doing with customers. Let people in the line organization define who the customers are. Everybody should then be meeting with or surveying customers.

▼ Assessing how our own people think and feel. Let managers and workers meet with people and ask them questions. We do not need third parties to diagnose our human problems. People will tell the truth to anyone they think will really listen. Attitude surveys, third-party interviews, and other tools of expert diagnosis are based on distrust of ourselves and actually get in the way of dialogue. If line people conduct their own data collection, they may miss out on gathering some bit of useful information, but our intent of keeping ownership and responsibility in the hands of those doing the redesign is much better served.

▼ Planning and communicating the redesign process. Those doing the work need to decide how and when to involve people, how and when to report on progress. Have work teams select consultants and other resources to learn the tools and tactics for bringing about the changes.

All these activities have traditionally been done by staff groups in the name of consistency and efficiency. We cannot afford to save money this way, the costs in terms of learning forgone and ownership lost are too high.

SELECTING LEARNING EXPERIENCES

Shift the emphasis from training to learning and put choice in the hands of the learner. Let different units choose their own way and place for learning. Let the agenda and environment for learning emerge, rather than be a cornerstone of the change strategy. We should not be teaching all people how to "Manage the Atlantic Way," or "Achieve Excellence through Quality and Accelerated Improvement." If we want each unit to design its own experiment to improve itself, then it also needs to define its learning requirements and choose its own means.

> *D*o not confuse creating a common language, which makes sense, with defining and creating common behaviors, or selling universal tools and techniques, which get in the way.

If a common language is required in some areas, hold meetings to establish the common language. Do not confuse creating a common language, which makes sense, with defining and creating common behaviors, or selling universal tools and techniques, which get in the way.

SUBSTITUTE RECOGNITION
FOR APPRAISALS AND REWARDS

As a community we need to acknowledge and recognize successful outcomes. Serving a customer, creating a new product, improving a work process, having our students score well on a test—all need to be valued.

A final caution, though. Many organizations are putting a lot of effort into giving more recognition for good ideas and good quality and service. Companies have team competitions for quality improvement. Many have awards for meeting quality criteria fashioned after the national Malcolm Baldrige Award. These are fine things to do. Praise for doing things right is a welcome relief. Recognition, though, does not constitute partnership. It is not political reform, or even a service orientation. What it represents is valuing and appreciation. It can too easily become an act of parenting at its best and an expression of the traditional belief that external rewards drive behavior. Keep the recognition systems, but don't act as if they will bring the changes we seek.

Feedback and rewards have a place in how we govern, but their place is not to drive and define change. We are not donkeys, and some of us do not eat carrots and we don't like sticks. As soon as we start paying and appraising for change, we place our hand on the lever of coercion. We want to keep coercion out of the change process because when we attempt to engineer behavior this way, we say goodbye to real accountability and ownership. Pay systems should not be changed until two to three years after a reform effort is begun; appraisals should be redesigned by each unit according to its own tastes. As soon as we tinker with appraisal and rewards as our first order of business the credibility of our offer of partnership is destroyed. Let our stance on rewards and appraisals become conspicuous by its absence.

Our stewardship strategy for political reform is clear on the destination but loose on the journey. Stewardship is not a stance against structure and control. It does aim to restrain the structures and controls that diminish the chance that others will act on their own account. Nothing in our strategy suggests that we forgo results and outcomes. The restraints we seek are to overcome the dysfunction that occurs when a future is predetermined by those in charge. Partners provide for each other a scaffolding within which each can then create their own more permanent structures as the means for determining their own future.

Steps toward Political Reform

There is something in us that likes a list. We want to translate everything in life into something that is practical. We sleep with our daytimer under our pillow and, when we wake, begin each day with a silent meditation on our seven most important goals, page 51 in the daytimer, revised quarterly, if you please. Lists become the diary of our compulsions, and we are too old now to change. We may not follow the list, but we would be lost without it. Recognizing this longing, and as a way of expressing the tactical stages of stewardship, here is another list. A summary of the steps toward political reform that have been sprinkled throughout the book. If you understand clearly where we are, and are ready for something new, skip this section.

STEP 1: DEFINE THE STEWARDSHIP CONTRACT

Define the stewardship contract for the reform effort. It includes the business reasons, the difficult issues, the unit's mission and value added to customers. It concludes with the principles for the redesign effort.

STEP 2: RENEGOTIATE CONTROL AND RESPONSIBILITY

Hold conversations about the renegotiated contract you want with bosses, staff groups, and subordinates. Here are a few specific tips.

▼ **Bosses.** The discussion with bosses is about their giving up control in exchange for our promise. We ask them to yield on their wish for consistency and let us conduct our experiment. In return, we commit to a set of results; we promise to honor the requirements of the organization, to keep them informed, and to live with the consequences.

▼ **Subordinates.** The discussion with subordinates is about purpose and responsibility. They join in defining what kind of unit this will become. They exercise more choice and control and in return claim ownership and real responsibility for the work process and outcomes. Self-management is a nice way to talk about this.

▼ **Staff groups.** We meet with staff groups to request an exception. Their jobs were created to insure consistency and control with respect to areas like personnel, technology, information systems, and finance. We want them to grant us an exception. Call it a pilot. In return they require that we understand the risks of deviating from the standard, and they want to be included in the planning and the learning. Our boss as broker may be helpful in getting this exception.

STEP 3: FULLY INFORM PEOPLE

Teach business literacy. This involves meetings about the core work process of the organization. How it all works, what is involved in changing it. What the business plan and economics of the unit are. How budgets are developed. Which financial measures are critical. Customer knowledge needs to be widely shared. The point is to help people understand the consequences of their choices.

STEP 4: CREATE A DESIRED FUTURE

Early in the game, many organizations are holding large group meetings with representatives from all their major stakeholders. Customers, board members, employees from all units and levels, key suppliers, community people, local politicians. A real cross section of the organization, broadly defined. The focus is on the future this group wants to create for the organization. No problem solving, no negotiation, strictly looking at the desired future. My friend Marv Weisbord calls these "Future Search Conferences." Searching for a common future. A good planning vehicle, this sort of meeting creates community and offers an optimistic context for the reform activities. Marv wrote a book about this called *Discovering Common Ground*. Buy it. If you have time, and are interested, read it.

STEP 5: TRAINING

Offer management training to core workers. This might be in areas like team skills, conflict management, communication skills, quality tools, and work process improvement. Most organizations create a menu that teams can choose from. Whole teams choose their agendas and attend the sessions together.

STEP 6: FORM IMPROVEMENT TEAMS

The quickest return often comes simply by having groups meet regularly to discuss improvement ideas. General Electric has something called a "workout," where whole departments meet to discuss and decide on how to simplify and streamline the business. It is their vehicle for creating a more entrepreneurial mindset. Quality circles were an early version of a team effort toward improvement. Many improvement teams cross functions and levels. Their focus is usually on cost cutting, quality enhancement, reducing cycle time, and satisfying customers.

STEP 7: CHANGE MANAGEMENT PRACTICES

Our redesign activity begins with customer requirements, which is the essence of the service orientation of stewardship. It begins to get more aggressive when basic management practices get redesigned. As we get clear what is valued by our customers, we address how to create procedures that make it easy for core workers to take ownership and responsibility for meeting those requirements. In schools this begins with a discussion of student outcomes and parent expectations. Next, school teams meet to rethink questions of curriculum, the structure of teaching within the classroom, cooperation among faculty. Procedures in budgeting, purchase decisions, hiring, and evaluations all come under the umbrella of changing management and work practices.

Many groups set up steering committees and task forces to shape this activity. Steering committees guide the whole effort, setting priorities, establishing study groups or task forces, making final decisions on changes, monitoring the effort. Task forces get set up to address specific changes and make recommendations. The spirit of the process is self-diagnosis and people redesigning their workplace for themselves.

There is much written about this part of the process that does not need to be repeated here. It goes under the name of work redesign, ecology of work, implementing high-performance work teams. For years it was hidden under the name of socio-technical work restructuring. Explain that to your nine year old. The name, of course, does not matter, the task is important. This step is where spiritual concerns become manifest in very concrete ways and the idea of stewardship begins to get institutionalized.

STEP 8: FIT ARCHITECTURE TO PURPOSE

You can change management practices and still not touch the basic structure of how work gets done. This step is about redesigning the structure or architecture of the organization. It usually involves structuring multifunctional units around a customer or a product. The roles of staff groups and supervisors also get redefined at this stage. If the structural change is major, this should be done early, around Step 5 perhaps.

STEP 9: REDESIGN THE REWARD SYSTEM

Changing the compensation system has to be done, but only after the other changes have begun to take hold. When we ask people to act as owners, we need to pay them more as owners. The pay system needs to be related to outcomes of the whole enterprise and to the outcomes of the smaller units that people are investing in, in addition to paying for outstanding individual effort. It doesn't matter whether your work is for profit or public service or not for profit. Each type of enterprise has measurable outcomes that are worth compensation dollars. Let different units design pay systems that fit the unique features of their work, yielding on the traditional demands for consistency across the board. Changing the pay system will not get us the end results we are looking for, but it needs doing for the sake of equity and to maintain credibility in the changes we are requesting.

These then are the strategy and the steps. They come roughly in the order presented, although taking them in that exact sequence is not all that critical. Managers have taken many different paths, all for good reason. Whatever the path, you will eventually come to each of these phases. I would suggest keeping the statement about the stewardship contract first and the pay system near the end.

The stewardship contract creates the context for everything that follows. The pay system, however, is such a hornet's nest that if you do not have some real success under your belt before you get into it, you may not come out the other end.

We have not even to risk the adventure alone; for the heroes of all time have gone before us; the labyrinth is thoroughly known; we have only to follow the thread of the hero-path. And where we had thought to find an abomination, we shall find a god; where we had thought to slay another, we shall slay ourselves; where we had thought to travel outward, we shall come to the center of our own existence; where we had thought to be alone, we shall be with all the world.

Joseph Campbell, *The Hero with a Thousand Faces*

▼▼▼

A Case Study Continued: The Answer to the Power Company Story, "Sometime Later in the Week"

This is the final answer to the story that featured Arthur, field technician; Mr. Phillips, supervisor; and a work process where the customer was left to make things happen and essentially fend for himself. The story is at the beginning of Part II, page 55. If you forgot, read it again. It's not that long.

There is no one solution, but if there were, it would focus on the stewardship contract, the management practices, and the basic architecture discussed in the book to this point. The elements would be:

1. Renegotiate the contract with Mr. Phillips and Arthur about the kind of response time, responsibility, and attention to customers that is now required. They are living in a marketplace and they do not know it. If they do not know it, then people above them do not know it either. They should invite customers to talk to them about what is not working. The new contract includes the fact that changes are needed to move toward the idea of partnership, internally and externally. We cannot have a partnership with the customer if we do not have one with each other.

2. Arthur and Mr. Phillips have to agree to be accountable for the new expectations and to commit to delivering results. No promise, no process. In the longer run, no promise, no job.

3. Hold meetings to explain how the whole system works. Everyone is going to be organized around customers, instead of functions, so they need to know how it all fits together. Include in these meetings a dialogue within each unit about of what kind of place they want this to be. What future they want to create for themselves. Something is needed to get Arthur feeling like this is his organization.

4. Eliminate the boundaries of the functional organization. Move from separate units of field technicians, construction, installation, and scheduling toward units organized around customers. Each new unit would expect all the members to learn all the jobs.

5. Change Arthur's role. Give Arthur the ability to inspect, schedule, price, and coordinate with other utilities, as well as locate lines. Give Arthur a cellular phone so he can talk to customers all day long. Arthur gets his performance reviews from customers and his peers.

6. Get the bosses working for their subordinates. Mr. Phillips becomes accountable to Arthur and gets his performance review from Arthur. He can coach Arthur for six months, but then he most likely will become a peer of Arthur, no cut in pay. The goal is to give Arthur the capability of responding the way Mr. Graham did in the story.

Promote Mr. Graham to president, and then have him and his shrinking executive team also be accountable to support Arthur and his team. Since Arthur's team is one of their customers, they need a conversation about how they can help the team. Start inviting Arthur and some of his team to the top group's meetings, so Arthur starts to get a feel for the larger picture.

7. Get Arthur and his team working on what practices and procedures they need to make this work. How they plan, schedule, budget, and deal with exceptions and cranky customers. How they want to handle appraisals, performance expectations, customer feedback. Each new practice must manifest partnership.

8. Get the staff groups billing their services directly to Arthur's team. Whatever support his team does not think they need from groups like finance, personnel, and systems, then the service is no longer offered. Any company policies or practices that interfere with Arthur's main mission, the team has the right to suspend, after dialogue and negotiation with the staff group responsible for enforcing those policies and practices. The team wins in case of a deadlock.

9. As for measures, the team defines what they will be measured on and how will they track them. The measures have to be dimensions that are important to customers, deal with costs and revenue, and with smart use of resources.

10. Have the team decide what additional skills they require and give them a menu of training options to choose from. The only conditions are that the training must be job related, 80 percent of it they take as a team, and they must stay within a certain budget.

11. After a year, change the pay system. Whatever system is in place for the top two levels, put in place for Arthur. Get Arthur together with a compensation person and have them decide together how to make this work. Arthur gets paid on how his department does, and how the power company does. Keep open the option of rewarding Arthur for exceptional contribution.

These are the elements of moving toward stewardship. Not complete, but they get at the fundamental beliefs about control and consistency. They change the architecture, the role of bosses and staff groups, where ownership and accountability reside, and they are relatively free of coercion and legislation. No universal prescriptions, delayed attention to the pay system.

▼ ▼ ▼

14

CYNICS, VICTIMS, AND BYSTANDERS

Every effort toward political reform runs into cynicism and doubt that any real change is possible. This doubt resides at every level of an organization and in every segment of our society. Whether we are getting out the vote for an election, working with schools to get literacy up, or getting our own unit to be stewards to our organization, we run into deep feelings of futility. Within each of our organizations there is a solid and seemingly unified contingent who wear tee shirts that say, "This too shall pass." Stewardship is an exercise of faith, responsibility, and commitment. As soon as we choose stewardship, we need a way of confronting doubt, helplessness, and indifference. When people do not buy partnership, empowerment, and service, it is not because it does not make sense or they think it will be bad for the business. It is more that they do not think it is possible or practical, or they don't trust us to make it work. Unattended, cynicism will carry the moment, and charisma, reason, and a compelling vision are not enough to get the job done.

Our instinctive response to resistance is to argue. To persuade the cynic that this change will be special. That we are indeed different from those who have gone before us. That our desire for stewardship is sincere and our choice to redesign the workplace and redistribute power is a long-term commitment.

These efforts to sell the new age through rational argument are generally futile. It is not possible to persuade or bargain with others for faith and responsibility. Yet we must do something, for without some faith and responsibility and commitment, stewardship fails.

THE POWER OF THE CYNIC

One verbal cynic in a room of fifty can set the tone and carry the day. It is not that we need every cynic to join our effort, but we want to contain the influence they have over others. To deal with the cynic we must have an understanding of their source of power. The basic position of the cynic is this.

The organization has been down this path before.
Our unit may be committed, but the rest of organization does not support it.
Prove to me that top management supports this. Have they taken the blood vow required of them?
And if we go along with you, how long will you (meaning us) be around?

These are compelling statements. The power of the cynics' position is twofold: first, there is truth in what they say and second, they speak for each of us.

THE TRUTH

Here is the rub. They are partially right. They often have history on their side. They have the data to prove that other attempts to change the organization have passed in the night. Top management does send mixed signals. We might be transferred sooner than we expect. Many of the programs that have been initiated over the years have failed to fulfill their promise. The reason it is so hard to argue with a cynic is that there is validity in what they say. Even if cynics do not have their facts exactly right, they are reporting on the way they have experienced events and there is an integrity to their experience that cannot be dismissed. It is the truth in the cynic's tale that is so powerful. If we refuse to recognize this truth, the cynic retains their power.

CYNICS EXPRESS EVERYONE'S DOUBTS

The second source of power in the cynic is that they not only have some history on their side, they also speak for us. They put into words the doubts that we all have. As committed as we might be to partnership, empowerment, and service, we all have our reservations. We have no doubts only about things we do not care about. Even if we do not have doubts about our commitment to the change process, the path to get there raises lots of questions. If that were not true, you would not be reading this book and I would not have written it. The cynic puts these questions into words for us, and does it in public settings, and for that we will never forgive them.

NO CONTEST

Because history is on their side and they speak our doubts, you cannot argue or barter with a cynic. You cannot talk them out of their version of history or make past disappointment smell any sweeter. And no concession on their part will satisfy the doubts we, ourselves, have. Even if they change their mind and get religion, our doubts will remain. The more we barter or argue with a cynic, the stronger they become. Cynicism is disbelief, a loss of faith in the sincerity or goodwill of others. How can you barter for faith? We can no more negotiate for faith than we can purchase performance.

The hero, whether god or goddess, man or woman, the figure in a myth or the dreamer of a dream, discovers and assimilates his opposite (his own unsuspected self) either by swallowing it or being swallowed. One by one the resistances are broken. He must put aside his pride, his virtue, beauty, and life, and bow or submit to the absolutely intolerable. Then he finds that he and his opposite are not of differing species, but one flesh.

Joseph Campbell, *The Hero with a Thousand Faces*

The cynic lacks faith and what they seek is a promise. In the context of an institution, cynicism expresses disbelief that management will do what it says it will do. The cynic in each of us demands to be convinced that this time it will be different. The cynic demands a promise as a cure to their lack of faith, and the promise they want is certainty. They want us to reassure them that we can provide a safe and successful future. We have to be very careful about the promise that we make, for if we do not deliver, the next round of cynicism will have been born. As much as we wish, we cannot promise a safe future and we cannot promise that the reform we are proposing will satisfy any one person or unit. The promise the cynic is looking for cannot be given. We cannot choose adventure, and then promise safety to get people to come with us.

Rescuing the Victim

The cynic in us has two first cousins, the victim and the bystander. When we ask those around us to join in the reform effort, the victim will claim that it is not within their power to make the changes required. Patriarchy breeds helplessness and victims are the product of the governance systems we live in. Bureaucratic behavior is the act of avoiding choice and giving control to some other person or some unchangeable policy. A good example is the sales manager saying, "Partnership can't work until we change the salary system for field sales people." Another favorite is, "We cannot contract as partners as long as I have to fill out the performance appraisal forms required by personnel." Or, "Nothing will change until my supervisor learns to listen and make eye contact." Somehow they would have us believe that the future of our institution hinges on the need for more cash, more permission, and more eye contact.

Our effort toward political reform needs a strategy to cope with this learned powerlessness. Where cynics are reluctant to have faith, victims do not want to take responsibility. Power is what victims want, and we are the ones they want it from. Victims believe that others, often us, hold the answer to their helplessness. If they were just given more power, or if our behavior would change in some way, then they would begin to take responsibility. In this way victims profess the belief that the people on top not only do

𝒫ower is what victims want, and we are the ones they want it from. Victims believe that others, often us, hold the answer to their helplessness. If they were just given more power, or if our behavior would change in some way, then they would begin to take responsibility.

hold all the marbles, but that they *should* hold all the marbles. Victims are strong believers in patriarchy, they are just angry that they are not the patriarchs. Victims do not want a change in the governance system, they just want a change in who governs. It is easy to be seduced by a victim's plea for more power, because the redistribution of power is one of goals of stewardship. The difference is that stewardship wants to redistribute power so that responsibility is taken and service is delivered, not as a persuasive device to get people to join the program.

Power gratuitously given is inevitably abused. Giving power to victims who do not want to choose responsibility is one of the reasons that revolutions often result in leaders who are more dictatorial than the people they replaced. Countries in crisis have wide swings in leadership from military dictator to left-wing socialists. Each regime promises to lead the country out of darkness, and each inevitably fails because they have promised prosperity that cannot be given. The people despair over their leaders because they have looked to them to give what the people have to take responsibility for themselves. Until people take the responsibility to lead themselves out of darkness, rather than expecting the government to do it, they will never become viable.

It is dangerous to offer power to people who say, "Until you give us what we want, we will not take responsibility for the success of the unit." This is not partnership and empowerment, it is entitlement and appeasement. We can no more barter for people to take responsibility than we can barter for them to have faith.

The resolution in dealing with cynics and victims is to reframe their stance as a choice, not as an inevitable outcome of their experience. More on this in a minute, after a brief discussion of one other form of resistance, the bystander.

FACTS WON'T HELP

Bystanders enter the game by withholding commitment. They want proof that stewardship works. Whatever form your revolution takes, whether it is site-based management, self-managing teams, or direct billing the services of staff groups, they want to know where it has been tried and what were the results and if it has not been tried, why would we "experiment" on our own bodies? Like the engineering manager who asked, "Has this been tried in a sixty-five person company in the packaging machinery business, and what were the results?" Needless to say, this manager ran an engineering group in a sixty-five person packaging machinery company. When an executive in Kansas City asked, "Do you have evidence that a company's stock price has gone up because they implemented empowerment?" what he meant was, "Give me proof, then I will commit myself."

Commitment is a personal investment or consignment in the face of an uncertain outcome. If the outcome were a sure thing, no commitment would be required. All the evidence in the world that other organizations have applied these ideas successfully does not mean that our attempts will work in our situation. Success stories are reassuring, but they do not constitute proof. Other people's experience is no final answer to the risk of creating an organization of our own choosing. Being a bystander is one more version of our wish for certainty and safety. We are constantly asking others to face the reality of our predicament, and when we make it seem safer than it is, we fool no one but ourselves. And we make an implied promise that we cannot fulfill.

Treating Caution as a Choice

Stewardship seeks the successful integration of the spirit, the marketplace, and politics. If the spirit is empty, or the marketplace is ignored, no political system or governance system can succeed. We need this three-legged stool to stand on. This means that each reform effort begins as an act of faith and gets built when responsibility and commitment are widely shared. Creating stewardship means we need to find a way to evoke faith and responsibility and commitment in those around us and at a minimum to keep the cynics, victims, and bystanders from controlling the emotional environment and undermining our efforts. We need a way of neutralizing their power. Something different from the instinctive act of arguing with them and trying to prove them wrong. Something different from bartering with them to purchase their support. If you ever hear yourself saying that this change effort is unique, this time top management is 100 percent behind us, the timing is right, the organization's commitment is genuine, stop it. The only one being moved is yourself. Persuasion and enrollment work only on the screen and the stage. If you hear yourself promising pay increases, greater freedom, more privileges, put these back in your pocket. What we need we can't buy.

INVITING A CHOICE

In place of persuasion and barter, we need to believe that faith, responsibility, and commitment are a matter of personal choice. Even though history may be on the side of the cynic, and their wounds are real, they can choose to have faith in the face of that experience. This is the invitation we make to them. We need to affirm their version of history and support them in their doubts. We replace coercion and persuasion with invitation.

At the same time we need to affirm the choice we have made. We choose stewardship and strive for political reform, in the face of our own wounds filled with our own doubts. We say to the cynic, "I understand what you say. The doubts and perhaps bitterness

The best definition of the gospel message I ever heard is that the gospel is the permission and command to enter difficulty with hope.

Donna Schaper,
A Book of Common Power

you express I, in some ways, share. I, though, have decided to have faith that this time we can do something here that will matter, and I hope you will make the same choice and join in this effort." This will not be persuasive, it will not change their position. What it does is neutralize the power they have over the community. They have a right to their own stance, they do not have a right to hold back others from investing.

The dialogue looks something like this.

1. Acknowledge the other's position. Do not label it cynic, victim, or bystander. Support them by acknowledging that part of you that agrees with their position. If you think you do not have your own doubts, think harder.

For the cynic, we can name other programs that have started and resulted in nothing of value. We can own the risks of the path we are choosing.

For the victim, we acknowledge their feelings of helplessness and their wish that people in power will not disappoint them. We have the same desire and the same doubt.

For the bystander, we support their desire for more data and more proof that this story has been written elsewhere and we will have a happy ending. We too have searched for reassurance and wanted more.

2. State the choice for faith and commitment in the face of our own reservations. What is critical in this whole process is that we make choices in spite of the doubts that we have. The safe path is to wait until the doubts have disappeared before we choose. This is the sorrow of the unlived life. The desire for top management approval, the search for places this has worked, the wish to measure and measure—all are hedges against the risk of redistributing power and purpose.

Our strongest response to the cynic is our own conviction. In expressing our decision to move toward stewardship, we affirm the belief that change is a matter of personal responsibility, not a response to the expectations of those above or below us. The statement is simply, "After all is said and done, I am going to do everything I can to bring partnership and ownership to every part of this unit."

3. Invite the same choice from the other person. Frame the issue as a choice. "I would like you to make the same choice." There is no promise in this invitation nor is there an immediate demand for acceptance. There is in the invitation a desire to keep the choice we are each making in the foreground and to keep the doubts and excuses in the background, where they belong. The final exchange of every meeting and conversation is a statement of wants and offers. This is the antidote to barter and debate.

The difficult question that always comes up at this point is, what happens if others do not choose stewardship and really want to maintain the patriarchy they signed on for in the first place? All they want is for us to become better parents, or if they are our boss, they want us to get with the program.

If we are talking about subordinates, they have a right to say no to our invitation. They may want a boss who will take care of them in return for hard work and loyalty. Their choice needs to be acknowledged, but it also has consequences. In the longer run, they will have a hard time getting what they want from this organization, and we may or may not have a place where they can contribute. Despite this, there usually is no need to force the issue at this moment. People need to be given time and support to make fundamental choices about faith and responsibility. The easy stance is to play captain of industry and tell people to either lead, follow, or get out of the way, but that is just business as usual. The truth is that we do not need everyone to choose stewardship, all we need is about 25 percent to commit and the way we operate will start to shift. Over time this 25 percent will pull the others along and another 20 percent will usually move on, out of their own discomfort.

BOSS EXEMPTION

EXEMPTIONS FROM BOSS AND STAFF GROUPS

The stakes get raised for us when our boss or someone in a key staff position is cynical about what we want to do. They often want to maintain tight control and consistency even after our best arguments have been made. Despite the risk, the process is similar to the one for dealing with subordinates and peers. We affirm the choice we have made and ask them to support what we are trying to do. When they lack faith or commitment, don't argue or negotiate. All we can do is communicate understanding to them—in a sense take their side—and ask to be treated as an exception, a human pilot program. We have to be willing to absorb all the risk. We will deliver results to our boss and if we do not, we expect to pay a price. In this case we are promising certain operational outcomes in return for the freedom to pursue a unique path.

The dialogue goes like this.

1. **Make the case for reform.** State the results you are seeking, the harsh realities the unit faces. Be clear about the principles you want to redesign toward and the constraints you have established.

2. **Acknowledge that you want an exemption.** You want an exemption from the normal requirements for control and consistency. Let them know that you understand the problem your request creates for them.

3. **Promise specific results.** In return for the exemption, you are committing to deliver specific results. You are promising that customers will be better served and that the business will benefit. Promising higher morale or better teamwork is not enough. Asserting your willingness to fall on your own sword if you are wrong is when you find out about your own commitment.

Remember, all you want from your boss is tolerance or indifference. You do not require sponsorship, commitment, or even deep interest. If you get enthusiasm, take it, but don't set it up as a requirement. If you think you need approval to create a place of your own choosing, go back to Chapter 3 and Chapter 6.

The process is similar for staff groups. We want to be a pilot effort. If staff groups such as personnel and finance and information systems will not make an exception for us, we may have to set up parallel procedures. Give the staff groups what they require, but operate internally as we choose. A simple example is the performance appraisal. If everyone has to fill out the same form, go ahead and fill it out and turn it in. We can still implement the process we want and have conversations we choose within our unit. Inefficient, frustrating, but workable. The worst thing we can do is to use resistance from staff groups as an excuse for not living out our intentions. The same with our boss. We are beginning our own voyage to discover the new world. We need to inform them what we are doing, we need the bankers to let us spend the money, but do not need their sponsorship to manage the way we choose. All we need is our own willingness to begin the adventure and live with the consequences. Besides, sleeping peacefully through the night is overrated.

▼▼▼

THE OPENING OF EYES

After R.S. Thomas

That day I saw beneath dark clouds
the passing light over the water
and I heard the voice of the world speak out,
I knew then, as I had before
life is no passing memory of what has been
nor the remaining pages in a great book
waiting to be read.

It is the opening of eyes long closed.
It is the vision of far off things
seen for the silence they hold.
It is the heart after years
of secret conversing
speaking out loud in the clear air.

It is Moses in the desert
fallen to his knees before the lit bush.
It is the man throwing away his shoes
as if to enter heaven
and finding himself astonished,
opened at last,
fallen in love with solid ground.

David Whyte

▼▼▼

15

CHOOSING FREEDOM, SERVICE, AND ADVENTURE

Write all the books you want. Give all the speeches you want. Run all the meetings, workshops, and conferences you want. Bleat out your longing for how the world should work, and you will get only one question back..."How?"

HOW

No one cares any more about why we should do something. No one cares about when we should do something, we are always beginning too late. We are in such a hurry, and so eager to copy what others are doing, that the question of whether we should act at all is a question that only delays us and wastes our time. Fire, no time and little interest in aiming. The question is "How?" You want to transform institutions, to empower them, to make them just in time, continuously improve them, excellentize customers and quality, do ethics, flatten them, shrink them, catalyze leaders to take us into the next millennium, the question that keeps coming up is "How do you do it?" This question becomes more interesting than the answer. This chapter is the answer to the question "How?" This chapter teaches you how. It is the ultimate how-to-do-it guide, taking only one chapter to deliver. Most how-to-do-it books give you instructions in one narrow area...cooking, home repair, communications, inventory control, customer service, leadership. This chapter accepts the challenge of teaching you how, regardless of your question. The original working title for this book was *How*. Not a question. An answer. How. This chapter is intended to put an end to the question "How?"

"How?" Is a Defense

There is depth in the question "How do I do this?" that is worth exploring. The question is a defense against the action. It is a leap past the question of purpose, past the question of intentions, and past the drama of responsibility. The question "How?"—more than any other question—looks for the answer outside ourselves. It is an indirect expression of our doubts. Our search for manuals, recipes, the practical is endless. The nonfiction best-seller list is filled with recipe books that have nothing to do with cooking.

I was with a group that wanted to know how to implement empowerment and participation. Who doesn't? I asked the audience how many of them had read the books *Thriving on Chaos, Seven Habits of Highly Effective People, The Empowered Manager,* and *The Fifth Discipline.* Most of the group raised their hand. In those four books there are over 925, count them, specific suggestions on how to move the workplace in high-performing and customer-centered directions. So if we have seen those books and others, and there are more practical suggestions than we can use in a lifetime, why are we still asking the question "How?"

What does it mean that self-help is what sells? Financial self-help, psychological self-help, spiritual self-help, food and exercise to immortality. So who wants to die with a healthy body? How many diets does it take to lose weight? How long does it take to stop smoking?

The experience of searching outside for answers expresses our doubts about being enough, having enough, doing enough.

The answer to "How?" takes us to three core questions that underlie the majority of our discussions about getting practical. The wish for concrete suggestions—tell me where it is working, show me how to do it, prove it to me—are the surface waves of these issues.

▼ Is it possible to discover, claim, and live out my freedom, in the midst of community and the marketplace?

▼ Is it possible to do something of real value and service to something larger than myself and immediate family?

▼ Is it possible to also be safe and secure while pursuing my freedom and searching for ways to be of service?

To serve. To be safe. To know what freedom feels like. These are questions for institutions as well as questions for individuals. These issues are what community, work, and organizations exist to answer. The problem is that the institutions we have inherited no longer deliver choice, service, or security. There is something in the nature of institutions that deflects them away from the service, freedom, and adventure that created them. Even as a nation, the founding instincts of life, liberty, and the pursuit of happiness have been distorted into materialism and outcomes of interest mainly to economists. As if the purpose of society is standard of living. At what point does the identity of a nation make the switch from the land of freedom to streets paved with gold? Standard of living, economics, profit are fuel to the organism, not its basic purpose. For us as individuals, our purpose gets deflected from what matters to what works. The intensity of the question "How?" is an expression of our having surrendered some part of ourself, our own struggle with purpose and destiny, by constantly kneeling at the altar of expedience.

If we took responsibility for our freedom, committed ourselves to service, and had faith that our security lay within ourselves, we could stop asking the question "How?" We would see that we have the answer. In every case the answer to the question "How?" is "Yes." It places the location of the solution in the right place. With the questioner.

Our organization, an embodiment of community, is the palette for discovering our answer. The underlying questions about freedom, service, and security carry their own answers within them. These questions are in some way irreducible. Our search for freedom, security, and service are explorations in inner space. Our common illusion is that these can be purchased at the mall or found in a classroom. That they can be created for us by strong leadership, or can be achieved only at other people's expense. A Darwinian rationale for self-centeredness.

The hope for stewardship and empowerment is that they provide a governance strategy which both serves a marketplace and honors our need to answer questions of safety, service, and freedom. It helps to realize that the answer to these questions is a package deal. You cannot answer one without answering the other two.

▼ My security is discovered by experiencing my freedom and using it in service of something outside myself.

▼ I discover my freedom through the belief that my security lies within and is assured by acts of congruence and integrity, which are the essence of service.

▼ I can be of real service only when I take responsibility for all my actions, which is the only safety I have, and when the choices I make are mine. Service out of obligation is codependency and a disguised form of control. Service that fully satisfies is done with no expectation of return, and is freely chosen.

Organizations are important, in part, because they become means to overcoming our isolation in finding answers to these questions. Organization, literally, is another word for interdependence. We need each other for a thousand reasons, both emotional and practical. That is why most of us live in communities. If you have doubts about this, fly across country, any country. It is open space with people huddled in small circles we call cities. The problem we face is that the organizational forms we have inherited and internalized do not nurture the realization of security, freedom, and service. In fact we have lost faith that these questions can be answered at the workplace. We have come to believe that to be productive in the marketplace we have to sacrifice our freedom, place our security in the hands of others, and bootleg our wish to be of service. Stewardship, more than leadership, offers hope that freedom, security, and service can be discovered in community, large-scale community, and still be productive in the marketplace. In fact, if we really care about cost, quality, and customers, this may be the essential path that will get us there.

The answer, then, to "How?" is to stop asking the question that way. Following action plans and prescriptions laid down by others often keeps us from moving ahead. It is the engineer in us that looks outside ourselves and wants to know, ahead of time, what steps to take. This is our desire for a safe and predictable future. Implementing changes of our own design is learning; acting on the designs of others is too often a form of staying stuck.

Ask instead these questions:

▼ What will it take for me to claim my own freedom and create an organization of my own choosing?

▼ What is it I uniquely have to offer? What do I wish to leave behind here? What is the nature of the unique service I bring to the table?

▼ When will I finally choose adventure and accept the fact that there is no safe path? That my underlying security comes from counting on my own actions or from some higher power, neither of which will be discovered via an engineering solution.

These questions become the context for the discussion on ways to move toward stewardship. Searching for ways to engage others in reforming our institutions faces us each time with our own limitations and our struggle to use ourselves productively. Saying yes to questions for freedom, service, and adventure, as an individual and as a work unit, opens up the possibility of beginning our own experiment in partnership and stewardship. It only takes one diet to lose weight, it only takes one instant to stop smoking, only one gesture to remove the crown from our own head. We know how. We only have to choose it and have the courage to live with the consequences.

> *L*ook for your own. Do not do what someone else could do as well as you. Do not say, do not write what someone else could say, could write as well as you. Care for nothing in yourself but what you feel exists nowhere else and out of your self create, impatiently or patiently...the most irreplaceable of things.
>
> Andre Gide

DEMOCRACY ON THE LINE

There is also more at stake than fulfilling our own personal destiny. Democracy is also on the line. There is an unmistakable contradiction between the democratic values of freedom and independence and the colonial and patriarchal strategies used to manage our organizations over the last forty to four thousand years. At nights and on weekends we cry out for human rights and freedom of speech, and then we go to work and become strategic and cautious about our every word for fear we will be seen as disloyal or uncommitted. Our newspapers take fierce and courageous pride in telling the truth in their communities and yet are managed in the most directive and aristocratic ways imaginable. Defenders of the First Amendment right of free speech, they will place a microphone in the face of all but their own employees. Freedoms demanded of others are denied to their own.

Democracy is the system of government that promises above all else to protect us from the abuse of power. We have as a society created mechanisms that are intrinsically self-correcting should our leaders exploit the power they hold. The constitution is the written form of these protections.

▼ We limit the tenure of our leaders. This means the leaders have some accountability to their followers. The selection process creates this accountability.

▼ Local control gets the benefit of the doubt. Any powers not specifically given to the central government belong either to the local governing unit or the individual.

▼ There is an explicit contract of protection called the Bill of Rights that makes guarantees to the individual. Freedom of speech. The right to assemble and hold meetings. The right to face our accuser and not be punished for the same crime over and over. The right to protect ourself physically by bearing arms.

▼ The creation of an independent entity to protect these rights. The judicial system. We know where to go when power is abused and rights are denied.

Despite our deep belief in these principles, we do not trust them to govern our organizations. To govern our society, yes; to govern our organizations, no. Many of the rights and beliefs we hold essential to democracy, we check at the door when we go to work. If you have doubts about it, consider this:

▼ How free do you feel to speak? Why is there such a predominant feeling at work that if you stand up you will get shot?

▼ What rights to assemble do you have? A small group talking about business, yes. How comfortable would you be to call a meeting of twenty of your peers, with only people at your level in the room and no bosses being informed about the meeting? And suppose the agenda for the meeting was how to get top management to change their way of operating?

▼ When you are given a performance review, how many of your accusers are in the room to be faced?

▼ How frequently have we had a voice in selecting our leaders? Why have we clung so tightly to management's prerogative to select leaders, define purpose, and determine what information is shared and withheld?

What interferes with our experience of democracy has nothing to do with politicians, public policy, legislation, or the electoral process. Democracy is much more complex than simply the right to vote for our leaders. Voting may be the dominant symbol of democracy, but it does not in itself provide the experience of democracy. Creating a living democracy has much more to do with the nature of our institutional experience. While we are members

We have no more a real democracy in the world today. Democracy in politics has in no country led to democracy in its economic life. We still have autocracy in industry as firmly seated on its throne as theocratic kings ruling in the name of a god, or aristocracy ruling by military power; and the forces represented by these twain, superseded by the autocrats of industry, have become the allies of the power which took their place of pride.

George Russell (1867-1935)

of a society that protects freedom of speech, choice, and the rights of the individual, the lived reality is that we work in places that are managed with beliefs that view the values underlying democracy with deep skepticism if not contempt. As an executive and managerial class, we are still convinced that for large groups of people to get work done and succeed in the marketplace, control, consistency, and predictability, engineered from the top, are absolute requirements. How many times have we heard at work, at moments of confusion or disagreement, the cry, "This is no democracy!" And we all nod and say, "Right, this is no democracy. Somebody make up their mind." I often wonder later, how did democracy get such a bad name? Our distrust of power in the hands of people other than at the top runs deep. This belief is what makes it hard for most of us to experience choice and freedom in our day-to-day lives.

Democracy is surely the most complicated form of governance and in ways seems so fragile. Perhaps not so fragile in the United States or in Western Europe, but certainly as we look around the world, we see countries constantly moving in and out of democracy. Visit Eastern Europe, Africa, South America, parts of Asia, or look at certain periods of U.S. history, and you begin to feel how attractive autocratic leadership is to us all, especially in hard times. The more economic stress we live under, the more a stable and democratic society gets confronted. It is people's sense of helplessness and powerlessness that first creates apathy and self-centeredness and eventually leads to extremism. If we are consistently breeding helplessness in our institutions, which is what patriarchy is good at, it will bleed over into our larger political process.

Democracy has as its essence a widely distributed sense of ownership and responsibility. Creating partnerships at work is a way of affirming and assuring the democratic experience. The marketplace has become the testing ground for how a society lives out its potential. Our experience inside organizations dictates the likelihood of our engaging in broader forms of participation in society. The learning place for our dependency has been the school and the workplace. We have swallowed the belief that organizations, and even communities, can survive only with enforcement of consistency and control.

As long as we continue to believe this, economic and political reform will never happen. So what we do in our workplace, with our marketplace, makes a difference. This is where democracy will revive itself, not in the voting booth. Our own unit becomes the place where the economic war will be won and democracy rediscovered.

This is what makes the choice for adventure worth taking. This is how choosing faith and accountability in our own environment becomes a broader act of service. It is our contribution to world peace and the secure planet we have been searching for.

LOST AND FOUND

The Lost and Found is where we reclaim what has once been ours, but has been inadvertently set aside. It is a place to begin looking when something is missing. This section is to help you find other places for learning. So if you still want more information, get ready for another list.

This section of a book is most often called a bibliography. A place where other writings are listed for further reference. The limitation of a bibliography is that it is restricted to the written word. People who are putting a set of ideas into action too often do not write about what they are doing and therefore never really get listed or valued adequately. The intent here is to recognize the action, as well as the written word.

Here is a list of pioneers who are acting on the ideas of stewardship expressed in this book. There are a few authors sprinkled among the pioneers, there are also some consultants who keep pushing the edge of the revolution and become my teachers whenever I am with them. The important people, though, are the supervisors and managers who are demonstrating that dramatic and enduring change can take place, regardless of our culture or where in the hierarchy we reside. This list becomes an answer to the question about who has influenced me, and I commend them to you.

If you want to learn more about what these people are doing, contact Designed Learning, 1009 Park Ave., Plainfield, N.J. 07060, and we will pass your message along.

ABELLA, CARN. Carn runs the Development Academy of the Philippines. Their primary client is the Philippine government and their purpose is to provide the tools to recreate democratic processes in their country. If you want to see what desire, commitment, and openness look like, visit them. A warning though, it will spoil you when you return to the indifference that so often surrounds us.

ARNOLD, JOAN. A Line Manager of machine operators, Joan has put the tasks of management back in the hands of those doing the work. So much so that she now spends a portion of her time on running a machine. Her unit has renegotiated the services received by staff groups and has integrated the notion that the business they work for is, in effect, their own.

THE ASSOCIATION FOR QUALITY AND PARTICIPATION. This is a biased recommendation, since I have been on their Board of Directors. They have chapters all over the country which provide support and information about the quality movement and managing change. Their conferences are among the best places to hear about innovative practices in participation and new workplaces. Plus they are very responsive if you call them with questions. Contact them at 801-B West 8th Street, Cincinnati, Ohio 45203, (513) 381-1959.

AT WORK: STORIES OF TOMORROW'S WORKPLACE. A bimonthly newsletter documenting innovative changes in organizations. It is about practice, not theory, and is a great place to read about other people's stories and to tell your own. If you have had it with reading, and are ready to write your own story, this is might be a good placed to start. Subscribe to the newsletter at Berrett-Koehler Publishers, Inc., 155 Montgomery Street, San Francisco, Calif., 94104-4109. To talk about having your story appear in the newsletter, contact the editor, Alis Valencia, *At Work*, 68 Sunrise Mountain Road, Cazadero, Calif. 95421.

BIEHAL, FRANZ. There is an Austrian consulting firm named Trigon that works on redesigning workplaces. Franz is a partner in Trigon and is working with staff groups that are experimenting with becoming autonomous service units which give choice to their internal customers and also sell their services to other organizations.

BLOCK, PETER. *Flawless Consulting: A Guide to Getting Your Expertise Used.* San Diego: Pfeiffer & Co., 1981.
BLOCK, PETER. *The Empowered Manager: Positive Political Skills at Work.* San Francisco: Jossey-Bass Publishers, 1987.

BREHM, JOHN. There are members of the managerial class who are initiating the revolution, albeit in a thoughtful and peaceful way. John is a senior vice-president of a midwestern utility, responsible for all the financial and administrative functions. He has decided to minimize the policing and watching role of staff functions and bet their future on service and creating capability within the line organization. It is a complicated, difficult path and takes time. But the choice has been made.

BUBER, MARTIN. *The Way of Man, According to the Teaching of Hasidism.* New York: Carol Publishing Group, 1990. Rich, condensed, almost poetic philosophical statement about hope and the human condition. I received this as a gift from a friend, and recommend it in the same spirit.

CAMPBELL, JOSEPH. *The Hero with a Thousand Faces.* Bollingen Series, vol. XII. Princeton: Princeton University Press, 1972. Campbell has brought mythology if not into the mainstream, at least into the bookstores. The first edition came out in 1949 and has some prose and ideas that latch on to you and will not let go, even though you may not fully understand them.

CHAPNICK, LISA. There are people in government who take the idea of public service seriously. One of these places is the Department of Inspectional Services for the city of Boston. They inspect for a living, have a very bumpy history and public image, and still are committed to bringing partnership and empowerment into how they govern themselves and work with their customers. Lisa runs the department and, having started below ground level, is demonstrating what is possible, even in a very tough environment.

COMMON BOUNDARY. This is an organization that explores the intersection between psychology and spirituality. They publish a journal and run an excellent conference in December in Washington, D.C. Contact is 4304 East-West Highway, Bethesda, Md. 20814.

DOLAN, PATRICK. Dolan and Associates has built their reputation on cooperative ventures between management and labor. Patrick lately has focused on education reform and has a series of videotapes to support that effort. There are several ideas in this book that come from him; he understands the hard edge of change as well as anyone.

DUPRE, VLAD. I have thought that among the professions, psychotherapists were some of the most patriarchal and paternalistic. There are, however, therapists who believe strongly in a balanced distribution of power and responsibility between doctor and patient. Vlad is an a good example of this. He has helped me see more clearly the hard stances required to help people take responsibility for their own actions, especially when their lives are not working. He creates in the therapeutic relationship what this book advocates creating in our larger institutions.

ELIADE, MIRCEA. *The Sacred and the Profane: The Nature of Religion.* New York: Harcourt Brace Jovanovich, 1959. Clarifying discussion of how cultures give meaning to people's lives. His perspective about the ways we symbolize our choice to make life sacred was very helpful.

FEDIGAN, COLETTE; KANE, KAYLEEN; NEWELL, JANET; SANFORD, JAYNE; TORKY, PAT. There are teams of people who are in traditionally low-power positions who have decided to make many of these ideas a way of life for themselves. The five listed here are a self-managing, administrative support group that knows about ownership, service, and responsibility, and also knows how to face difficult issues and work things out.

FRANCK, FREDERICK. An artist, a teacher, and a writer who leaves a compassionate fingerprint on all he touches. He and his wife, Claske, conduct drawing workshops which teach people to see. What we can see, we can draw. What we see and draw, we are compelled to care about and love, and so this wise, Dutch dentist goes quietly about changing the world. They have created a sacred space in New York state, open at times to the public, and they have a newsletter. Contact Pacem in Terris, 96 Covered Bridge Road, Warwick, N.Y. 10990.

GIBSON, TREVAR. The empowerment and service ideas are being embraced more and more in small businesses. Edson Manufacturing, in Canada, makes packaging machinery and they are writing the book on renegotiating the social contract. There are struggles, but the book is being written. A small example. They recently had a layoff and peers voted on who should stay and go. Three months later, they needed to rehire seven employees. Again peers voted on whom to bring back. Trevar used to run this company, now he is just president.

GOGOLL, WOLF DIETER. The ideas about stewardship are growing in Germany. Wolf Dieter, through patience and being a trustworthy human being, is part of bringing partnership to a truck tire division of a large tire company. It is another example of change starting in the middle and expanding outward.

GREENLEAF, ROBERT K. *Servant Leadership: A Journey in the Nature of Legitimate Power and Greatness.* New York: Paulist Press, 1977. Greenleaf originated the idea of the servant leader and embodied it in his work with AT&T and afterwards. He wrote widely and his work is being continued by the Robert K. Greenleaf Center, 1100 West 42nd Street, Suite 321, Indianapolis, Ind. 46208. They offer booklets, videotapes, and other resources for those interested in the ideas.

HART, CHRISTOPHER. I heard about service guarantees in a talk by Hart. They are also described in Chapter 6 of *Service Break-throughs: Changing the Rules of the Game,* by James L. Heskett, W. Earl Sasser, Jr., and Christopher W. L. Hart (New York: Freedom Press, 1990).

HENNING, JOEL. Joel has been my spiritual partner in working these ideas. He makes the ideas concrete and practical by his will and willingness to set aside all else, in service of long-term, in-depth commitments to his clients. Nobody does it better.

JACOB, RICHARD. Briskheat, in Columbus, Ohio, is another small manufacturing company that is redesigning itself. Rich has initiated a process where core workers make major decisions, teams manage themselves, the managers keep wanting to change more quickly. I asked a maintenance technician in the plant what had changed in the last three years. He said, "If I need a part, now I can buy it the same day. Before, it took two weeks of paperwork, and then I still might not get the part. Now they trust me."

KNOWLES, RICHARD. Dick is one of many manufacturing managers in this country who are initiating a transformation in their own unit. By consciously changing the roles and relationships and moving the responsibility and accountability to those doing the work, the Belle Plant can compete with any in the world. The process is also creating the opportunity for meaning and dignity in what could otherwise be a grinding and alienating operation. Contact Plant Manager, E.I. Du Pont de Nemours & Company (Inc.), 901 West Dupont Avenue, Belle, W.Va. 25015.

KOESTENBAUM, PETER. *The Heart of Business: Ethics, Power, and Philosophy.* Dallas: Saybrook Publishing Co., 1987.

KOESTENBAUM, PETER. *Leadership: The Inner Side of Greatness.* San Francisco: Jossey-Bass Publishers, 1991. Continuing to be a world force, Peter talks and writes of leadership in a way that illuminates the soul. I have not yet met a wiser man.

LEZOTTE, LARRY. One of the strongest efforts at school reform goes under the name of Effective Schools Research. Larry is at the center of this effort and can frame the issues with great clarity and humor. I would show up to listen to him anywhere. His organization works with schools, distributes booklets on school reform, and supports educators all across the country. He is a terrific talk show guest, and will soon be making the rounds, so watch for him. He is Executive Vice President, Effective Schools Products, Ltd., 2199 Jolly Road, Suite 160, Okemos, Mich. 48864.

LESTER, BUD. Dr. Lester writes fiction and non-fiction. He also writes database programs. He offers personal computer systems support and specializes in consulting with home-based professionals. He knows what service and integrity and patience are about. I am one of his customers. Contact him at P.O. Box 86005, Plano, Tex. 75086.

LYLE, JOHN. If you want to talk to someone who knows how to create new entrepreneurial operations, John is the one to talk to. He is very clear about the social contract needed to create ownership at every level. He is very willing to experiment and has a keen sense of what to control and what to let go of. He continues to start up new businesses and has his hands on five of them.

MARTIN, BOB. Bob led the AT&T Phone Centers, part of which experience is referred to in the body of this book. He is a true innovator and knows how to place a theory into a business practice. There is a set of audiotapes of an empowerment seminar Bob and I gave in Japan, in which he talks about what he did with the Phone Centers. If these are of interest, contact Designed Learning, Plainfield, N.J. Bob now has his own consulting firm.

MARKOVITCH, VICKIE. An educator and school superintendent, Vickie is making stewardship work in public education. Public schools have such a complicated set of customers and regulators, it is sometimes amazing that any learning takes place. In the face of this, Vickie knows how to create partnerships and how to raise expectations in a useful way.

McKEE, MARIE. There are not enough human resource executives who have a clear idea of what the function might be and how it might offer real service and get out of the policing and conscience role. Marie works for Corning, Inc. and is one of those executives who offers a ray of hope for those of us in the profession.

McKNIGHT, JOHN. *The Professional Service Business.* Evanston, Ill.: The Center for Urban Affairs and Policy Research, Northwestern University, 1976.
McKNIGHT, JOHN. "Do No Harm: Policy Options That Meet Human Needs." *Social Policy* (Summer 1989): 5-15. McKnight writes with precision and radical insight about the politics of the helping professions. His ideas have discomforting relevance to those in staff roles in organizations. Most of his work is published through the Center for Urban Affairs and Policy Research, Northwestern University, 2040 Sheridan Road, Evanston, Ill. 60208-4100.

NIETZSCHE, FRIEDRICH. *Thus Spoke Zarathustra: A Book for Everyone and No One.* Translated by R.J. Hollingdale. New York:

Penguin Books, 1969. Nineteenth century philosopher who mistakenly gets associated with the Third Reich in Germany. A book of vivid aphorisms which massage our wishes for greatness and purpose.

OSBORNE, DAVID, AND GAEBLER, TED. *Reinventing Government: How the Entrepreneurial Spirit Is Transforming the Public Sector.* New York: Addison-Wesley, 1992. Well-written book documenting successful public sector efforts to bring the entrepreneurial spirit into government. Many of the ideas apply just as well to private and not-for-profit organizations, especially when you look at internal service units.

PACE, HUGH. Conventional wisdom says that you cannot implement partnership and empowerment when the business is in crisis, is shrinking, and you have a culture with a strong patriarchal and autocratic legacy. Hugh proved this theory wrong by literally reforming, and bringing to life, a tire company in Argentina. He is now introducing these ideas to another company in Mexico. In another book, I stated that I wrote for people who wore pinstriped suits and had a radical heart. Hugh Pace was whom I had in mind.

PIERSANTI, STEVEN. He has decided that his publishing company will be built on stewardship and an equitable balance of power. Radical thoughts in his industry. He coaxed this book into being, and so in that sense it is his fault.

REDBURN, RAY ET AL. *Confessions of Empowering Organizations.* Cincinnati: Association for Quality and Participation, 1991. Want some examples where partnership and empowerment are working? Interested in self-managed work crews? Self-directed reorganizations? Here are ninety-two case studies, with names and phone numbers. This book was written for bystanders and others who want proof.

Ross, Doug. There is an organization known as Michigan Futures that has the vision to create community on a state-wide scale. The ideas of quality, participation, and widely dispersed power and responsibility are the basis upon which this coalition is being built. It represents a new kind of politics based on partnership and service rather than power and self-interest. Doug is creating this process. Their address is Michigan Futures, Inc., 30400 Telegraph Road, Suite 370, Bingham Farms, Mich. 48025.

Sachdev, Anil. There is a network of human resource people and line managers in India who are pushing empowerment and inventing more democratic institutions. There are organizations in this Third World country that are far ahead of most U.S. companies in creating high quality, quick response, service-oriented delivery systems. Anil is a director of Eicher Consultancy Sevices in New Delhi, India, and is at the center of this network. The comments about Gandhi, early in the book, came from Anil.

Schaper, Donna. *A Book of Common Power: Narratives against the Current.* San Diego: Lura Media, 1989. A good book about theology, social justice, and political reform.

Shorris, Earl. *Scenes from Corporate Life: The Politics of Middle Management.* New York: Penguin Books, 1981. A hard and sometimes harsh, but enlightening, look at totalitarianism in organizations. Well written, with passion. To me it is a classic.

Stephen, Leslie. Leslie has edited two of my books, my first one and this one. When I have needed an image of someone who has chosen service over self-interest, she comes to mind. She is an advocate for the reader, can reshape a book, drain out edginess and boredom, and still be faithful to another's voice.

Vandegrift, John. Another middle manager who, starting with strong convictions and a deep concern for the survival of the total business, has created a division of empowered, service-driven people. He works for a large, unnamed document company, which itself has undergone a major transformation. John is living out a hopeful story, even with all the reservations that go with knowing how much more is possible.

WEISBORD, MARVIN R. *Productive Workplaces: Organizing and Managing for Dignity, Meaning, and Community.* San Francisco: Jossey-Bass Publishers, 1987.

WEISBORD, MARVIN R. *Discovering Common Ground: How Future Search Conferences Bring People Together.* San Francisco: Berrett-Koehler, 1992. Marv has spent the last twenty-five years redesigning workplaces and writing about it. He always has a way of seeing situations that are illuminating and action-minded. Recently he has been documenting these efforts on videotapes, which are available through Blue Sky Productions, 5918 Pulaski Avenue, Philadelphia, Pa. 19144. Marv has also set up SearchNet, a network of consultants learning to run "future search" conferences by donating their services to non-profits in their own communities. Network members work on issues such as the environment, homelessness, AIDS, education, and housing. Contact Workplace Revolution, (215) 951-0300.

WHYTE, DAVID. *Songs for Coming Home.* Langley, Wash.: Many Rivers Press, 1989. We become so immune to language that words lose their meaning and dialogue takes us in circles. Words like continuous improvement, empowerment, participation, and leadership all lose their impact. Poetry is a form of profound speech, and when spoken with conviction and surrounded with a little explanation and insight, it can be a wake-up call. David Whyte makes his living as a poet and has eagerly entered the world of business. He has brought poetry into our empowerment workshops in a way that is relevant and touching to all. He has written several books and offers tapes of his readings. His poem at the beginning of Chapter 15 is used with his permission. Contact Many Rivers Press, P.O. Box 868, Langley, Wash. 98260.

WINOGRAD, MORLEY. Sales organizations used to be the holdout when it came to innovative ways of managing. If you wanted to bore a sales group, talk about partnership, participation, and teamwork. If you wanted to excite a sales group, talk about redesigning compensation systems and creating justice in defining sales territories. That has changed now and Morley is pioneering the change. He is bringing partnership, teams, and empowerment into his field sales organization, and that is a radical act.

WOODMAN, MARION. *Addiction to Perfection: The Still Unravished Bride*. Toronto: Inner City Books, 1982. A wonderful writer and speaker, she offers a archetypal and mythological frame to understanding human beings. She offers powerful ways to see our struggles without judgment. Plus, with other book titles like *The Owl Was a Baker's Daughter* and *The Pregnant Virgin*, you have to pay attention.

WORLD BUSINESS ACADEMY. This organization is committed to giving business leaders a forum for applying human values to the mainstream workplace. It conducts conferences and publishes an excellent quarterly journal about the transformations that are taking place in businesses around the world. Contact the World Business Academy, 433 Airport Blvd., Suite 416, Burlingame, Calif. 94010.

A LAST ACKNOWLEDGMENT

One final word of appreciation to Frank Basler. He was one of the reviewers for this book and, at times when I was losing it, put precious energy into suggestions that became my life raft in pruning and ordering the book into its somewhat readable form.

THE ARTIST

John Nieto, whose painting "Archer III" is on the dust jacket of this book, is one of America's most renowned painters. He concentrates on capturing in his work his vision of the subject through vibrant, electric hues. The bold imagery is the essence of his art.

The personal philosophies of Nieto are a vital element of his style. He says, "I employ a subject matter that is familiar and express it in an unconventional manner. Art is not mere technical representation but communication of feelings, emotions, values, and culture." The combination of his sensitivity and his technical versatility becomes the vehicle that allows him to transcend the ordinary. While his career is in a state of constant progression, he is acclaimed as one of the most significant artists of our era.

John Nieto lives and works in the Sangre de Cristo Mountains east of Santa Fe. His cultural heritage is of mixed Spanish and Indian blood. His family roots are firmly planted in New Mexico, as it has been the birthplace of his ancestors for three hundred years.

For more information about Nieto's paintings and exhibitions, or to see examples of his work, contact John Cacciola, at J. Cacciola Gallery, 125 Wooster Street, New York, N.Y. 10012. The phone is (212) 966-9177.

THE AUTHOR

One of the defining elements of Peter's work life has been the twenty-plus-year connection with two businesses. Initially it was the creation of Block Petrella Weisbord, a consulting firm that has from the beginning been a major contributor to workplace transformation. The firm still thrives and manages to stay near the leading edge of organizational change. They can be contacted at Block Petrella Weisbord, 1009 Park Avenue, Plainfield, N.J. 07060.

More recently Peter has also been a partner in Designed Learning, a training business that offers workshops for companies committed to developing widespread ownership and responsibility. The ideas in Peter's books underlie the skills taught in Designed Learning's workshops on stewardship, empowerment, building relationships, and consulting skills for staff people. Residing in the same building as the consulting company, Designed Learning can be contacted at 1009 Park Avenue, Plainfield, N. J. 07060.

The second major current in Peter's work has been writing what is now three books. The first was entitled *Flawless Consulting* and has been a best-seller for internal and external consultants. The second book, *The Empowered Manager*, has also been a best-seller and helped bring the idea of empowerment to our consciousness. The books have become, for Peter, a vehicle for expressing a deeply held set of beliefs and a certain amount of alarm about the way organizations and our society function. His writing becomes a political statement in content and style, which addresses the distribution of power and compassion, and the desire in each of us, author included, to find useful ways to express our freedom.

Peter and his wife, Barbara, live in Connecticut.

INDEX